What Else But Home

# WHAT ELSE BUT HOME

*Seven Boys and an American Journey Between the Projects and the Penthouse*

## MICHAEL ROSEN

**PublicAffairs**
*New York*

Published in the United States by PublicAffairs™, a member of the
Perseus Books Group.

PublicAffairs books are available at special discounts for bulk
purchases in the U.S. by corporations, institutions, and other
organizations. For more information, please contact the Special
Markets Department at the Perseus Books Group, 2300 Chestnut
Street, Suite 200, Philadelphia, PA 19103, call (800) 810-4145, ext.
5000, or e-mail special.markets@perseusbooks.com.

Designed by Timm Bryson
Text set in 10.5 point Berling

Library of Congress Cataloging-in-Publication Data
Rosen, Michael (Michael Louis)
  What else but home : seven boys and an American journey between
the projects and the penthouse / Michael Rosen. — 1st ed.
    p. cm.
  ISBN 978-1-58648-562-7 (hbk. : alk. paper) 1. Rosen, Michael
(Michael Louis)—Family. 2. Foster children—United States—
Biography. 3. Foster parents—United States—Biography. 4. Extended
families—United States. 5. Social class—United States. I. Title.
  HV881.R67 2009
  362.7092'27471—dc22
                                            2009018734

ISBN: 978-1-58648-562-7
First Edition

10 9 8 7 6 5 4 3 2 1

# CONTENTS

*"You needn't be afraid he'll leave you this time."*
*"Home," he mocked gently.*
*"Yes, **what else but home?***
*It all depends on what you mean by home.*
*Of course he's nothing to us, any more*
*Than was the hound that came a stranger to us*
*Out of the woods, worn out upon the trail."*

*"Home is the place where, when you have to go there,*
*They have to take you in."*
*"I should have called it*
*Something you somehow haven't to deserve."*

—ROBERT FROST, from
"The Death of the Hired Man" (1915)

# INTRODUCTION

Afterwards, they went to college.

That happens all the time—no startling triumph because we build homes for kids to grow up safe and nurtured, and help them to make their way in the world from there.

But our home was accidental, from random circumstance, at first without expectation. Nine of us, in what became the great adventure of our lives, lurched and wobbled as an improvised family to the moment each of the boys did have the opportunity to make a life mostly free of the burdens he'd been born into.

Parenting, for Leslie and me, became a joyous, trying, rewarding, often uncomfortable and messy process in which we found new ways to make mistakes almost daily. Other parents, anyone parenting, knows the same. Nutritionists, educators, counselors might despair at our inadequacies. Yet along the way, without preamble or forewarning, often after some calamity on a baseball field, on the street, at school or around the kitchen table, we were graced by a transcendent moment, a miracle not on Thirty-fourth Street but one lifting itself up from the accidental mix of our lives; New York's public housing projects on the Lower East Side and a penthouse.

Ripton has grown to be the biggest of us, enormous and strong. We hadn't expected him to be. He sat with Ricky at the kitchen table on Ricky's first night home from finishing his first semester at a community college in Pittsburgh. The two, practicing manhood, were smoking Cohiba Extra Vigorosos, gifts from a friend.

Ripton would hear from his favorite college in spring, but he'd been accepted that afternoon to another near-favorite choice. That school, lovely to Leslie and me, was in North Carolina, fine for learning and in good enough baseball country. Ripton would be graduating high school from Brooklyn Friends and going to college. He hoped to be a baseball walk-on wherever he went. The same with rugby or football.

"Those Tompkins Square games, when we was kids, that was the best time of my life, man," Ricky told Ripton.

"I'm not gonna argue with you about that," Ripton answered.

The two of them thought between puffs, young men behaving like old troupers.

"That summer, too, in Stuyvesant with Jeff; we rocked people," Ripton started again. "I felt sorry for kids. I hit two or three home runs, a 600 batting average. It wasn't fair to have you and me on the same team."

Ricky nodded. He tapped the half inch of ash away to ember. "You remember when I struck out almost the whole team? Like, no one got a hit?"

"You were amazing."

"But everythin I hit, I kept pullin. All summer."

"You never were a hitter."


I drove Carlos up to Stamford, Connecticut, to meet Bobby Valentine (a hero to the boys in our extended family). After he left home, Carlos played two seasons in Missouri, one poorly and one well. He was recruited on a full ride to a four-year college in St. Louis, but came home because he thought the coach was biased against Latinos. He decided it wasn't worth attending class if he wasn't playing ball, because that's what he was out there for. He moved back in, depressed, uninterested in ball and other things. His sadness grew more acute at draft time, when too many of his summer ball teammates were given that big chance, but not him. Then the St. Louis team he'd left, where he was to have been a leader, made it to the College World Series.

I told Carlos he had to play baseball. He said he was finished. I explained that he was depressed. He explained that he was as good as those teammates who'd been drafted, and certainly not worse. "You don't want to look back when you're forty and think maybe you'd have been drafted the next year, but you quit," I said.

"I didn't want to be forty, lookin back thinkin I should'a played," Carlos explained to Bobby Valentine as we sat in the waiting area of his training center. He and Carlos were breathless from batting practice, Valentine dressed in a black tee, CHIBA LOTTE MARINES, JAPAN SERIES CHAMPIONS, OCTOBER 2005 in English across the front.

To qualify for Queens College, Carlos had to make up for a semester of failed courses by attending Borough of Manhattan Community College for one semester and then a winter session; he took six courses and got five As and one B. Other than phys. ed, he'd never before earned an A. Leslie did the reading for each class. She and Carlos lived at the table; together they made sure he got the grades he needed. He was accepted at Queens College and became a captain of the baseball team.

Carlos was keeping the door open.

Kindu completed Morrisville, was accepted to the four-year undergraduate program at SUNY Farmingdale and moved home. He played center field at Morrisville, was a team leader and made the baseball team at his new school. But he also made dean's list his last semester at Morrisville, an extraordinary accomplishment, and decided to pass on playing baseball thereafter to focus on his grades and future. He wants to work in the management of the game after he earns his bachelor's degree.

Phil transferred from Borough of Manhattan Community College to join Will and Juan at Mohawk Valley, Upstate, but none of them stayed long. Angie, Will's girlfriend, became pregnant two or three semesters into Mohawk Valley. Though Leslie and I argued that his best route to support his daughter was to stay there and earn his degree, Will decided to come home, finish an associates degree at BMCC en route to a bachelor's somewhere, and raise the daughter he and Angie would have. He moved in with us for the first semester, till Kaylee was born and he went back to his mother's.

Juan left Mohawk Valley almost when Will did. We started paying for a few classes at BMCC, because he had to raise his grades to requalify for financial aid a second time. He did well, started another semester of classes to improve his grades further and, with Will, disappeared the Wednesday after Thanksgiving 2006.

It took a week before we discovered that they were in boot camp in the Naval Training Center in Great Lakes, Illinois. They'd joined the navy to pay expenses, to help care for Kaylee, to get money for college later. The Iraq war was on and I told them they'd end up in it. They told me the navy wasn't fighting there. I showed them a newspaper article about USN soldiers being sent into combat.

Their navy recruiter was slicker, more relentless and smarter than I. Will thought he was joining the military as a fireman, Juan as a guard; the recruiter called the Monday after Thanksgiving and told them that to serve at a Virginia base together they had to sign new papers and leave that Wednesday. So they did, arriving in Great Lakes to be told they'd signed on anew as corpsmen. That meant nothing to them until the commanding officer told the eight hundred gathered boys that they were enlisted medical specialists. Ninety-nine percent of them would be attached to marine units doing combat tours in Iraq.

Neither Will nor Juan wanted to die there. They called me repeatedly; I phoned our US congresswoman and the base commander of the Naval Service Training Command in Great Lakes, accomplished nothing, but both boys were home for New Year's of their own accord.

Since then, Will has been working at a gym for the past two years. He's studying to be a personal trainer and plans after that to return to college full time.

Juan's been working at a restaurant. He's taking two courses each semester at BMCC and trying to figure a way back into a full-time student life.

Phil stayed one semester at Mohawk Valley after the other two bigger boys came home. Then he also left, started at BMCC, quit with the story of dental school in the Dominican Republic, became a union construction worker, quit to take courses part time at BMCC and is being . . . Phil. He's bright. He'll land on his feet.

All the boys will.

Morgan, too, is in high school at Brooklyn Friends. He and Ripton played on the varsity baseball team together last spring. Morgan's fast. He has a great arm and great balance. He'll play left and center fields. He still skates and skateboards. He has a poet's heart.

Leslie is still a partner in her medical practice. She's still calm and centered, much more than the rest of us.

Mr. Jenkins is still fine. He's a little fatter, a little slower. He and I are alike that way. We both have a little arthritis, too.

Our story, then, is about an accidental family navigating its way through our slice of America. It starts on a baseball field in the Lower East Side. Ripton brought us there. "Some baseball is the fate of us all," Robert Frost wrote. Then, "I'm never more at home in America than at a baseball game, be it in park or in sandlot." This book is about a home we made after a baseball game.

# CHAPTER ONE

# THE SANDLOT | *June 1998*

Ripton led us into the park to play baseball on a Saturday afternoon in the middle of June in the summer of 1998. We'd spent that morning in the primary colors jungle gym in Tompkins Square, much as we had weekends since the park reopened, regardless of season, except for hard rain or when it was covered in snow. Ripton, seven, and Morgan, two and a half years younger, were growing up on the slides, swings, hanging bridges and bars.

Nine months after Ripton was born, in the cool of an early June morning, Tompkins Square Park had been cordoned off then occupied by hundreds of police on horseback, marching in riot gear, in troop carriers and protected by the force's few tanks. More than two hundred homeless were routed onto the streets as their shanty homes were crushed into Department of Sanitation garbage trucks. In our community's mind, expelling the homeless blends with the riots two years earlier when people gathered in the park to protest gentrification as the police hid their names and badge numbers with tape and bloodied artists and community activists, pounding some unconscious.

We watched from the top terrace of our home across the street, in the Christodora, and from the building stoop.

When Tompkins Square reopened a year after the expulsions, the city had put thought and money into the children's playground. The park had been a place people with young children avoided. "Works, works" men assailed passersby hoping to sell needles and syringes. Heroin and crack came from a myriad of dealers. Men with gauzed looks from lifetimes with alcohol, bloated faces and blackened hands shared bottles of Thunderbird and Wild Irish Rose in brown paper bags. "There's always ten drops at the bottom of a bottle," one said in a sandpaper voice to another as I passed by one morning.

The new playground was an urban refuge surrounded by a wrought-iron fence with gates wide enough for carriages and children on bikes with training wheels. The neighborhood was in the midst of a wrenching gentrification—Leslie and I were among the newly arrived very-middle-class parents pushing young ones on tire swings and running with them through mist jets on the hottest days.

But, a few weeks from eight, Ripton had enough of the jungle gym playground. He wanted us to walk home, get his new baseball glove. The pickup game was in a section of the park left untouched by the planners. Ripton had noticed boys playing baseball there from morning till evening on a blacktop field across from the playground, along the Ninth Street pathway.

Leslie, Ripton, Morgan and I turned through the gate in the chain-link fence and walked along the right field foul line towards a line of benches. The boy at bat hit a bloop towards left field and the third baseman, a tall Black kid neither thin nor fat, hustled after it. He was one of the oldest and it seemed the tallest boy playing. The ball bounced fair past the base, rolled across the foul line, then hit and stopped at the base of the chain-link fence paralleling the third base line and Tenth Street. The tall kid got to the ball and made a two-bounce throw to second base. The runner slid feet-first across the infield skim coat of concrete.

"Safe!" the runner bounced up screaming. "Out, out," the second baseman hollered. The tall kid from third base ran, arms flailing, wailing towards second base. Players from both sides rushed into the fray.

We stood near the benches. The tall kid reached second base, players giving way till he was pushing chest to chest against another boy, whom I recognized from the neighborhood, shorter, a few years older, a young light-skinned Puerto Rican probably in his early twenties, broader. "Nigga safe," the older one shouted, "you couldn'ta seen."

"Fuck no," the tall kid bellowed, "out!"

Other players watched. The tall kid lifted both arms, a supplication, exasperation. He looked at us across the infield. "Mister! Mister!" he yelled, "Kid was out, rah?"

I watched him, then the young man, then the others. "I didn't see," I yelled back. "Lady?" the third base kid looked to Leslie. "You saw?"

Leslie shook her head.

"You blind, that nigga OUT," the tall kid swung his glove over his head and slammed it to the cement at the feet of the older one. But somehow a decision was made—seemed to come into existence as much as made—that the batter was safe. Tempers and flamboyance disappeared, players walked back to where they'd been, the next batter hit a single, the runner from second scored, then he and his teammates shook a little strut. We'd walked into a tied game at the bottom of the last inning. The defense abandoned the field and kids from both teams pooled around home plate. The tall kid and the young man started to pick sides. Ripton, without a word from us, walked into the mix.

Most of the boys standing at home were eleven or twelve, a few were in their mid to later teens, a few were Ripton's age. The bigger boys, faster, stronger, certainly better, were picked quickly, before the captains hovered at the edge of Ripton's group.

"The White nigga," the older one pointed to Ripton, choosing him before any of the other boys who seemed his age. Ripton was tall. His team took the field and Ripton wanted to play first base. He owned a first baseman's mitt and saw no reason not to expect he'd play the position he wanted.

"Yo, dogs," the older captain yelled, stopping at the "X" painted to mark the pitcher's spot, tossing the ball up and down in his right hand.

Ripton didn't realize he was being called to. Another boy intending to play first, older and bigger, stood beside him.

"Yo, White nigga," the captain called again, impatient. Ripton realized he was being spoken to.

"Take right," the captain commanded, pointing his gloved hand to the hinterland.

Ripton hesitated; he didn't want to take right.

"Yo, nigga, right field," the kid beside him hissed. "You stuuupid?"

Ripton didn't move. "I want to play first," he answered.

"It's mine, nigga. I play first," the older kid told him.

"Right field, dogs," the captain commanded, wagging his glove again that way.

Ripton's shoulders drooped, and he started away from the painted base then stopped, his face flashing to indignant. Right field is the great emptiness in children's baseball, the place for unknown and bad players; balls are rarely hit there.

The Tompkins Square infield was a skim coat of concrete across blacktop. The X-marked diamond was grayish blue and two citrus-wedge-shaped pieces of base path between first and third were Mets orange. The outfield was blacktop. Left field ended in a string of basketball half courts filled with Black and Latino youths, like the baseball players, but older. Center field ended in a few more half courts running into an American elm, a century and a half of grandeur, its canopy catching any balls hit that way; center field, for the home run hitter, didn't exist.

Clear of basketball half courts and trees, the right field fence was nearest to home plate. The ballpark belonged to natural lefties and good switch hitters, all the more because skateboarders and inline skaters had taken over right field as if baseball didn't exist. The clack and fall of boards, nose manuals and olies accompanied fly balls and base hits.

Leslie and I were the only parents watching the game, the only ones guarding a child. The other adults were Polish-speaking destitutes, all of us sitting on the park benches backed against the chainlink fence along the first and third base lines. The men were the park's newest poor, bearing the same blackened hands, puffed and veined faces, sweating and unshaven. Flies settled on the newspaper Leslie was reading. Their bellies were Day-Glo green and it took me a little time to follow the path of their buzzing to a swarm on the ground in back of the bench we sat on, a green blanket undulating on a pile of human excrement—probably why the men around us had left this bench open. They were swapping brown paper bags with bottlenecks barely visible, paying no attention to us. We started to smell the urine then.

The boy at bat, a round-faced Latino kid, hit the ball slowly back towards Ripton's captain, who scooped and threw it to the boy on first two steps before the runner reached base.

"Out!" the captain shouted again, blowing on his raised index finger as if cooling a revolver.

"Didn't touch!" the runner hopped up and down pointing at the white box painted onto the skim coat, crazed, dervish, to the first baseman and anyone else who'd hear.

"I tagged you, idiot!" the first baseman argued.

The batter had closely cropped hair, almost shaved, an eleven- or twelve-year-old cherub wiggling his foot onto the white paint of the base against the foot of the boy playing there—who pushed back.

"Nigga Phil," another boy practicing swings without a bat groused loudly, amused, to his teammates. He was shorter than cherub-faced Phil, his skin lighter, also eleven or twelve years old. His face was longer, black hair knit in tight geometric designs against his scalp, hanging free in narrow lines to near his shoulders. He jogged broad shouldered to first, hugging an arm across the batter's back, "Phil, son, nigga got you by two steps."

Phil smiled and pirouetted away from the base, walking to his friends at home.

Leslie and I moved to a bench farther from the men. "Mommy," Ripton called to Leslie from right field, then "Mommy!" again because she hadn't looked up from her newspaper. "I'm bored," he shouted, no longer paying attention to the pitcher in mid-windup. "I'm bored," Ripton said again.

"Are you hungry, Sweetie?" Leslie asked.

"Can I have a Gatorade?"

"What color?"

"Red."

"What do you want to eat?"

"Skittles."

"Anything else?"

"Chips."

Leslie walked to the deli across Avenue A.

The taller, younger captain lined a hit to first base—the first baseman caught it. The next batter popped up to the second baseman and Ripton survived his first half inning. Some of his teammates dropped their gloves when the third out was made, and started trotting home. Others handed their gloves to the boys replacing them at their positions or to a buddy. The kid playing first base for the other team trotted up to Ripton, blocked him and held out his hand. Ripton stopped, uncomprehending that half the boys didn't have baseball gloves. A useable glove wasn't cheap and a special one like his first baseman's, a Rawlings, cost far too much. "Give it," the kid, older than our son, finally said.

Leslie was still across the street. Ripton didn't look to me. I hoped he'd hold his own.

Then Ripton looked.

"Nigga, give it," the older kid repeated, wagging his receiving hand. Then he looked at me with nearly the same expression as Ripton's. I reached for the glove I'd brought, an aging and mediocre utility mitt, and handed it to him. Ripton would come to learn the ways of the game.

———

We first learned about Ripton when his mother was seven months pregnant, visited a doctor's office and decided to place him. Leslie and I had been looking to adopt for almost a year. We picked his name while pouring over a Vermont state map. I'd grown up there. Robert Frost, the poet laureate of my youth, had been from Ripton.

Our Ripton was born on September 1, 1990. His birth parents changed their minds about adoption and took him home the next day. We gave away the baby belongings that had quickly filled our apartment; clothes, a crib, bassinet, high chair, infant formula, bottles, medicines, toys and storybooks. Leslie was inconsolable. I knew we'd find another child, and if a boy, we could name him Ripton, but that we shouldn't. There wasn't an interchangeability. We hadn't experienced a death, that a child who was going to be our son was alive, but felt a deep hollowness from his disappearance. I wanted to be his father.

Our adoption lawyer called a week later. "Do you still want to be parents?" she asked Leslie, telling us that the baby's parents—in our talk he'd been "the baby" though we'd picked "Ripton"—had called to ask.

"We do," Leslie answered.

In that case, our lawyer went on, she and the parents had scheduled a time later that day to bring the baby to her office. They'd sign the adoption papers and she'd call us afterwards to come get our son.

Leslie cancelled her patients and I cancelled meetings.

The lawyer called a little later and told Leslie that the baby's parents had changed their minds—they were keeping their son.

She called the next morning, asking if we still wanted the baby. She'd set up a new time for the parents to bring him to her office.

We did want him.

They called and cancelled a while later.

The back and forth went on for a week until Leslie decided she couldn't take the pressure. We needed to get on with our lives. We'd find another child. She wanted me to call the lawyer and tell her our decision. I called and asked the lawyer to contact me instead of Leslie if the parents changed their minds again.

Our lawyer called a couple of days later. She asked and I told her we wanted this boy. She called a few hours later—the baby was in her office. She'd reviewed the adoption papers with his parents, answered their questions and they'd left to walk in Central Park to decide finally if they would sign. She believed they would. They'd be back in an hour. "He's healthy and happy, everything'll be fine," our lawyer said.

I waited the hour, then more as the baby's parents decided whether their son might be ours. The lawyer called and said the parents had come back from the park, hugged their son, signed the papers and left. I could not imagine what they felt: they had conceived this boy, lived the miracle of the mother's body changing, felt the baby's heartbeat, the first kick and many others, delivered him healthy into the world and signed papers giving up the right to be his parents. They hugged him, of course they hugged him, and cried.

"We need to pick up our son," I told Leslie on the phone.

He was wearing a baby blue jump suit. We signed papers; I don't remember. I held him in the backseat while Leslie drove home through Central Park. We bought formula, bottles and diapers at the drugstore on the corner. We rang Leslie's parents' front doorbell and showed our son to Leslie's mother, Ria—we lived across the hall from them. It was early evening and she invited us to dinner.

We spread a bath towel on the floor by the side of our bed that night, nestled Ripton on it and covered him with a dishtowel. His breathing was loud and nasal. That's the way it has stayed.

---

"Thanks, Mister," the kid playing first base reached for my glove.

Before he took it, Ripton shouted, "Here," and flung his Rawlings on the ground beside the kid.

Who scooped it up. I walked back to the bench, Ripton to home plate, where his teammates had gathered and the older captain stood scheming over the batting order. He designated Ripton in the seven slot. Ripton was thrilled; seven was his favorite number.

The first batter got on base with a single through the gap in the second baseline. The second batter swung at an outside pitch and missed. He lunged at another and hit it foul. "You suck," the boy with the braided hair and broad shoulders playing shortstop shouted to the batter. "You gonna strike out, Will," the shortstop taunted him.

Will, almost thirteen years old, didn't show if he noticed the heckling. He let the next pitch pass and the next, both outside. The shortstop kept silent. The captain's next pitch was fine. Will lined it to a space between shortstop and third baseman but the shortstop ranged fast to his left, backhanded the ball and gunned it to first. The kid with Ripton's Rawlings "FOR THE PROFESSIONAL PLAYER" did his job but Will, fast, narrowly beat the throw.

A young kid, Ripton's age and even a little taller, batted third. His skin was a dark mahogany and geometric braids lined his scalp then hung to his shoulders, like the shortstop's but not as tight. He swung at the first pitch in the way young boys do— impatiently—popped it foul but his swing was sweet and beautiful. He swung at the next pitch and got only a little of it. The ball rolled towards the shortstop; it looked like an easy play. The shortstop charged and the batter with the sweet swing was slow in that way of boys tall for their age, with muscles not yet honed to bone. The shortstop pulled the ball from his glove and rifled a throw to the first baseman, faster than the last. The first baseman froze, made no effort and the ball hissed past and rebounded off the high bar of the chain-link fence. "Run!" Jason and the other boys at home screamed. "FuuCK!" the shortstop bellowed, his face in rage. "Run, Ricky!" the kids at home plate yelled and the batter launched himself off first, his arms pumping and braids lurching, a Tex Avery contradiction of thrashing arms, face in determination and long legs striding in slow motion. The ball flew where only the right fielder had a chance, but as he ran he collided with a skateboarder engrossed in a kick flip. The two fell and the skateboard kept rolling with the whirl of ball bearings and wheels across blacktop. The ball bounced and rolled farther outfield. "Bastard," the skateboarder shouted. "Get it! Get it!" the shortstop shouted at the right fielder, floundering for the ball around the trunk of an American elm in center field. "Run, Ricky!" Ripton and his teammates shouted. The shortstop sprinted for the braided boy, caught and tagged him out—a run batted in and two away.

"Carlos, yo Carlos, sorry dogs," the first baseman yelled across to the shortstop.

Who lost his scowl. "S'okay, nigga," Carlos, twelve years old, yelled back. "We got these niggas, we got 'em," showing the ball in his hand. Smiling. While the tall kid was captain likely on account of age, Carlos was clearly the strength of this team. He had presence.

The older captain walked to the plate. He tapped the bat around the circumference of home in a jerking way. He turned on the first pitch, jerking that too into a foul off third. He batted stiff in every way the young kid Ricky was smooth.

Leslie walked back carrying two black plastic grocery bags, one sagging and the other puffed full. She took them to Ripton, who was behind the fenced-off dugout benches near to the swarming flies and his teammates, listening to Will, wonderstruck. Leslie handed him a red Gatorade from one bag and reached into the other for Skittles and bags of nacho chips. Ripton gulped the Gatorade, tilting it back like a television commercial. He ripped at the snacks. Will said something, Ripton took another drink at the Gatorade then handed it over. Will drank, handed it to another boy, then another and the drink was gone and then the snacks. The older captain was still at bat.

This part of the park did have a water fountain, at the end of the benches along the third base line. The indigent men washed themselves at it, and ran water through their hair, dripping down their faces and necks. Some brushed their teeth, rinsed, spat back into the fountain, scrubbed their hands and drank.

None of the boys went to the fountain for a drink.

"Ripton's still thirsty," Leslie walked back and told me.

"He shared everything," I said approvingly. "The kids were thirsty."

I assumed those boys didn't have more than a little money for the store, assumed most of them were from nearby public housing, then thought I was being presumptive, then thought I was probably right. Ripton was the only white kid in the game. He went to a private Jewish day school on the Upper West Side where everyone was white except the janitors. Unlike the ballplayers, none of the kids at his school lacked money for snacks.

I bought bottles of water, Coca-Cola and Gatorade, bags of potato, corn and plantain chips, cartons of cookies at the bodega across Avenue B. The proprietors the past several years had been East Asians newer to New York. These are the small neighborhood groceries that used to cover their windows side to side, top to bottom with boxes of cereals and laundry detergent, stacked rolls of toilet paper and other nonperishables, sight blocked because drugs were dealt inside. But the stores had changed with the transition of our neighborhood; the newer proprietors tried to make a go of it with open windows, though they still had a limited range of foods, very little that wasn't fried or sweetened and wrapped or bottled in plastic, nothing fresh save for blackened plantains and withered tomatoes.

"Ten cents each," the man at the cash register looked down on me, counting out the twenty plastic cups I'd asked for.

The tall captain was at bat again when I walked, bags in hand, back into the park. The game stopped as boys from both teams came to home plate, leaned and sat against the backstop and some on the benches. "Thanks, Mister," a few kids said one way or another. Most ate and drank, dropped their plastic cups and empty chip bags to the blacktop around home plate and went back to the game. The captain hit a ball over the right field fence with enough arc to hit someone in the playground. Boys chased after it, Ripton with them, but they came back empty handed. Ripton walked to us, asked for one of the baseballs we'd brought and took it to his captain, milling at home plate with most of the others.

"Sir, can I use that glove?" Will, the boy Carlos had tried to intimidate at bat, walked over and asked before play began again, pointing to my glove on the bench, holding up the one he had, its webbing shredded, stitching ripped and a crease line where a pocket should have been.

I gave it to him.

"Yo, son, what's your name?" the older captain asked Ripton when they passed each other at the inning's end. Extra baseballs were scarce.

Ripton told him.

"Ripken," the captain repeated. Our son was still in right field the next inning, but he was Ripken out there. The game ended when the heat came off the day, before dusk but into dinnertime. Boys gathered around home plate to pick up their tees and backpacks. Ripton came to us. Will walked over with my glove, put it down on the bench while looking at the ground. "Thank you," he said softly.

"You want to come over?" Ripton asked. "I have Nintendo."

"Dogs, I don't know," Will hesitated, perhaps because a seven-year-old asked him, perhaps because parents sat there, perhaps he had other things to do.

Ricky brought the baseball. "Thanks, Ripken," he said, handing it over.

"You want to come and play Nintendo?" Ripton asked Ricky.

"Sure," Ricky answered. "Where you at?"

"Over there," Ripton pointed across center field, past the half courts and chain-link fence to the other side of Tompkins Square, to the one tall building coming through the canopy of American elms.

"That big one?"

"Yeah," Ripton answered.

Ten boys started home with us, Will among them. We asked the two youngest if they should let their parents know they were coming. "It's okay," Ricky answered for them both.

# CHAPTER TWO

# THE ROCK

We served orange juice and milk until we ran out of both and I went down to the corner grocer for more. We heated frozen macaroni and cheese, bagel bites, chicken fingers and pizza in the microwave until we ran out of these. Then we ordered takeout from the Chinese restaurant down the block.

Most of the boys were in the TV room, down the hall past the kitchen from the front door, watching Ripton and taking short turns at Mario Brothers 64. Ripton had been encouraging Mario, Mario's video brother, Luigi, and their dinosaur horse, Yoshi, through kingdoms in quest of saving the imprisoned Princess Peach since he was three or four years old, starting by watching my then business partner play while sitting on his knee.

When other players lost, Ripton took back his controller and tried to play a game or more before allowing another boy a chance, except for Will, whom he kept handing the controller to. "Jump," he coached. "Spin."

"It's time to go home," Leslie announced at nine o'clock. She started to bed early, by 8:30 or 8:45 on a regular night, loving to bathe, read and sleep. We had a claw-foot tub in the top terrace's green-house, eighteen floors up in a neighborhood of low-rise nineteenth-century tenements; the military had used the terrace during World War II to scan the East River for U-boats. She read the *New York Times* in the bath and in bed afterwards. Our bedroom was the old water tower.

"Already?" Ripton pleaded.

I felt a cascade of eyes. "It's late, Sweetie," I answered, and asked the boys to take their cups, silverware and dishes to the sink. They filed out silently; as boisterous and free as they'd been on the base-ball field, the boys avoided looking at Leslie and me now. There were no handshakes or thank-yous except to Ripton as he held open the front door. Some of the boys sat on the hallway carpet, others leaned against the walls, as they laced up their sneakers. I wondered and smiled at the idea of our next-door neighbor, a gangly quantita-tive hedge fund manager with the means but no interest in a rich man's life Uptown, far neater than us, coming out of his apartment then.

"Ripken, you comin to Tompkins in the morning?" Ricky asked. Snow-filled woods at night, stone fences, Robert Frost's rural New England poetry was meaningless to these boys. But Cal Ripken was a legend.

"Yeah," Ripton answered.

Then I realized we were sending two young children onto night-time streets alone. "Guys, hold on for them," I said to the others.

Ricky and the other boy walked back in but reluctantly, as if I were going to reprimand. "You should call your parents. Is it okay for you to walk home alone?"

"Yeah," both boys answered.

"I think you should call."

"I don't have to," Ricky insisted for himself and the other boy.

"Just to make sure," I urged, "you should call."

The other boy did, and handed the phone to Ricky after he fin-ished. Who also spoke to someone in Spanish. "She's good," he said.

"Your mother?"

"Yeah. I can go."

Then our home was normal, from twelve boys to two.

Ripton screamed at a moment in Mario. I turned off the faucet, wanting to listen to Ripton cooing encouragement to the controller and characters. Morgan played with his GI Joes. The elevator bell rang in the hallway, probably our neighbor coming home. The Con Edison electric plant along the East River began to hiss. I went to the window to watch steam escape from a cooling tower. I looked a few blocks north to the concrete towers of Campos then to Haven Plaza, public housing projects where some of the boys who'd been here lived. Our worlds barely touched. We passed in the park, were momentarily side by side at the corner store.

---

Leslie grew up with her mother's mantra that a child can't take care of itself but an adult can; meaning that Leslie's children received her absolute attention, getting and doing much as they wanted and adults were on the sideline. My parents let their children know their relationship came first, my brother and I there but as supporting cast. Leslie and I have circulated into, through, back into and out of hard marital times. I acquiesced to Leslie's lead in raising our boys, initially unaware of doing so but eventually resenting my dismissal. When I disagreed about one or another aspect of parenting, Leslie countered with expertise. The space around her computer and the floor beside our bed was stacked with books and magazines about adoption, the developmental stages children pass through and sensory integration dysfunction—most prominently Carol Kranowitz's *The Out-of-Sync Child*.

As a toddler, Ripton took a test determining he had sensory integration issues, a condition causing difficulty processing sense information. He wouldn't keep his hands off the heads and necks of his classmates. He was disgusted by the smell of bananas, basil and other scents. He had trouble moderating his voice, sitting still and with small motor skills. We started taking him to an occupational therapist, who also spoke with his toddler program teachers and re-built his physical school environment—we supplied a beanbag chair for him to squirm in, equipped his pencils with squishy gadg-ets that let him hold them more easily and made other professional accommodations.

Ripton had serial "best friends" rather than children he bonded with for more than a couple of weeks or play dates. We invited his Heschel School classmates and their families for Saturday night din-ners but were only once invited in return. So, in the park, I didn't have the heart, and I'm sure Leslie didn't, to suggest a limit on the number of boys coming to our house.

Ripton didn't know it was unusual to invite a crowd home, kids who didn't look like him, spoke and dressed differently, lived under different circumstances. He didn't have the language for race. "That brown boy," he'd said of another in the jungle gym the week before he brought us to the baseball game.

---

The next morning we took more baseballs and our gloves back to the field. The same boys were there. "What up? What up, nigga?" the boys softly grazed clenched fists, lightly tapped open palms and wig-gled fingers against each other greeting Ripton, who slipped into the game. He joined a team with the older captain, Ricky and Will, and this time with Carlos.

The lead jockeyed and only changed when each team sent up its older boys, who swaggered like upperclassmen.

I happened to look up while Carlos came to bat that second day and paid attention to his first swing, grazing a ball but beautiful. I watched a second pitch, nestling his feet into what would be the batter's box, focusing on the tall captain readying, holding his bat back rocking at the wrists, hands cocked and loose then sliding fast through the batting zone sure, level and strong. Carlos showed more than an inkling of possibility. I didn't dare dream. That would be silly. I didn't know the boy. But I did. He stood in a stadium, waiting for the next pitch. Kicking his feet into the batter's box. Sensing what had to come.

Leslie and I walked to the store together and bought bottles of juice and water, plastic cups and bags of peanuts, potato and plantain chips when the first game ended. We brought back four boxes of pizza from Nino's across the street. The older captain gave Ripton an inning at first base after the food. It became too dark to play and boys asked Ripton if they could visit after the game. Ripton made sure Will was coming, who convinced Philippe to also come, the boy who'd tried to trick his way onto first the day before. I watched Carlos flick and clasp hands, tickle fingers and tap shoulders goodbye with the two captains, then with Will and Philippe. Younger boys came to him for the same. Then he walked out of the park without a baseball glove or company.

The boys who came home were mostly the same, more familiar this time, less formal, louder.

"Carlos—" I started with Will then stopped. "The shortstop—" and stopped again.

"What about him?" Will answered softly, watching me, fidgeting that I was speaking with him.

"He's intense."

"He's a beast, that's what." Then more confidently, "He can't lose. You see that."

"Who?" Philippe heard us. He was smiling bigger than a cherub, more evil, sweetly, probably knowing.

"Carlos, nigga! Who else?" Will answered.

"A beast," Philippe flashed his look from Will to me, not breaking the smile.

"A beast," Will repeated, warming to the telling. He, Philippe, Carlos and Juan, another boy from the game, always quiet and who'd not yet visited, were best friends at PS 56, Corlears Junior High School, Will explained.

Leslie made sure the boys left earlier; our children had camp the next morning. Leslie took them each morning except Tuesdays, my day. Otherwise, I was out of the house at 5:40 a.m. Ripton and Morgan went to camp at Friends Seminary, a Quaker meetinghouse a few blocks from home. They were happy there. We were happy that it was an accepting place. The Quaker beliefs in simplicity and peacefulness attracted us.

"Ripton doesn't want to go to camp," Leslie called me at 8:00 a.m.

"What's wrong?"

"He wants to play baseball with his friends."

"And?"

Leslie lowered her voice, Ripton must have been nearby. "I think we should let him stay home."

That was our dance—contesting what our children wanted. I believed what they asked for and what they received shouldn't always be the same. Starburst candies for breakfast, ice cream for dinner, as many fishing rods and reels as Ripton wanted. He had wanted us to enroll him and his brother in the Friends camp before summer began—I believed he and we should honor that commitment, a part of how we would teach, and he would learn, responsibility.

"Can Jonny come?" I heard myself ask. Jonny McGovern was our babysitter, hired a year and a half earlier, when we had to fire the woman who'd been taking care of our children and Ripton wanted a male replacement. Jonny worked long hours the first year, but now he picked our boys up from camp or school and spent a couple of hours with them before Leslie or I came home. If Jonny couldn't help, I knew from Leslie's voice that she'd want to cancel her patients, at least the morning ones, and she'd ask me to come home early.

"He's free," Leslie said.

"But, Les—we paid for the camp," I pushed myself to say, "because Ripton wanted to go. He should play baseball after camp."

"Then you talk to him," she was impatient, handing the phone over.

"Hello?" Ripton's voice was soft.

"Hi, Sweetie."

"Hi, Daddy."

"Mommy says you want to stay home?"

"I'm not feeling good," he drew these words out.

"Oh? What's wrong?"

"I'm just not feeling so good."

"I'm sorry. Mommy says Jonny can come. But you should stay inside today, okay?, if you're sick."

"What if I feel better?"

"If you feel better, how about going to camp and playing baseball afterward? If you feel sick, Mommy or I can come get you."

"But maybe they won't be there."

"Who?" I lost him.

"My friends."

"Sweetie, they play every day. You can invite kids home again for supper."

After camp, Jonny took our boys to the park. "I have a problem," Jonny said to Leslie before he went home. "Those kids scream gay slurs all the time. 'Fuck you, faggot,' 'You gay.'" Jonny was the Gay Pimp in *The Wrong Fag to Fuck With*, a cabaret show he'd written and had been directing since graduating acting school a couple of years earlier. He was nearly six and a half feet tall and muscled in an Abercrombie & Fitch sort of way. "Hypercharismatic," one theater review described him.

During the next few weeks Ripton's passion for baseball never slacked. Morgan played a few innings some days, the older boys indulged him, but he liked just as well to ride his new bicycle in unhurried loops around the edges of the field. Morgan, whose normally straw-blond hair by mid-summer had bleached to translucence, did build constant relationships and as the days of baseball turned into more he argued strongly for returning to the jungle gyms and his friends there. Leslie and I started to split our oversight. When only one of us could be in the park, we made sure Will watched over Ripton.

A dozen or so boys kept coming to our home, the kids changing to include Carlos and Juan after Will's and Philippe's invitation. Jonny became fixed on convincing us that these older boys, in particular, were using Ripton. "It's not like you think," he said. "They talk back to me. They're not nice to Ripton when you're not around. You don't see." They wanted our baseballs and gloves, he explained, the food and drinks we took to the games. They wanted the home we had, the video games, televisions, computers, stereo, food, drink and the space of our apartment.

Of course they wanted these things. Boys came hungry and thirsty the first time, knowing of but never playing with Nintendo, telling us they didn't have computers at home. We gradually heard their stories, of larger and extended families in public housing, crowded homes. They hinted at sometimes going hungry. It would be fantasy to think the boys wouldn't be influenced by what we had, or that the boys a few or more years older than Ripton would be coming principally as friends. Ripton took to calling Will "Posada," after the Yankees' young catcher, whom he resembled with close-set eyes, a long face and Romanesque nose. Will addressed Leslie and me gently, always with deference, and Ripton grew increasingly attached to him. They were comfortable particularly when they sat on the sofa beside each other taking turns with the controller, lost in the story, colors and sounds of Mario Brothers and Donkey Kong.

"Ollrrot," Will whispered when I asked how he was or for his help with something.

"Ollrrot," Ripton whispered when I asked how *he* was or for his help with something.

Ria and Mike, Leslie's proper parents, asked if they could come on a Sunday and watch Ripton and Morgan play baseball in the park; Ripton had been telling his grandmother—who was "Ria" at her insistence—about the game and his new best friends. We agreed that I'd barbeque on the terrace afterwards, a king mackerel the wholesale monger allowed me to pick from his back refrigerated room for the blackness of its eyes and the strength of its flesh. I made hamburgers and hotdogs for the boys.

"Are you comfortable with those children?" Ria asked Leslie the next day, on a phone call thanking her daughter for dinner. "Are they Ripton's friends? They're quite a bit older, aren't they? Do you think it's good for Morgan? Do you know their families? It was a little noisy."

It had been very noisy. Leslie's parents had not liked what they'd seen any more than my parents would have. My father demanded order and quiet.

Ricky's mother, a smiling, shorter and thickset woman wearing a flowered housedress in shades of brown and tan, came to watch part of one game on a Saturday afternoon, sitting on a nearby bench. We smiled back and forth, trying to understand each other between Spanish and English, stuck between those smiles with nods, pointing to our children, the others and our home. "*Gracias,*" she said a few times. No other parents, aunts, uncles or older siblings ever came. The dangers of city life, the reality of kidnapped children, black and white pictures posted on the sides of milk cartons, a possibility we addressed by making certain Ripton and Morgan were watched, didn't carry over to the others.

The World Wrestling Foundation crept deeper into our lives, Ripton insisting we allow him to stay up later some nights to watch his favorite matches on TV; then that we should buy a poster of The Rock, his favorite character, which he and Will taped to the wall beside our dining room table, then that he needed a life size cardboard cutout of The Rock, which he and Will stood beside the pullout sofa Ripton shared with Morgan on the second floor. Then Ripton needed The Undertaker, an even larger life size man in a black wife-beater pulled tight across a bulging chest, a bad-guy black leather jacket draped to his knees, full beard, greased and curling hair to his shoulders topped by a black flat-brimmed Stetson Royal Flush, ready to haunt any sheriff in white.

"Undertaker's stuuupid," Carlos said, a few boys sitting on the pullout sofa bed between the cardboard cutouts, pulling at the frayed webbing of my baseball glove. "He and Stone Cold beating Kane and Mankind, then loosin, that was stuuupid."

"He was champion," Ripton defended.

"Nigga, the tombstone pile driver's stuuupid. You know that. The People's Elbow, that shit is hot."

"They're both good," Ripton said.

"Yo, Carlos, you be The Rock, I'll be The Undertaker," Will said, and the two started to wrestle between the bed and bookcase, their heads slapping close to metal and wood.

"Guys, guys! Someone's gonna get hurt. Go down to the living room," I said, putting a book back onto the shelves, my way to keep on eye on them. They hurried downstairs and started to wrestle.

"I'm The Rock," Will called in the living room a few days later.

"No, dogs! I'm The Rock," Carlos disagreed. "You're Triple H."

"I'm Stone Cold," Ripton tried to be in the fight. "It's me and Will's turn," he said.

"Yo, nigga, it's my turn, you Stone Cold last night," Carlos protested. He was right and Ripton backed down. "Will, nigga, you The Rock this morning," Carlos persisted. The boys had taken over the living room for this game, warring across the floor as Mankind, The Rock, The Undertaker, Triple H and the others. They watched a differently named match on TV each night; Hell in a Cell, Raw, the Survivor Series.

"Fuck you, faggot, I weren't," Will complained.

"Stop the gay comments," I reprimanded.

"Sorry, Mike," Will said softly.

"It's my turn. You The Rock—" Carlos tried.

"You stuuupid. Phil was, you whack," Will pushed, his voice back to loud.

"You tight, nigga. Tight tight," Carlos crouched, squinted, stepped towards Will jabbing his finger, taunting but smiling; a snarling dog wagging its tail.

"Tight you tight, nigga, tight," Ripton mimed Carlos, agitating, too loud.

"Shut up, faggot!" Will yelled at Ripton.

"Remember what I said," I shouted from the other room.

It was a short time before Ripton convinced Leslie to buy the WWF's Smackdown authentic championship belt. I wasn't told until it arrived in the mail because the belt cost more than I could stomach. Its center was a heavy metal medallion, oblong and coated to shimmering gold, the middle a baby blue earth held aloft by a kneeling Atlas. Cherry red lettering arched above the world, *WWF* and *Smackdown*, surrounded by eagle's wings. Two smaller medallions flanked the center, tapering to ends studded with eight shining gold-colored metal button snaps. Open, the belt was a fat, enormous wristwatch and band to be held aloft the instant of victory. The boys knew how to use it.

Astonishingly, our downstairs neighbor never complained. The cement floor had to reverberate with the boys' poundings. Ripton was buying Official WWF CDs and we let the mob turn the stereo volume to explosion. The vaulted space of the living room seemed to quiver and ripple, my ribs throbbed, an involuntary sounding board to bass, and the boys worked themselves to frenzy. They lined the edges of the room, Philippe strobing the lights. Will and Carlos pulled off their shirts. Carlos reached for a pair of Ripton's aviator glasses on the table beneath the mezzanine, next to The Rock poster taped to the wall. The floor undulated.

> *Livin' easy, lovin' free*
> *Season ticket on a one-way ride*
> *Asking nothing, leave me be*
> *Taking everything in my stride . . .*

SummerSlam 1998's theme song, AC/DC ripping metal.

Will swigged water from a clear plastic bottle. Carlos pranced, ducked and weaved, flexing his muscles and throwing the aviator glasses onto the sofa. He hoisted his right eyebrow, squinted his left eye and cradled his chin in his right hand, cocking his head. Then he jumped onto our ottoman screaming, "Do you smell what The Rock is cooking?" The boys cheered, knowing the script, mimicking The Rock.

Will clenched both fists above his head, flexed his pecs and biceps with the strobe of Phil's lights and blasted out a firm and fine spray of water—Triple H's way.

*And I'm going down, all the way down*
*I'm on the highway to hell . . .*

beating his chest to the lights, to AC/DC.

The two boys circled each other in the way of wrestlers, looking for a weakness. Forget that the WWF is scripted, that its heroes and heels are picked for TV appreciation, each slam to the canvas a practiced pirouette with a partner. Our own Triple H and The Rock circled. Will lunged at Carlos and handfuls of boys shouted death and destruction, Ripton and Morgan a part of them. Carlos let himself be thrown to the cushions and the boys screamed even louder. Carlos sprung loose, tripped Will, rolled on top and pinned Triple H.

Ripton, the referee, ran into the imaginary ring holding the American Eagle championship belt, the second to have arrived, costing more than a full week's gross salary for someone earning minimum wage.

"Off, nigga!" Will shouted, beyond play, but Carlos held him down. "Fuck off," struggling, "Triple H was supposed to win."

"I don't want to lose," Carlos answered, but let Will up.

"We agreed."

"I don't lose."

"Let's both win," Will said. "Ricky, Dakota, you be Stone Cold and Mankind, run into the ring and steal the belt, we'll fight you off then share."

Ricky and Dakota, the right fielder who'd crashed into the skateboarder, were four or five years younger than Will and Carlos, the same age as Ripton.

"Jump from there," Ripton pointed to the mezzanine knee wall, fifteen feet up. "We'll pile the cushions, and the dogs." He meant the cushions and pillows from the sofas and chairs, and three enormous stuffed dogs piled on top of each other beneath the spiral staircase. The dogs were trophies from an adoption carnival, where Ria was the high bidder three years running because Ripton insisted on having them.

The boys stripped cushions off the sofa and chairs then piled the stuffed dogs on these. Ricky and Dakota climbed the spiral stairs to the mezzanine and perched themselves on the knee wall while boys adjusted the cushions where they thought their friends would fall. Ricky launched himself, screamed and landed, the boys cheered and Dakota hesitated. Another young boy climbed and jumped, then Morgan, then boy after boy including Dakota until the WWF was forgotten for the moment and the knee wall covered in hand and heel prints. They decided to try frog splashes and body slams from up there.

Ripton and Morgan's summer camp ended the first week of August. We asked Jonny to start coming in time for Leslie, and for me on Tuesdays, to leave for work. He agreed and arrived, hardly hiding his disdain with the newly constant companions. In the park, the boys offended him, but their after-game visits in our home were completely intolerable. All the more on rainy mornings, wet for baseball, when the doorman called from the lobby by nine-thirty if not earlier with any of Will, Philippe, Carlos, Juan, Ricky, Dakota, Junito or others there asking if Ripton were home and if they could come up and play. Jonny took our children shopping, mostly when Ripton tired with one video game and wanted to see what else he could play, or when an important game was being released. But with baseball and the school year starting at the end of August our boys wanted, and Leslie suggested, Jonny shop with them for equipment and clothes. Ripton wanted Will and Philippe along. The bigger boys knew which soft core baseballs were best. They knew which stores sold the best clothes—Ripton no longer wanted to wear Kmart, Gap or Lands' End. He wanted to look like the other kids in the park, the boys coming to our home.

The shopping crew came from one trip with new clothes and two pairs of the latest Michael Jordan leaping man sneakers. The design and release date of Nike's next in the line of Air Jordans was near to the Yankees and the World Wrestling Foundation as a topic of passion among the boys.

Will and Ripton sat on the sofa playing Mario that evening, other boys walking in and out to watch but not asking to join in, spending time in front of the TV and near me in the kitchen as I sat on the exercise bike while the Yankees played. Will wore an ash blue oversized tee, a mustard tiger springing across its front and wrapping around his shoulder and sleeve, a smaller sky blue tiger across his chest with ROCAWEAR and then DENIM SPECIALISTS stacked below. Ripton wore an oversized black tee decorated across his chest by a rhinoceros armed with an automatic weapon walking beside a small monkey bearing a red flag of the ecko unltd. rhino brand, the flag fluttering on expedition. Will and Ripton wore similar jeans hanging to below the bands of their patterned boxers, yellow stitching along the seams of denim, the large red tag of "mecca usa since one day" sewed onto the back hip.

"You gay, nigga," Philippe shouted at Will.

"You stuuupid," Will shouted just as loudly.

"Homo," Phil taunted.

I got off the bike and walked into the TV room. Will was working the controller, Phil facing him. "What are you guys talking about?" I asked.

"He's retarded," Phil answered. "He can't play," broadening his smile.

"You wanna try?" Will asked, not pausing from jumps and spins.

"Look at that, you're retarded," Phil said as Mario was crushed beneath a roaming mushroom.

"You're a faggot, you play," Will held out the controller to Phil as Ripton reached for his turn.

"Stop the gay comments," I said. "We don't want it in our house."

"Sorry, Mike," the two answered.

Will handed the controller to Ripton, then, "But Mike, it's against the *Bible* to be gay. I know what you and Leslie say, but it is."

I imagined Will was reciting Father Julio, the priest he'd grown up with, Church doctrine, his mother and friends.

"Jonny's a good person, that's all that matters, not hurting anyone," I said.

"Yo, Mike, he's a nice guy and all, but that's fucked up," Philippe said. "Being gay, it's wrong, that's it, that's it. It's not natural."

"It's a sin," Will kept his conviction.

"We don't believe that, Will," I answered. "Leslie's partners, some of the doctors in her office, they're gay, and friends of ours. In this house, no 'nigga' and no 'gay' this-or-that. It's no different than racism. I don't want to hear it. It's no different than people in a store picking on you because you're Spanish, because they don't like Spics."

"It is different, Mike, it's a sin," Will argued.

"There are people who legitimated slavery by saying Black people weren't as human as Whites, and who look down on Latinos for the same reason."

"That's stuuupid," Philippe said.

"It's not the same, because it's not right," Will insisted.

I left the room.

Slowly, in small part, the WWF lost a bit of hegemony to the "gun game," hide-and-go-seek shootouts with plastic M-16s, Kalashnikovs, UZIs, rocket-propelled grenade launchers, Lugers, 22-caliber Colts, Day-Glo futuristic water weapons, broken reproductions of pirates' pistols and one Springfield load-and-lock Mauser action World War I rifle. The game was all players and no audience save Leslie and me. It demanded devastation. One side, half the boys, died for the others to win; not to mention deaths on the winning side. The boys no longer limited themselves to a ring of pillows and stuffed dogs and hurling themselves from furniture and our mezzanine. They claimed the whole apartment.

They liked best to play in the dark. Philippe taped a flashlight to the barrel of an M16 when he was on the seeking side. Morgan imitated the idea, strapping a red laser pointer to the barrel of the air-pump rifle. A boy saw a point on his body and knew he was dead.

Philippe, a captain, picked Will, Ripton, Dakota and Morgan, who started as a mascot but, lithe and quick, held his own. In our family of oblong faces, Morgan's was round, freckles and alabaster skin, blond hair spilling from two cowlicks across his head. His eyes were hazel. He was on the moderate size for his age and disarmingly solid.

He started jumping from chairs and tables soon after he learned to walk, landing on two feet. He progressed to standing on the wide wing chair dressed in a Batman costume, cowling and cape, jumped a handstand onto the ottoman and finished his flip into the stuffed dogs and sofa cushions on the floor, a model for the knee wall launches. In social grace and wisdom, Morgan was not the younger brother.

The other team ran off and the hunters counted to sixty. Leslie and I were instructed not to open the refrigerator because the light might betray a soldier. Nor to open the coat closet door, which was triggered to a lightbulb. Nor to turn on the televisions or computers. We sat in the dark. I mumbled about the absurdity and Leslie countered with the "quality time" of being with our children, even if they were pretending to shoot us.

We called our bedroom, the old water tower, off-limits. We also forbid children to go out on the terraces, afraid of their falling. The top terrace, at the level of the greenhouse where Leslie bathed, was a half floor below that bedroom. Kids in the gun game hid behind the door into the greenhouse, listening for soldiers climbing the stairs, trying to time a kill. It was hard for a seeker to keep silent carrying a weapon climbing a long, steep and winding stair in the dark.

Boys hid in Leslie's claw-foot bathtub, kneeling, eyes accustomed to the city's night of dusk, gun barrels pointed toward the door, waiting for the enemy to turn the corner. The advantage stood with the hunted.

The middle level of our apartment, below the greenhouse and top terrace, was a warren of hiding places. Two rooms, each half a greenhouse, opened onto a long terrace facing mostly east, across the East River and into Brooklyn. The five major bridges accessing Manhattan—the Triborough, Queensborough, Williamsburg, Brooklyn, Manhattan spans—glittered north to south at night. The sun rose over Brooklyn, red up from a skyline still of tenements, forsaken factories and warehouses turned to condominiums, church steeples the tallest sights into the skyline, what Whitman saw.

The larger room on the middle level, originally our living room before we bought the adjoining apartment, turned into Ripton and Morgan's bedroom when we pulled out the sofa—they were young enough to need to be within our hearing at night. Disheveled comforters, blankets, sheets and pillows provided gun game cover for hiding either in bed or underneath. The smaller room had closets starting seven feet up. Whole teams of boys fit inside these aerial caves, hoping for a rear attack. A bathroom off the hallway ended in a secret shower. A smaller bathroom, doubling as my clothes closet, offered more cover. I'd said this room was off-limits to no effect whatsoever.

"Bam!Bam!" two bams overlapped.

"You dead!" Carlos cried.

"YOU dead!" Ripton cried back.

"You dead, Juan," Will shouted.

"You stupid!" Juan hollered back. "I been dead, Ripton kilt me."

The stairway lights turned on. The boys were coming back, plastic guns banging into walls, automatic weapons firing. Then they appeared, soldiers slipping into camp after battle, kids who'd watched more than one Vietnam War movie; bandoliers, an armory of weapons.

We microwaved food and passed out cups of orange juice and water. A break in the hostilities.

"Yo, Ripton, you always gonna be at Heschel?" Will asked.

"They stop in eighth grade," Ripton answered.

"They don't got high school?" Carlos asked.

"That's a Jewish school, rah?" Phil asked.

"Yeah," Ripton answered. He was starting second grade, already his fifth year there.

We'd picked Ripton and Morgan's school in part because its namesake, Rabbi Abraham Joshua Heschel, a scholar at the Jewish Theological Seminary in New York, taught the sanctity of compassion. Asked why he marched with Reverend Martin Luther King Jr. from Selma to Montgomery, Rabbi Heschel answered, "When I march in Selma, my feet are praying."

"Ya niggas have-ta wear those round hats?" Phil smiled, patting his head.

"Yeah," Ripton responded, "but we wear baseball hats."

"In school?" Will asked.

"Sure," Morgan answered. He was going into kindergarten, his third year at Heschel. "And kids have Yankee kipas, Mets kipas—"

"'Key' what?" Phil asked.

"You like that school? Carlos asked.

"Yeah," Morgan said.

"I hate it," Ripton answered.

"Your dad says it's deep," Carlos said. Heschel was on the Upper West Side, I thought too far from our house.

"Yo, like, what are Jews, really?" Carlos asked. "Do you believe in God?"

"Sure," Ripton answered. Morgan's brow sank, one side deeper than the other, hazel eyes retreating for a moment, confusion.

"Are you White? I don't understand. You're White, but a different race, rah?" Carlos tried to figure an understanding.

"Dogs, you'all don't believe in Jesus, so you can't believe in God," Will was certain.

"Are you Israelis, is that the same?" Phil asked.

"We don't believe in Jesus," Ripton explained.

"We're not Israeli," Morgan answered, "but my Grandfather Mike has a house in Israel."

"You have to believe in Jesus to go to heaven," Will insisted. "Or—"

"Shut up, nigga," Carlos was firm.

"You do," Will persisted.

"Are your real parents Jewish?" Phil asked.

"My mom was Christian," Morgan answered. He was curious about why and how he'd come to be with us, who his birthparents were, wanting to know as much about his mother as we knew.

Ripton was silent. The boys waited for him. "You, Ripton?" Will finally asked.

"My dad was Jewish," Ripton halted, "and my mom was Italian." That was near all he knew. Where Morgan sometimes called himself "Brock" after his birthmother's surname and kept a photograph of her with two daughters and a son on her knees, his half siblings, Ripton asked no questions and had no mementos. He avoided talking about his adoption. Then more smoothly, "When I go to Heschel, I'm Jewish, but when I come home, I'm a kid. I don't like it there. It's rich kids."

Carlos looked at the rifle he was holding, then aimed it at Mario on the TV screen. "Ya hear about Robinson?" he asked. Robinson was another of the kids on a baseball team with the older boys in an East River league. He didn't often come to Tompkins Square, but I'd met him, a tall pitcher, sweet natured and from the same projects as Carlos and Juan.

"What?" Will asked, twisting his shoulders and face into a jump he wanted Mario to make.

"His brother killed a guy on Avenue D," Carlos answered.

"Word?" Philippe answered. "What happened?"

"Nigga was in a fight. Nigga pulled a knife and Robinson's brother shot him."

"Police got him?" Will asked.

"He's run," Carlos answered.

# CHAPTER THREE

# PARAGON

*August and*
*Early Autumn 1998*

Ripton, Will and Carlos, still strapped in machine-gun-bullet bandoliers, in dark clothes best for hiding, came to us after the gun game. Will and Carlos wore du-rags, black nylon tight over their heads and tails dangling down their backs, Ripton a black bandana folded as a kerchief fashioned by Will as a stand-in. "They want me to go to the game tomorrow," Ripton told us.

"What game?" I asked.

"The Tides," Carlos answered.

"Ray's team," Will explained.

"Baseball?" Leslie asked.

"Yeah," they answered.

"Where, what time?" I wanted to know.

"The East River—we're the East River Tides," Carlos stressed the place.

"Nine-thirty," Will answered.

This was their local team, more serious than Tompkins Square. "Who plays?" I asked, feeling that I ought to know more.

"Me, Will, Phil, Juan, Robinson, all of us. Other kids, too," Carlos answered.

"Can I go?" Ripton was impatient.

"To play?" Leslie asked.

"It's just big kids," Ripton answered—what was supposed to be obvious.

"He's too young, Leslie," Carlos said. "But he can watch. He can meet Ray so he can play pony next year. Playin wif us, he's gettin good."

"That's what we done, played pony, Ray's cool," Will said.

It's a twenty-minute walk to those fields—past Avenue D where Robinson's brother killed the boy, through the housing projects to a footbridge over the expressway, then south. I used to run through the projects to the river. Boys hanging out taunted and threw things sometimes, though I was rarely alone and nothing more serious happened. But I was fearful for Ripton—Leslie and I glanced at each other.

"Nothin's gonna happen," Will understood. "He's wif us."

"Nobody gonna mess wif my White brother," Carlos puffed himself.

"We'll bring snacks," Leslie said.

"Mommy, just me and the guys, okay?" Ripton insisted. "You take Morgan to the playground."

"Dogs, we playin, you don't wanna be by yourself," Carlos said to him.

Ripton thought a while. "Okay," he answered.

By nine o'clock the next morning we were ready with drinks, sandwiches and because Ripton didn't eat sandwiches, cans of Chef Boyardee ravioli in single-serving-size containers with red plastic lids made for microwaving. Ripton preferred the congealed globules of tomato sauce and ravioli squares at room temperature. He was dressed and covered in sunscreen. Will didn't arrive, so we went to the lobby. Leslie finally called him from her cell phone.

"*Disculpa, no entiendo, esperate un momento,*" a woman said to her.

"This is Ripton's mother," Leslie repeated.

"*Esperate,*" the woman responded and called to someone in Spanish.

"Hello?" a young girl answered.

"Hi, this is Ripton's mother, Will's friend, who is this?"

"It's Miriam, Will's sister. That was my mom."

"I'm sorry to bother you, but is Will there, we're supposed to go to a baseball game?"

"He left with Carlos."

"How long ago? He was supposed to pick Ripton up at our house."

"It was, like, fifteen minutes ago."

Leslie told us the news. Will lived around the corner. "Let's go, we'll meet them there," I said.

Will and Philippe walked into the lobby wearing cherry red Tides tees, red caps, gray baseball pants and black Jordans, Philippe with his tan Wilson glove. "You're late," Leslie said to the bigger boys' smiles.

"Phil was showering. You know Phil," Will answered, and Phil's smile grew larger and embarrassed.

"Where's Carlos?" Leslie asked.

"Carlos?" Will repeated.

"Your sister said he was with you."

"Damn, Leslie, you callin my house? We like that?"

"You said twenty minutes ago, you were supposed to be here."

"I had to get Phil. Carlos gone to his mom's, he left his uniform, we gonna pick him up wif Juan."

"You're going to be late," Leslie said.

"We all right," Phil said, "trust me."

We started across Tenth Street into Jacob Riis, red-brown brick buildings made as rectangles and crosses six and thirteen stories tall, sidewalks, bushes, lawns and parking lots between, Le Corbusier's tower in the park style, four Whites and two Latinos. "Guys, which building is Carlos's?" I asked Will and Phil six steps ahead with Ripton between them, Morgan weaving among us on his bike. Young kids, young couples, middle-aged women alone pushing shopping carts, most Black, a few Latino, eyed the crew of us as we went. Some of New York's worst tenements stood once where we were, photo-documented by Jacob Riis in 1890's groundbreaking *How the Other Half Lives*, demolished to open nineteen buildings with 1,700 apartments stretching from East Sixth to East Thirteenth streets, named after the journalist. Another sixteen buildings with 1,857 apartments adjoin Jacob Riis from East Houston to East Sixth, named for the social activist Lillian Wald. These thirty-five buildings, developed by the New York City Housing Authority, were initially enclaves of Irish, Jewish and Italian Americans, changing with our neighborhood to overwhelmingly Latino, Black and decidedly poorer. "Davon, nigga," Phil was suddenly loud, clasping hands and touching shoulders with a boy who sometimes played in Tompkins Square.

"What up, my nigga?" Will too greeted Davon, grasped and slapped.

"Tides?" Davon asked.

"You know it," Phil said. "Ripton, son," making sure Davon knew him. "And his parents, and Morgan," biking around us slowly.

"What up, I know Ripken," Davon said, clasping hands and bending to touch shoulders with our son. "Nice to meet you, you brings us pizzas and all," Davon nodded to Leslie and me.

"We gonna be late, we gotta get Carlos and Juan," Will said.

"All right, peace my niggas," Davon said. "Nice to meet you," he looked to Leslie and me, starting away.

"One," Phil said to his friend, tapping a fist to his chest, swinging his hand away and opening his index finger.

"One," Davon did the same.

"I remember him. He not on the Tides?" I asked the older boys when we'd walked a little along.

"He played but he didn't like it. He don't like things organized," Phil answered.

We reached the footbridge crossing the FDR, the roll and motor of cars. We walked down along the river, past men from Chinatown casting long rods bending with lead and lures into the tidal flow for striped bass running from Albany to the Atlantic, joggers and in-line skaters passing in both directions along the pathway built as a bul-

wark then finally under the stone and steel span of the Williamsburg
Bridge, which, in 1903, was the longest suspension bridge anywhere,
cars, trucks and subway trains making a waterfall of noise overhead.
We turned towards Field Six. At 10:45, only a few Tides were there
and a few others in green and yellow Athletics tees and caps. Leslie
and I were the only adults; no umpire, no Ray, no Athletics coach.
We sat on a decaying concrete bunker. "What can I do?" Morgan
asked a few moments later; he didn't want to ride on the road
around potholes, trucks, cars, vans, bicycles and runners. There was
no place to ride inside the gate, only dirt.

Other players came and then Ripton tucked among Carlos,
Philippe, Will and Juan in their uniforms. Juan held a left-handed
glove passed down from his godparents. A natural rightie, he was
born with the index and middle fingers attached on that hand. Sur-
geons tried to separate the fingers when he turned two but the
blood supply to the middle finger wasn't sufficient and it had to be
removed. Pins were inserted to straighten and strengthen the index
finger. These were pulled out one at a time as he grew older and they
poked through the skin. His index finger is arced to the side. Juan
keeps that hand hidden and learned to be a leftie.

A heavy umpire walked in, a navy blue tee sticking to his back
and pressed against his belly in the rising heat. The Athletics coach
came, then a four-door dented and dusty red Honda pulled close and
stopped against the chain-link fence, its motor sputtering and refus-
ing to stop before a final bang. The Tides players went to it, carrying
equipment bags from Ray's trunk and seats back to their dugout.
Ray, the Athletics coach, the umpire and all the players I could figure were Latino, though perhaps a few were Black. I felt the absurdity of these distinctions again. Ray unpacked squeeze bottles of
water, two bats, balls and gloves. Carlos and Will rushed for gloves.
Will got one. Carlos didn't.

Leslie walked with Morgan to the road because he couldn't sit
any longer and I followed the umpire onto the infield as he dropped
bases onto undulations of sand. There was no grass. What should
have been the pitcher's mound was a pile of dried mud cut with

rivulets. Pebbles mixed into sand marked the beginning of the outfield. Center field was an expanse of pebbles turning to small rocks
and occasional brown and green shards of broken bottles.

I pushed against the chain link of the backstop when the game
started, close as I could into the mud churn of the batter's box, the
umpire, full-dress catchers and batters bending together into each
pitch, timing break, movement, ball and bat through the hitting
zone. The speed of the ball frightened me, its hiss and whack into
the catcher's glove. A hit was like the hammer I used to swing into a
steel wedge splitting firewood as I grew up. "I see great things in
baseball," Walt Whitman wrote. In this East River hardball I saw a
spit and fury, a place our four older boys knew and I didn't.

Ripton was against the fence beside me but as the game wore on,
as the heat and humidity closed in, we went back to the concrete
bunker. Leslie had returned with Morgan. Ripton lost interest in the
game and took his brother to ride. Carlos came to bat. "I want to buy
gloves for him and Will," I said to Leslie.

"Who?" she asked, into the *New York Times*.

"Carlos."

Leslie looked up. "Okay," she said. She didn't ask how much baseball gloves cost. I would have; they're expensive. I sew my socks and
underwear. Leslie buys new. She's not worried about money.

"*Vete*," Tides screamed as Carlos hit a strong ball to center field.
"*Vete*," watching it carry. "Go," I screamed, Leslie looking up from
the paper. The center fielder turned and ran but had no chance, the
ball hitting high on the chain link a few feet from a home run. Carlos was on third base standing, tempted towards home but held by
Ray, clapping, smiling the deepest I'd seen him.

The first time he came to our apartment, Carlos asked for shrimp
fried rice and fried chicken wings when Leslie ordered Chinese food.
He drank glass after glass of milk. I went down to the corner grocer
because he asked if we had more. Seven people lived in his apartment—his older brother Jesus, three younger brothers, him, his mom,
her current boyfriend—and when a gallon of milk was finished there
probably wasn't another, especially near the end of the month when

the assistance money was gone. He thought himself lucky if he could get two glasses from a gallon. He'd never been in a place where he could drink as much milk as he wanted, where there was as much food as he could eat, where he didn't have to fight about anything. At home, with his mother for the last eight months since they'd left the homeless shelters, they'd done nothing but fight.

That's why he almost never went home. Carlos slept at Will's or Philippe's most nights. Though their apartments were also crowded, they did have their own bedrooms. He had to share their beds, but that was better than sleeping in his own bed in the room he shared with Jesus at home because there wasn't the fighting.

The Tides finished beating the Athletics. Juan caught the final out, a fly ball to left field. Tides jumped, squealed, ran to home plate, drank and spat, lined up to pass by the Athletics and touch hands. Carlos called over to Ripton. Ray brought his team to the dugout. Ripton went between his friends and Ray reviewed the game in Spanglish, pointing and nodding to different of his smiling, tired, dirty boys. "*Este es mi amigo,*" Carlos introduced Ripton. "*El juego primera bueno.* He wants to play pony next year."

Ray reached for Ripton's hand. We'd been encouraging him to shake; to hold firmly, not too little or much, to look into the other person's eyes and say "thank you," "nice to meet you," "hello" or some such. "Hey, Ripken, the guys'll tell you in the spring, when we start practicin."

Ripton shook well. "Thank you," he answered. "I'm hungry," he said to us a few moments later. We sat in the sun and ate sandwiches, Ripton his individual serving sizes of Chef Boyardee. Then he wanted to leave with the bigger boys, going home to their homes to change clothes, to our house for baseball equipment and finally to Tompkins Square. The usual crew came home after the game. We bought drinks from the corner grocer and ordered Chinese again from the restaurant in Red Square. The woman answering the phone there had come to recognize my voice.

I made an omelet for Leslie and myself, frying onions and tomatoes from the Sunday farmers' market in Tompkins Square, adding

Chinese hoisin sauce and Pakistani pickled garlic relish till the mix caramelized, folding this into the eggs with old English cheddar. Leslie cut and toasted slices of bread. We'd not sat and eaten alone together in weeks. "Where are the kids?" I realized the silence. They weren't in the TV room or the living room. I heard muffled voices and climbed the spiral stair to the mezzanine, a space I could barely stand in, bent lower to get beneath a beam and came to the black Magic Marker writing on the closed white door into the hidden room beyond: MANAGER, PRIVATE! NO ADULTS ALLOWED! MOM AND DAD—STAY OUT! I knocked. Voices stopped.

"Who is it?" Ripton asked.

"Your father," I answered.

"You're not allowed," he said.

"Does Mom know you wrote on this door?" I asked. Not that Leslie would object, but I did, sort of.

"She said it was okay," Ripton answered.

"I told them it was okay," Leslie called from below.

"Is everyone there?" I asked.

"Yes," boys answered.

"What are you doing?"

"Making teams," Ripton answered.

"For what?"

"Tompkins," he said.

I'd been using the room for storage. "Let me see," I said to silence. Then Morgan opened the door dressed in his Batman costume, Ripton behind him. I looked inside, boys sitting on children's chairs and the floor, holding flashlights, crowding around a children's table covered with magazines and sports pages. The Rock and The Undertaker were bent, pressed against a wall. I hadn't noticed the wrestlers weren't in our boys' bedroom. "We're managers and wrestlers," Ripton said.

Ripton closed the door while I stood there. Leslie called to them when the delivery man arrived. They ate and went to wrestle in the living room. Ripton and Morgan came to us at the kitchen table, Ripton holding the Smackdown belt, Morgan still in his Batman suit.

"Can the kids sleep over?" Ripton asked.

"Who?" I asked.

"Sure," Leslie answered.

"Our friends," Ripton said.

"Who?" I asked again.

"Everyone," Ripton answered. He'd never had a friend sleep over. He'd never been invited to stay at anyone else's.

"Sure," I answered.

Ricky and Dakota called their mothers for permission to stay. The four bigger boys insisted they didn't have to. Leslie and I opened the futon sofa in the TV room, pulled out the living room sofa and a third in the room beneath the secret manager's office. We put on sheets and didn't worry about blankets. Leslie went to bed and I ran a bath for our sons—they bathed together most nights and I read while they sat in the tub and again when I took them upstairs, lying between my boys to the pages of Dr. Seuss or *Frog and Toad*. They liked *Berenstain Bear* books, where Papa Bear was the family idiot and Mama Bear was wise and tolerant of her husband. That dynamic struck close. Ripton was captivated by *The Old Man and the Sea* and Morgan was patient with it—something magical in Hemingway. Both boys allowed the first half of John Hersey's *Blues*, a book about blue fish mixing poetry and literature, but nothing further.

"Don't say about me and Morgan," Ripton said when he heard the bathwater.

"Okay," I answered, sad that a time had passed and an awareness come, seeing the line of life and proud of the man he'd be. I sat with Ripton while he hurried through washing his hair with no-tears shampoo. Our boys didn't use soap—Leslie insisted it dried their skin and sitting in bathwater mixed with shampoo was sufficient. I rubbed a wet hand over their bodies. I wondered what mistake Papa Bear would make over soap and cleanliness. Ripton didn't want to be read to, nor did Morgan.

I asked the boys for last snack requests—glasses of milk, orange juice and water, toast with butter, toast with cream cheese and jam, toast with peanut butter and jam, bowls of Cinnamon Toast Crunch, Lucky Charms and Frosted Flakes. I called Morgan and Ripton to brush their teeth. I didn't have toothbrushes for the other boys. I didn't talk with them about washing. Ripton wanted to share the TV room pullout futon with Will. The six others went three to a bed. They promised to go to sleep. I turned out the lights, locked the front door and went upstairs.

Rain against the metal roof of our water tower bedroom woke me sometime in the night. Winds sucked one side then another of the sheathing, tin buckling in a snare and we were the drum below.

The eight boys were asleep in the living room when Leslie and I came down in the morning. Ripton was lying between Carlos and Philippe on the sofa bed. Morgan, Will and Dakota were on and woven beneath the stuffed dogs. Juan and Ricky nestled into the blue overstuffed chair, their legs stretched to the ottoman. The boys kept sleeping as Leslie and I brewed our individual cups of coffee—she preferred hot skim milk, less coffee and four sugars, I preferred strong coffee, a bit of whole milk and no sugar. Leslie made herself an English muffin lathered with butter and jam.

---

"Do you guys wanna get baseball gloves this morning?" I asked Will and Carlos, managing to get them aside.

"What you mean?" Carlos asked.

"There's not going to be baseball, with the rain," I pointed outside. "I thought we could go to Paragon and get you guys gloves."

They looked to each other. "For real?" Carlos asked.

"Yeah," I nodded. "It makes sense."

"Sure," Will agreed.

"I don't care," Carlos answered.

On the street, beneath umbrellas, I hailed a cab on account of the rain. As the yellow car slowed, I thought that a dad should take his son to buy a first baseball glove, his second and third. Carlos' biological father was alive but the man wanted nothing to do with his son.

Will's father was falling deeply to alcohol and depression, starting to move out of their home. None of the bigger or younger boys, except for Dakota, seemed to have dads deep in their lives.

I recognized the Paragon salesman as Carlos and Will picked through gloves hanging on the wall. I was willing to buy good but less than particularly expensive ones; they ranged from forty to over two hundred dollars—Wilson, Easton, Louisville Slugger, Mizuno and brands I'd not heard of.

The salesman was doting on a father and son, my age and Ripton's, a shopping basket filled with *Rawlings Official Major League* baseballs at ten dollars or more per ball at their feet. He had both wearing Rawlings' top glove, black deerskin, tossing a ball to each. The boy dropped a gentle lob. The three went to size Louisville Slugger's aluminum TPX bat, the one the salesman had earlier mentioned to Ripton was best and we unquestioningly bought. The way he said Rawlings was the best first baseman's glove.

In his late fifties, slight, white haired, soft faced and shouldered with dark and damaged eyes, the salesman had told Ripton, Morgan and me about his season in the minor leagues, how much he now enjoyed selling baseball equipment after his career in electronics, how kids needed the right equipment but most salesmen didn't know enough to work with kids. He was quick to fix his baby blue stickers on Ripton's bat, our two gloves and the shopping basket of soft core baseballs.

"You see that?" Carlos whispered, holding the black Rawlings, showing us the price—$249. "YoMike, we gonna get these?" he smiled.

The salesman finished fixing his stickers to the father and son's cache and walked to us. "You guys looking for gloves?" he asked.

"Yup," I answered. "Yessir," Will said softly. Carlos said nothing.

"Do you play a lot?" the salesman asked my boys.

They hesitated, then, "Yessir," Will said. "Everyday," Carlos said. "Where?"

"Wif the Tides," Carlos answered, "and in the park."

"The Tides?" the man asked.

"Little League, along the East River," I said, "and pickup in Tompkins Square."

"Okay," the salesman said and it was clear he didn't know about baseball along the East River or probably where Tompkins Square was. "What do you play?" he asked the boys.

"Shortstop," Carlos said. "Infield," Will said.

The salesman held out a hand for the black deerskin Rawlings the boys were wearing and pulled two gloves from the wall. "Try these," he said. The boys held the new gloves, black and brown leather SSKs, a brand I didn't know, flexed them, turned them over and pushed and pulled their hands inside. Their faces were blank. "What do you think?" the salesman asked.

"It's small," Carlos said and Will nodded.

"Close it," the salesman said. Each did and disappointment showed—I was going to cheat them out of real gloves. "Looks right," the salesman said. "You're infielders, you'll have more control." He took an SSK, pulled it on and took a baseball from his pocket, walked down the aisle surrounded by bats and uniforms, wagged his gloved hand to Will from twenty feet away and threw a fast groundball. Will hurried in front of it, fielded and tossed the ball gently back. "Your turn," the salesman said to Carlos, who cleanly fielded the grounder and tossed it back. The salesman hurled a fast overhand. I froze. Carlos caught the ball. A customer could have been hit. The man smiled, pleased, and threw equally hard to Will. "You guys are good," he said. "SSK is new, you're going to hear a lot about 'em. I played for a year with the Dodgers, Double A, I wish I had this glove, between price and quality."

I hadn't seen the price.

"What did you play?" Carlos asked.

"Second base."

"Why you stop?"

I reached for one of the SSKs, twisted it so I could see the price and fixed on its "Pro" label, not a good sign, then saw it was $119.99. Less than I'd feared.

"I ruined my knee," the salesman pointed. "Ripped it. Now they could fix it with those scopes. But it never got better. I didn't have the speed anymore."

"What you bat?" Carlos asked.

"Two ninety-five, till I got hurt. I was getting better picking up the slider—that was hard."

Carlos and Will nodded.

"That's advice for you. When you get older, and pitchers get better, you gotta learn to pick up the slider." He spoke through a callus, but the splinter was evident beneath.

"What do you think?" I asked, nodding towards their gloves.

"Ollrrot," Will answered, cradling his, grinning slightly. "Whatever you think," Carlos looked at the floor.

"We'll buy them," I told the salesman, who slipped the baby blue stickers from his pocket and put one on each of the gloves.

"Are you their coach, or teacher?" the salesman asked.

"A friend," I answered.

"You bought some gloves a month or so ago, right?"

"For my sons."

"And a bat."

"Yeah."

"I don't forget. I'd dampen the gloves, tie a ball into the pocket and put it in the dryer for ten minutes, like I said last time," the man told us.

"I remember," I answered.

The cashier dropped the boys' new gloves and a half dozen soft-core balls into a large plastic bag, folded the receipt over the top and stapled it shut so we couldn't slip stolen goods into the bag on our way out. She handed it to Carlos, who tore it open when we got to the street, took the gloves, handed one to Will and the bag to me. The boys didn't seem to notice that the clouds were gone, rain drying from the sidewalk and street.

"Thanks, Mike." Will held out his hand and we shook as he looked away down the street.

"Look me in the eye, Will," I said and he looked to me instead of the distance. "Let's try again. In the eye, and firm."

"Okay, Mike," he said and we did.

Carlos, smiling at the lesson, hugged me. He was large but I'd never realized quite how. His breath was warm. "Thanks, Mike," he pushed his chin into my shoulder, his mouth against my ear.

The boys stepped off the curb and two paces into the street, looking up Broadway. "Let's walk," I said, with no intention to pay for a cab.

"YoMike, the guys are gonna be in Tompkins," Carlos said.

"We can walk, it's not raining," I answered.

"We gotta get there, the guys gonna need us," Carlos insisted.

"Then we gotta walk fast," I said.

"NiggaMike," Carlos said, patting me on the back. "I never met anybody like you. Let's take a cab, I'll pay."

"You have the money?"

Carlos smiled. "YoMike, why you like that? Want me to beat you up?" He twisted me around again and lifted me off the ground in a bear hug. "We gonna take a cab?"

We walked to the park in fifteen minutes. A few boys were there, a few skateboarders and in-line skaters but not my family and the other boys who'd slept over. I called Leslie, who said they were coming out. "How was the shopping?" she asked.

"Whaddayagot?" The older captain saw the Paragon bag and fresh gloves, reaching for Will's, who let him take it. "SSK, seems nice," he said, turning it around, trying to put his hand inside. "But it's kinda small."

"It's for infielders," Will said. "You have better control."

"Ya gotta break it in," the captain said.

"No shit, genius," Carlos said. "Ya want us to break 'em in now?"

"Well, tonight."

"No shit," Carlos answered.

"Ya niggas ain't changed clothes. Ya go home last night?"

"We stayed at Ripton's."

"Sweet," the captain said, seeming to understand the three of us together, the gloves and Paragon bag.

More boys came in ones and twos, walking slowly, gloves down till they turned the corner and saw there were others on the field, lifted their gloves and leaned onto their toes.

Then in a Spaghetti Western one thin line spread across the pavement, a dozen boys walked and rode low-slung bicycles onto the field, stopping to face the older captain at the pitcher's "X." The boys who'd been playing gathered beside him. Both sides clutched their bats.

"Who are they?" I asked Morgan, who'd come to the field because none of his friends were at the jungle gyms.

"Campos," he said and shrugged, having overheard the others. Campos meant nothing to him.

The high-rise public housing buildings of Pedro Albizu Campos Plaza are lifted on pillars one floor above the ground and set with slabs of concrete to the sidewalk. There's no grass, no flowers, no trees, only piles of dog shit owners are obliged to pick up but don't, cigarette butts, crumpled newspapers and discarded gum wrappers. It's an austere place some urban planner miscalculated, named for the twentieth-century Puerto Rican intellectual who advocated liberty from the United States by any means necessary and died in a U.S. prison after suffering a stroke and possibly poisoning from radiation experiments.

The Campos kids moved to take the field and our boys stepped away to bat. Ripton yelled and waved to Morgan, who joined in.

A bantam, angry boy circled the perimeter on his bike, rolled along the first base line around the puddles and through the few skateboarders, in-line skaters and the Campos boy playing right field, away beneath the intersecting lines of half-court basketball backboards marking deepest center field, through left field, returning along the third base line, behind the batter, starting again around the loop. He smiled and nodded each time he passed, flashing his tongue with a two-edged razor blade resting there, flipping the blade in a roll, sliding his tongue back into his mouth, never breaking eye contact with us, around and around, slowing to smile, darting his tongue and rolling the blade. "What should we do?" Leslie asked.

The sun and humidity seemed suddenly unbearable. I told myself that the Campos boys were no different than our Lower East Side boys. "He's showing off," I said, not very sure.

The score ran against Campos. Carlos, switch-hitting, yanked a home run over the right field fence. He slammed Ripton's bat to the pavement, sliding his hand up onto the sweet spot of the barrel, raising his arm to hammer it down. Aluminum slapped against concrete and the bat bounced one end to the other back and forth. Boys ran off in search of the ball and Carlos circled the bases. I reminded a few not to throw the bat when they asked for another ball on the way back.

Will hit a home run and the knob of the TPX rolled one way and the bat another when he slammed it to the ground.

I jumped.

"Michael," Leslie cautioned.

"But—"

"We can get another one," her eyes set on me, her voice stern—Paragon's expensive bat. "Let them play."

One boy went after the knob. Will pushed the broken bat to the side and grabbed a replacement aluminum one.

The score grew increasingly lopsided and our boys' swagger set me on edge. I'm not sure if Leslie noticed. Morgan swung into a soft pitch, Jesus' bat too heavy and lofted a slow fly toward first, tossed the bat angrily and ran but the first baseman caught the ball before he was a quarter way there, the third out of the inning, stranding teammates at second and third. Morgan slapped his side, kicked the ground and grimaced. A Campos kid, our bigger boys' age and Will's size, kinky hair in braids to his shoulders, green eyes, brown skin, picked up Jesus' bat and came at Morgan as our son went back for his glove. The Campos kid said something and Morgan said something back. The Campos kid shouted. I stood and started towards them. Morgan said something else and the Campos kid raised the bat above his head and closed the distance between them. I rushed in front of the kid, Morgan at my back. "Put it down," I lowered my voice, words clear the way my father was when he was most angry, the way I did with Ripton and Morgan where they'd stop. The Campos kid fixed on me, grinned and brought the bat down at me. I cringed. He stopped, green eyes cold and grinned more. "Put it down," I said. Our boys were in back of me, the Campos boys behind the kid who'd gone at Morgan.

"Michael," Leslie's voice tapped from the outside, her rising tone of fear.

The Campos boy brought the bat down again. I wondered how I'd be hurt. How we'd get out of this. If there were knives or more and the boy stopped, raised the bat, started again and stopped. Jesus grabbed it from him, Carlos spun me around, boys came behind and beside pushing me out of the ballpark. "YoMikeletsgohome," Carlos said.

"Nigga Mike nigga Mike," Phil kept singing in his flat nasal voice, smiling at me.

I was shaking. "I want the kid to apologize."

"YoMike, it's over, let's go home," Carlos said, putting his arm around me again.

I saw the boy and started after him. Carlos and the others stood and stopped me. Will, then Philippe, started laughing. Morgan clung to Leslie. "Nigga tight," Philippe said about me, "tight, tight," laughing.

We gathered our belongings and Will's new glove was gone. "Campos, we'll get it," Carlos consoled him, but we never saw that glove again.

———

On the walk home, perhaps to calm us, Leslie suggested going to Chinatown for dinner.

No one responded.

"Should we go to a restaurant tonight?" she asked more loudly. "In Chinatown?"

"Where?" Ripton asked.

"Chinatown, dogs, your moms said. You heard?" Phil answered.

"With the guys?" Ripton asked Leslie.

Leslie meant the Chinese restaurant on Canal Street near the Manhattan Bridge. Ripton liked the place, where we took him and Morgan each weekend before we met the other boys in baseball. After that he didn't want to leave his friends. For Leslie and me, it was one thing to feed boys in the park, to have and feed them in our home. But taking a crew out to a restaurant was a step beyond. Leslie and I looked at each other. "Of course," she answered, "if everyone wants to go."

Everyone did. We went upstairs to drop our things, use the bathroom and get cash. Mr. Liu, who worked for me in the Wall Street firm but quit to go back to the restaurant business, did not accept credit cards.

Math and parenting preferences worked against the twelve of us getting conflict-free to Grand Sichuan. New York City taxicabs legally take up to four passengers. Some drivers risk the fine and allow a fifth to ride in front beside the driver, but no matter how Leslie and I practiced seating arrangements we needed three cabs and one wouldn't have an adult. We'd never sent our boys off without us, other than with their grandparents, Jonny or the babysitter before him—and certainly not alone with other children. Leslie scoffed at parents who put their children on airplanes to fly alone. Parents who entrusted their children to unknown cab or car service drivers were beyond careless.

"It's me and the guys," Ripton announced when we came down the stairs of our building and crossed to the far side of Avenue B. Tourists and recently arrived New Yorkers hail cabs from the sidewalk, or when slightly less timid, one step from the curb. Ripton attacked oncoming traffic, choking the lane, waving at any cab, occupied or ready. A cab slowed and pulled over. Ripton rushed the bigger boys to it. The driver, an older man with a white beard against dark skin, a tired face and modest white turban, turned around and saw the first of the boys climbing into his backseat. He rolled down his front window. "An adult must come, yes?" he said to me as boys kept climbing in.

"We have younger children we have to go with," I answered.

"You or the lady," the driver looked to where I pointed, seeing Leslie.

"They're my sons, they're good kids," I nodded towards the boys in his backseat.

"Move, nigga," Juan erupted. The driver and I turned to see Juan trying to get a seat, pushing Ripton over. "Nigga, sit on Will's lap," Juan strained. Will, Phil and Juan were already in.

"Only four," the driver looked at me.

"Can he sit in front?" I pointed to Juan.

"Not allowed, Mister. I cannot afford fine," the driver said.

Juan, the most remote of the bigger boys, pushed his hands into his pockets, slumped his shoulders, set his face elsewhere and walked to the curb. Ripton pulled the door shut.

"They're going to Christie and Canal," I told the driver. I reached through the open rear window, across Ripton, and handed Will twenty dollars. "No screaming, guys, and tip fifteen percent, okay?" I said. Will took the money but only Ripton acknowledged what I'd said, nodding. I knew he hadn't learned fractions. Fifteen percent was also probably beyond the older boys, though it shouldn't have been. "They're bright," I'd been saying to Leslie, filling a worry I shouldn't have had—I wouldn't say such a thing about a group of Heschel kids. Malcolm X wrote that the Black ghetto bookie would be a banker in a different world. "It'll be about six dollars, so give the man a dollar tip and give me the change," I said through the open window. "You'll get there first, so wait for us on the corner."

I put my arm around Juan's shoulder, but he walked away. "It's not you, the cab was full," I said.

Leslie hailed a second cab and left with Morgan, Ricky and Dakota.

"No, Mike. I see how it is," Juan answered, "That's how it always is. I'm one of the guys, but I'm not one of the guys, see? I'm friends with Will, we're tight but I don't count the same. I'm not Carlos. You guys treat him one way and me different."

"The cab was filled, Juan."

"You coulda told Ripton to move over."

"You heard the driver, he'd only take four."

"You coulda told one of the other guys."

"They were in already."

"You took Carlos and Will for gloves."

"You have a glove."

"Mine? It's terrible. It's not like Will and Carlos got. Will don't even take care'a his."

Juan, two brothers from the park and I took a third cab. The others were at Christie and Canal when we arrived, standing on a street of slow-roasted ducks hanging head down, threaded by their feet in restaurant window after window, brown-red with light from neon signs, from sauces and cooked skin, closed eyes and tight beaks, hanging quarters of pig the same, tilapia, carp, perch, freshwater eel and whitefish stirring round and round, some listless and drifting sideways in greenish aquariums waiting for a diner to pick fresh fish, what could be a corner in Hong Kong with sidewalk stands, street hawkers and passersby on a Saturday night. Carlos handed me eleven dollars; the fare was nearly six and they tipped three. Ripton was giggling. "There's four girls at Houston Street, Phil shouts—" and broke in laughter. "Phil shouts, 'Yo baby, you hot! Where you live, girl?'" pointing at Phil, his lips pulled back to gum with the nibbed white teeth of children, all of us caught in our son's smile and laughing in his moment. Ripton couldn't talk anymore, then, "Where you live, girl?" he snorted. Phil, Will and Carlos huddled in budding adolescent conspiracy.

We encouraged the boys into Mr. Liu's, down this block where Chinatown was still a bit raw, less touristed. Customers entered Grand Sichuan through a narrow glass vestibule beside the large storefront window. Dakota, Carlos, Juan, Will and Philippe pushed into it, a swarm of brown-skinned boys, then hesitated, milling, fish caught in a corner. Mr. Liu, stooped on his worn wooden stool close by, straightened to the commotion. He stood up, his face suddenly tight, and started for the door. He was a good man, who'd left my firm when his stockbrokerage department failed and his boss ran away. "Go in, go in," I said from the street and the boys filed by Mr. Liu. Morgan and Ripton walked in, Leslie and me and Mr. Liu smiled, his bang of bone black hair glistening against his forehead. He took my hand and shook too strongly, smiled awkwardly as he always did. He'd been a teacher, a kind man in broken health who'd suffered an intellectual's breaking labor and humiliation during the Cultural Revolution. He encouraged the halting Chinese I'd learned. "Are those boys with you?" he asked in Mandarin.

"Yes. They're our friends, our sons' friends," I said.

Mr. Liu kept ahold of my hand, kept his smile but his eyes weakened. I'm certain he would have preferred the boys weren't with us, able to tell them to leave.

Both types of Mr. Liu's customers, Cantonese-speaking locals and English-speaking visitors from Uptown and elsewhere, inspected our group as Mr. Liu showed us to the back of his main dining room, next to a large-screen TV and the steps down to the kitchen and bathroom, to his one banquet table, set with a lazy Susan. The TV was tuned to videotape loops of Chinese couples at ballroom dance in tuxedos and pastel taffeta gowns swirling through variety stageshow sets. The audio was turned off and Chinese subtitles scrawled beneath. We'd often sat at a table for four nearby.

"Sit here," Ripton urged Will, rocking, slapping the back of a chair beside him till Will started his way and Ripton began slapping the back of the chair on the other side, "Phil, Phil."

Morgan sat next to Dakota. Leslie and I were next to each other, opposite our sons. Carlos was on my left. A waiter asked what we wanted to drink and handed out menus. The boys ordered Coca-Colas and Sprites. Leslie ordered a Coca-Cola, I wanted a water, we both asked for tea.

"What do you get?" Phil asked Ripton, spinning the closed menu around in his hands.

"Fried dumplings," he answered.

"Do you want help with the menu?" Leslie asked the boys.

"Na," kids said, shook their heads and looked through their menus.

"Do you know what you'd like?" Leslie asked after a while.

"Chicken wings and shrimp fried rice, like always," Carlos smiled.

"Me too, with pork fried rice," Will said. Philippe and Juan wanted their fried chicken wings with pork fried rice. Dakota wanted his with shrimp fried rice.

"Do you want to try other things? They have great food," I said.

"Like what?" Carlos asked.

"Chicken with broccoli. Orange-flavored chicken."

"What else they got?" he asked.

"Red braised pork," I said.

"Fucks that?" Carlos asked too loudly.

Grand Sichuan offered an oversized menu of American favorites, Sichuan specialties, a hot pot selection printed only in Chinese and a hit parade of "Mao's Favorites," odd for an owner who'd suffered so deeply from Mao's time. I explained red braised pork, squares of meat and thick fat sautéed in more fat and simmered with water chestnuts in a sweetish brown sauce. "It's like roast pork," I finished—the bigger boys had spoken about roast pork.

"That's nasty," Juan said.

"My dad eats everything," Morgan said, drinking his Coke.

"Cockroaches, grasshoppers, it's disgusting," Ripton said. "He went to a dog restaurant, and he ate snake hearts. They were still beating."

The waiter took order after order of fried chicken wings, fried rice with variations and fried dumplings. Leslie and I ordered other drinks.

"How do you use these?" Phil tore open his envelope of chopsticks, split the pieces apart and started waving them.

"Michael'll teach you," Leslie said. The other boys tore open their chopstick envelopes, including Ripton and Morgan, who'd never shown an interest in using them. I went boy to boy around the table, showing in my hand, taking each boy's hand and placing the sticks as they should be.

"Yo, waiter!" Carlos yelled across the restaurant.

A young couple on TV was waltzing amid champagne bubbles. The tables around us froze. I wanted to disappear but was amused at the same time. The waiter kept walking into the front room. "Sshh!" I said. "Don't yell. You don't yell in a restaurant."

"But I'm thirsty," Carlos answered.

"You need to catch his attention. That's what you do in a restaurant."

"That's what I'm doin," Carlos answered.

"You can't yell," Leslie said.

"That's what you do in a Spanish restaurant," Phil said. Other boys agreed, though I'm not certain most of them had been in a place other than Kennedy Fried Chicken or McDonald's.

I turned, looking to catch a waiter's attention. Morgan put his Coke can and glass on the lazy Susan and rocked it back and forth. Dakota put his on and turned it, completed a rotation, grew braver and spun it more quickly, testing gravity. Cans and glasses started to slide. "Stop," I said. The boys ordered another round of sodas.

"YoMike, like, what's this really for?" Carlos pointed to the lazy Susan.

"Sharing. Right? You put your chicken wings here, I put my fried snake here, or dog sausage, we turn it and everyone shares, like a banquet."

"What's a 'banquet'?" Will asked.

"A big meal, a celebration, like a christening."

"Damn, nigga, I'm starvin like Marvin, I ain't sharin MY food," Phil said.

"Me too," Carlos said. "Unless you and Leslie want chicken wings?"

"Suckup." Philippe punched Carlos in the arm, who punched him back harder.

"Stop it! Guys," Leslie said.

"Guys, guys," Ripton sang in falsetto. "Guys," Will started singing and others joined in. Leslie made a sad face.

Soup came, then spareribs, a chili-spiced eggplant dripping in red oil and a bowl of mixed vegetables. The waiter set bowls and

Chinese-style porcelain soupspoons in front of each of us and ladled broth and wontons as he went. Boys ignored the mixed vegetables and eggplant, finished their wontons and broth, spun the spareribs to each other till these were finished and we ordered more.

"Try the eggplant," I said. "We like it."

"That looks nastEE," Philippe said. The other bigger boys and Ripton agreed. "YO!" Philippe yelled and waved to the waiter across the room.

"Phil," Leslie hissed.

"Sorry, sorry Leslie, sorry Mike," Phil said. "I forgot."

"What do you need?" I asked.

"The wontons didn't come," Phil answered.

"YoMike, why's it a 'lazy Susan'?" Carlos asked, spinning the plate.

I remembered the first time I ate charcoal-grilled steak, more than my parents could afford, gathered beside a family friend's pool where we'd spend afternoons and evenings, the meat cut into bite-size pieces for us kids and put on the lazy Susan with summer ears of corn. That was the year JFK was murdered. "Like a mother who doesn't want to walk around the table serving everyone. Spinning the food is easier," I said.

"That's lazy, dogs," Phil said.

"It's sexist, only the mother cooks and she's 'lazy' if she doesn't walk around the table serving," I said.

"That's how it is. I ain't cookin, that's wifey's job," Phil said.

"My mom doesn't serve. She watches TV wif Jose and drinks beer. She's not goin out of the house, since we got here," Carlos said.

"It's hard, son," Juan said.

"In our house, Michael cooks, you see him."

"My mom doesn't know how to cook," Ripton said.

"For real?" Will asked.

"We had maids, I never really learned," Leslie explained evenly.

"Was they Spanish?" Carlos asked, all the boys watching for her answer.

"Sort of. When I was young, they were Brazilian, because my mother came from there," Leslie answered.

"So you're Spanish, sort of?" Phil asked.

The boys were rapt.

"My grandmother was in the Holocaust. My grandfather, too," Ripton said.

"He was in the Battle of the Bulge," Morgan said. Morgan liked armies.

"What's the halacast?" Phil asked.

None of the other boys seemed to know.

"That was killing Jews, in World War Two, rah?" Juan finally said.

"Yup," Leslie answered.

"And Gypsies, gays, intellectuals, Catholics, Jehovah's Witnesses—" I started.

"Damn? Catholics?" Phil stopped me.

I nodded.

"But most Jews," Ripton said.

"Your mother was in that?" Carlos asked. "That Holocaust?"

Leslie nodded.

"That's Oh-Dee," Will said.

"How many niggas they killed?" Phil asked.

"Six million." Ripton knew from the Heschel School.

"Jews, and almost as many others, five million," I said.

"YoMike, that true?" Carlos asked.

"It is," I said.

"Like eleven million people?" Juan asked. "Mike, how many people we got in New York?"

"Eight, I think, eight and a half million."

"So that's, like . . . more than New York," Carlos figured. "Every person."

"All of New York, then almost half of it again," I said.

"After the war, my mother and her family went to Brazil."

"But Leslie, I been thinking, why don't your moms cook?" Carlos asked.

"Nigga, they rich, that why. You rich, you don't gotta cook," Phil said.

"She does know how, sometimes she did," Leslie answered. "But the maids really cook."

"They do, it's Oh-Dee," Ripton said. "In white dresses and my grandmother rings a bell."

"For real?" Will asked.

The four of us said it was.

"My moms knows how," Carlos said. "In the Bronx, before, she makes the best *arroz con gandules*, chicken with *adobo* and *sofrito*, not these vegetables," nodding towards the mixed vegetables, "and that, what's that—it's nasty," pointing to the eggplant.

"Eggplant," I said.

"Only White people eat that," Carlos said.

"It's Chinese, Carlos. We're in a Chinese restaurant," I said.

"Yeah, genius," Ripton chided.

"Yous stupid, Carlos. But that stuff does look nastEE," Will laughed. "Carlos is right, gotta say that."

"Ching chang chong," Phil burst out.

"Phil, stop it," I said, dismayed.

"Ting teng tong," Phil laughed and the boys with him.

"Ching chang chong," Ripton mimicked.

"Sshh! Stop, it's racist," I whispered, embarrassed and angry.

"Sshh! Stop, it's racist," Ripton repeated, smiling to his buddies in abandon, his gums glistening.

I leaned over the table towards the boys. "I won't allow it—not making fun of anyone else," I hissed, loudly enough for our table and probably others to hear. "These people work hard, harder than you can imagine, they're trying to make a living, not sitting in an apartment collecting government handouts."

The teasing stopped.

"My dad loves Chinese people," Ripton said.

The main courses came in a flourish of four waiters skimming a dozen filled plates to the lazy Susan. Ripton picked a fried dumpling with his left hand and pried it open along the seam, scooped out the kidney-shaped minced pork and scallion, stuffed the newly emptied envelope with white rice, ate his creation then stripped, stuffed and ate another and another till he was full with rice and dumpling wrappers and eight kidneys of minced pork and scallion oozed on his plate. "Rats' brains," he said to his friends, spinning his plate to me on the lazy Susan.

"That's nastEE," Phil said as I ate the rats' brains.

"I told you Dad eats everything," Ripton said.

Boys held fried chicken wings and pushed chopsticks into the joint between the humerus and radius. They held their new skewers and ate, tried to use their chopsticks regularly for fried rice until Leslie asked for forks, talked about the Yankees dominating the season and their baseball in Tompkins Square.

"Where's the bathroom?" Juan asked.

"I'll show you," Ripton answered. He and the bigger boys stopped eating and walked down the narrow steps beside the TV.

"You stupid . . ."—"Nigga . . ."—"He's a bum . . ." we heard in bursts from the cellar. The bigger boys and Ripton came back and Morgan, Dakota and Ricky walked downstairs.

Mr. Liu brought a dozen orange wedges and fortune cookies and placed the bill beside me with only the thinnest façade of a welcoming smile. "Could I have some more tea?" Leslie asked him. Ripton and the bigger boys refused the oranges, crushed the cookies and read their fortunes. A waiter came and poured tea. Leslie ripped open and emptied four packets of sugar into the small cup, spraying white granules onto the stained tablecloth as her hand trembled, stirring the bottom with a chopstick.

"YoMike, what does this mean?" Carlos held his fortune in front of me, pointing to "suitably." "Your talents will be recognized and suitably rewarded."

"In a way that fits, like, if your baseball talent is really good, people will recognize that, and recruit you. Being recruited 'suits' good talent. Does that make sense?"

"NiggaMike," Carlos shook his head.

"Does it make sense?"

"Well, yeah, but I'm not sure about 'suitably.'"

"Ya wanna go outside?" Ripton asked the bigger boys. "Can we go?" he asked us.

"Sure," Leslie answered.

"But stay on this block, near the restaurant," I said.

There was one fortune cookie left—Leslie and I agreed to share it. I counted the cash for our bill.

They hurried out and Leslie showed me our fortune—"Love is like paint, it makes things beautiful when you spread it, but it will dry up if you don't use it."

"Excuse me," a man nearby called over. He was in his midfifties, roundish with thinning white hair moussed back. "Excuse me, but are you with Big Brother, or Fresh Air, or some program?" He was wearing a long-sleeved, blue-and-white-striped button-down shirt. He and his wife, white haired also, were comfortably tanned.

"I hope we weren't making too much noise," I said, but of course we were.

"No, not at all," he said smiling, and his wife the same. "Are you counselors?"

"We're just friends—our sons and their friends," I said.

"Oh, how nice. Bless you," the woman said, drinking plum wine.

"Mr. Rosen, so many boys?" Mr. Liu held my hand again by his stool.

"I'm sorry we were loud," I answered in English.

"They're boys," he said. "But so loud."

Leslie and I looked left and right when we got outside and the boys weren't there. Truck transmissions and air brakes screeched as long haul and short riders slowed to the red light on the Manhattan Bridge exit in front of Grand Sichuan. I couldn't hear but saw our boys playing tag on the raised island between the crowded feeder street in front of us and the main stream of traffic coming off the bridge beneath the triumphal arch and colonnade at its footing, Paris and Rome, an ignored treasure by the architects who planned our Forty-second Street public library. "Let's go," I yelled to the boys, who weren't supposed to be on the other side of the street and couldn't hear me, running beneath the bas-relief of four Plains Indians at full gallop, bows drawn and arrows flying, one buffalo falling, one calf helpless beside her, others fleeing terrified. Buffalo and lion heads, swords and shields, the bows and keels of galleons in low re-

lief lined the sides of the arch. The boys were standing and looking
when I got to them. A half-naked Indian woman stood beside a half-
naked pioneer boy halfway down the column. "YoMike, you see?"
Carlos pointed and smiled, a bit bashful and a bit brazen, only us
guys. The boys smiled, watched me, pointing to a matching couple
on the other side of the arch, different symbols, the same breasts and
nipples.

"What you think?" Phil smiled. "Are these decent?"

"They're art, women have breasts," I answered. "There's nothing
wrong with that."

"But Mike, Iiiii . . ." hesitating. "Would you like to see your sister
up there?" Will asked.

"Dad doesn't have a sister," Ripton said.

"Or—some woman in your family?" Phil asked. "With nipples,
that's decent? I don't like to see that, not wif my family."

"It's art. That's art."

"That dude's *brolic,* that's all I got ta say," Juan said of the winged
man, chiseled. "What's that, up there?" he waved at the arch and
colonnade.

"Suckup, you lookin at the girl," Phil said to Juan.

"I don't know, I've never been here," I said.

"You never been here, you?" Phil asked.

"It's a bridge, genius," Carlos jabbed.

"It's beautiful, but I've never seen it. We'll look this up when we
get home."

"That's okay," Phil answered.

"Let's go, Leslie's waiting," I said.

Ripton started looking for a cab when we got to the other side of
the street.

"Let's get ice cream," Leslie called Ripton back from the street
and the boys together on the sidewalk.

"Where?" Ripton asked.

"Ben and Jerry's," she answered—nearer our home, on Third
Avenue.

"Let's take cabs," Ripton argued.

"Let's walk," I answered.

"Cabs," Ripton insisted.

Will went to Ripton. "Listen to your dads, it's not far," he said.

Twenty minutes later, walking into the ice cream store, lining up between the ropes, I was acutely aware of how un-White we were, the only Spanish and Black people in Ben & Jerry's. This place of friendly Holstein cowherds, shining stainless steel countertops, childlike graphics and eccentric ice creams named for an assortment of chic middle-class concerns wasn't made for inner-city people without money means. Wholesome college-age boys and girls with the gleam of limitless possibilities smiled and said hello, asked what we wanted, scooped, sprinkled and poured for us. Customers glanced at us, courteous in looking away and back to their conversations when I made eye contact, except for one man in one couple. He gaped. The boys joked and poked. "He keeps lookin," Carlos said in a gentle voice, licking his double-scoop Chocolate Fudge Brownie in a sugar cone.

"We're unusual," I said.

"Now you see," Carlos said.

"What?"

"What it's like."

CHAPTER FOUR

# BOOKS | *Autumn 1998*

I nodded, feeling the boundary between the sidewalk and front door of the boutiques, restaurants and cafés that had opened around us the past years, made for the people moving and not those born here. We started home, an August evening with the heat retreating, young people crowding the cafés on Third Avenue, NYU students back for the new semester, pigeons cooing from their first- and second-floor building ledges, little brown birds hunting for discarded donuts and pizza crusts. Half a block away we passed the windows of St. Mark's Bookshop. Bill Bryson's *A Walk in the Woods* was on display and I remembered that I wanted it—I planned and never got around to hiking the length of the Appalachian Trail. "Finish your ice creams," I said, which were anyways mostly gone.

"Why?" Leslie asked.

"Everyone should pick a book, something they like," I said. I wanted Ripton and Morgan to want to start our reading again. I wanted the other boys, as many of them as possible, to fall in love with books.

"No," Ripton said.

"It would be good. Everyone can find a book they like."

"We want to go home already," Ripton said.

Perhaps passion would be unleashed in a book.

"It's a good idea," Leslie agreed with me.

"Are you going to read to everyone?" Morgan asked.

"No, Mor'n, Dad means alone."

Morgan looked to Leslie. He couldn't read well enough alone. "I'll read to you," Leslie assured him.

"We'll both read to you," I said.

"Do we have to?" Ripton asked. The other boys stood disinterested.

I nodded. "We should."

A few of the boys dropped their plastic sundae cups, spoons and paper napkins on the sidewalk, getting ready for the store. Everything scattered. Passersby stared.

"Guys, what's with the littering?" I asked.

"You told us to finish, we done."

"No no no, you don't drop things on the street. That's littering," my voice rose.

"But we done, you told us."

"You don't litter. There's trash cans on every corner. Everywhere. This isn't ghetto."

They bent for their discards and started off to the trash can on the corner. "YoMike, don't embarrass 'em, you don't do that, not in public," Carlos said when they were gone.

"But you don't litter."

"Don't shame nobody, not on the street."

"Then don't litter."

"YoMike, this ain't no joke. Maybe here, but not on Avenue Deez. That ain't right."

"I'm sorry, I didn't mean to pick on you," I said to the three when they got back. "But it's not right to litter."

Leslie and I had book ideas for the younger boys when we got inside, because they were close to Ripton's age.

"That's really good," Morgan said of the Berenstain Bears' *The Big Honey Hunt*.

"That's for little kids, Mor'n," Ripton chided.

"I like this," Ripton showed the kids *Frog and Toad Are Friends*.

I devoured Hardy Boys and Pippi Longstocking stories sitting in a tree one summer. But Pippi, Frank and Joe Hardy were decades out of date and certainly middle class, foreign to these boys, who knew discrimination, hunger, shootings and more.

We wandered the stacks and didn't come across anything I could convince the boys they wanted. I'd heard some of them mouth the newspaper headlines and first parts of the sports pages and they were halting at best, nowhere near grade level.

Having them in our home had our children reading less, cutting into what Ripton did on his own and what we did aloud with him and Morgan. I'd asked the bigger boys, and none of them remembered being read to at home when younger. They didn't own books. They hadn't walked through bookstores with adults. Nor, for that matter, had I heard them speak about fathers.

"*Pimp*, by Iceberg Slim," the lady behind the information counter recommended. "Kids love it. And *Trick Baby*, also by Iceberg Slim."

I'd never heard of Iceberg Slim, but a large portion of a shelf in Literature was dedicated to him. Will and Philippe wanted his books. I tried to sell Carlos on *The Giver*, a perennial on assigned reading lists among New York's private schools. I leafed through its pages and told him what I knew, but he'd have none of it. I hoped he'd pick a book about love, courage, liberty, freedom, security and happiness. Carlos wanted *Shiloh*, the story of an eleven-year-old boy fallen for an abused dog he tries to rescue.

Juan slipped Walter Dean Myers' *Fallen Angels* from the shelf, about a combat unit in Vietnam told by its Black protagonist. "We read him in school," Juan turned the book over. "Not this, another book, it was good, about Malcolm X."

"We should have reading time when we get home," Leslie said.

"What you mean?" Will asked.

"Half an hour, when we get home, with the TV, video games and computer off."

"That's not fair," Ripton said.

"It's a good idea," I said.

"It's a good idea," Leslie said.

We walked past the new restaurants and cafés built to draw customers from around the city and suburbs. It was hard to imagine that the population plummeted by 70 percent here in the seventies. The last gasp of the Jewish community fled Latino and Black immigrations, fearing loss of safety, plummeting property values, Puerto Ricans, Dominicans and Negroes. Landlords set apartment buildings on fire in hope of insurance money or abandoned them to the tax collector. Cars were overturned, burned and left for weeks. Dealers took control of buildings and blocks and eight police were executed on the streets. We walked past designer boutiques and gift stores thriving beside trendy restaurants, bars and clubs. I'd developed Red Square, where we ordered Chinese, in the late eighties, and had kept a construction-progress photograph taken from beside Mrs. Zawin's liquor store on the corner of Avenue B, looking down five hundred feet of empty lot along Houston Street where we'd started building. Our residential tower was coming out of the ground. One mess of a man near the lens carried a brown bag, Thunderbird or Wild Irish Rose from Mrs. Zawin's. Another, his back to the camera, was urinating against the fence. No one else was on the sidewalk. A decade later and a decade after that pedestrians, bike riders, skaters, skateboarders and kids on scooters are constant. During our first winter in the Christodora, I took a photograph standing on the corner at Tenth Street and Avenue B in front of the greengrocer looking towards Avenue A. Ripton was one and a few months old, Leslie pushing him in a stroller towards me. Not a car was parked or traveling along Tenth Street. A decade later and a decade after that, cars fill the streets and there's no room to park.

At home, we gathered in the living room. "How long we gotta read?" Will asked.

"Half an hour," Leslie said. She walked to the kitchen and set the oven timer.

Carlos, Will and Philippe sat on the sofa with a formality of students in a school library. Juan sat on the stuffed dogs and Ripton on the arm chair and ottoman. I sat with Bill Bryson at our table beneath the mezzanine. Leslie read to Morgan in the TV room.

"'You shoot its head clean off?' Dara Lynn asks. She's like that," Carlos read quite aloud and slowly. The other boys didn't seem to notice but I couldn't concentrate.

"Carlos?"

"Dad chews real slow before he answers. 'Not quite,' he says, and goes on eating. Which is when I leave the table." Carlos doesn't hear me.

"Carlos?" a bit louder.

He and the other boys looked at me. "Can you read silently?"

"I can't, Mike, you know that, rah?"

I didn't.

"How you not know that? You seen me."

"What's 'inevitably' mean?" Will asked.

I explained.

"YoMike, what's 'slightest'?" Carlos asked.

Juan and Ripton didn't ask about vocabulary. The others went on word after word until I went to the kitchen, sharpened pencils and handed one to each boy. "Circle the words you don't know, we'll go over them afterwards."

"I don't need it," Ripton answered.

"Me, too," Juan said.

"Just take it, in case," I said, holding out pencils.

The oven timer rang and the boys closed their books. Not one seemed to finish a sentence, paragraph, scene or chapter—they stood and left for the TV room, tossing their books and pencils near me on the table. No one asked the meaning of words. I turned off the timer then looked at their books. Will had read four pages with eight or more words circled on each. Carlos and Philippe had done essentially the same. Juan read nine pages and circled two, three or no words per page. I couldn't tell how far Ripton had gone in *The Korean War*, a children's history, but he hadn't circled any words. From one of her child-rearing books, Leslie told me that a person is beyond their level if there are three or more words she or he doesn't know per page.

Leslie and Morgan came to the living room to finish a chapter.

The boys had started a video, *The Sandlot*, one of our favorites, about an endless summer baseball game, and Ripton and Phil were laughing uncontrollably. Their laugh was the same, exploding in fits, bordering on awkward, the type others laugh with because it's infectious—but too much. I wondered if Philippe had the sensory issues Ripton supposedly did.

I wondered why Juan, silent in his hurt way, could read much better than his friends. I hoped Ripton and Morgan didn't learn to distance themselves from reading—that it wasn't cool, because only sports, video games and girls were.

The four bigger boys slept over that Saturday night, then the next Friday and Saturday nights. Ripton and Morgan's summer camp ended and the bigger boys moved in. It's nothing we planned or spoke about, only that our children didn't have to wake up for camp the next morning. The boys were hours from bed when Leslie went upstairs each night. They were sound asleep when I left in the morning and still asleep around 8:00 a.m., when Jonny came and Leslie left. Jonny poured bowls of cereal and milk, scooped out ice cream for breakfast, served The Rock's chocolate chip cookies Leslie had learned to make from the WWF's new cookbook.

By the end of August, the bigger boys went home every couple days to change clothes. I noticed newer clothes on Will, Philippe and Juan, new Jordans they left in the hallway. If Carlos had them, he was saving his new clothes for school.

The boys woke up early the Saturday before Labor Day, hurried through breakfast and insisted we get to the park. Enough kids were there by 8:30 to make teams. They played until we brought pizzas, drinks and cookies for lunch. We suggested Mr. Liu's for dinner, but our crew insisted on staying in the park. They wanted McDonald's. Leslie called the one on First Avenue from her cell phone. The person on the other end of the line refused to take our order, insisting McDonald's couldn't deliver to a park. Leslie tried to explain the baseball game—McDonald's would have none of it. We bought more pizza and drinks on Avenue A.

We were back in the park early the next morning. Leslie and I insisted on Chinatown that night. The boys, unwilling to admit exhaustion, reluctantly agreed to break at seven.

"We'll be quiet," I told Mr. Liu when the same twelve of us walked in. The kids ordered the identical foods and no one disagreed when Leslie and I suggested ice cream at Ben & Jerry's.

"But no books, rah?" Philippe needed to make sure.

I'd been a failure at enforcing reading time, Leslie much better, but reading had drifted anyways.

The boys turned on the baseball highlights as soon as we got home. The Yankees had lost to the White Sox in Chicago while we'd been out. "A bum," Carlos shouted when sports TV showed the Yankees' Hideki Irabu on the mound. Irabu was supposed to have become a hero when the Yankees signed him as an ace pitcher from Japan. He hadn't been terrible but he was no Cy Young. "Bum," Carlos yelled more energetically.

"He made it to the majors, he's not a bum," I said.

"A bum. I get bigger, I pipe that nigga," Carlos said.

"Anyone who makes it to the Yankees—"

"A bum."

"If you make it to the Yankees—"

"A bum. YoMike, I been thinkin, seriously, let's make a barbeque tomorrow. Labor Day and all, that's what we done in my house. When my father was alive, we always had a barbeque."

"Yo, that's good. But it gotta be Spanish," Phil was excited. "Not Mike's food, no salmon and crazy spices."

"We gotta make *moro*," Will said.

"I ain't eatin *moro*," Carlos said. "I hate black beans, black rice, I ain't Dominican. You and Phil eat *moro*, you almost Black, nigga."

"*Moro*'s the best. What wrong wif you? You want *arroz con gandules*?"

"My moms makes pick beans and yellow rice," Carlos corrected. "*Gandules* is pigeon peas, stupid."

"*Moro*," Phil said, "two against one."

"No, nigga, Juan's Puerto Rican, he gets to vote, two against two."

"Juan's Black. Your father's Black, rah?—you're Black," looking at Juan. "Look at him!" Phil insisted.

"Bullshit, you stupid. Juan's moms' Puerto Rican. He don't live with his dad, he don't see his dad. Juan, you Black or Puerto Rican?"

"Puerto Rican," Juan answered.

"Bullshit, you don't know Spanish. Your Spanish sucks. Speak Spanish!"

"I can understand. I can talk, good enough."

"Bullshit. *Los Yankees no saben jugar pelota. Los Red Sox son los mejores . . . ganarán este año!* What did I say?"

"The Red Sox suck," Juan smiled.

"You Black, son," Philippe said. "You can't vote. *Moro.*"

"I can't eat black beans, nigga, no joke," Carlos said.

Ripton changed the channel. Carlos and Will called their mothers for recipes. I looked over their lists to see what we had and what we needed to shop for. "*Jamón*" was on both lists—that wasn't chicken. "Ja-mon?" I said.

The bigger boys laughed. "Ha-mone," Philippe corrected.

"YoMike, you got Spanish kids, we almost livin here and you don't speak no Spanish? What you learnin Chinese, I don't see no Chinese kids here?" Carlos asked.

"Ham, right? Leslie doesn't eat ham," I said.

"I don't eat what?" Leslie walked into the TV room.

"Ham, we're planning a Labor Day dinner," I said.

"We're makin Spanish food," Carlos said.

"You're making ham?" Leslie asked.

"No, for rice and beans," Phil said.

"Can you leave it out?" Leslie asked.

"We can use pork," Phil said.

Not that Leslie kept kosher, but she grew up in a home that was and nonkosher animals were beyond her stomach. "How about putting it on the side?" she asked but told us. "I don't like it."

"My moms said you cook it wif the rice, for flavor," Carlos answered.

"Then make some for me without it," Leslie finished.

The boys and I went to the supermarket in the morning for bottles of Goya's adobo and sofrito, cans of Goya's pink beans. We bought a bag of yellow rice, chicken pieces, green peppers, onions, garlic, ham, hotdogs, hamburger meat and buns. I went to the fish store and bought fresh salmon and jumbo shrimp.

When the boys finished baseball we sat at the kitchen table slicing onions and green peppers. I peeled and crushed garlic. "Smaller," I said, looking at the chunks of onion Phil was leaving.

"Nigga, this is Mexican work," he waved his knife.

"Stop it, no racism."

"Racism? It's not racism, it's true."

"It is racist. We're the same."

"YoMike, if we're the same, look in a restaurant, who you see cuttin vegetables and washin dishes?" Carlos asked.

"And cleanin toilets?" Phil asked. "Mexicans aren't the same, they do anything. If it's true, it's not racist, rah?"

"That's economic injustice—because they come over the border, risk their lives for a better life, send money home. Just because it happens, that doesn't mean it's right."

"Mexicans do anything, dogs. They work for nothin, ruin it for everybody. You know it's true," Phil said.

"It's true," Ripton agreed.

"Listen, Ripton—"

"Listen, Ripton," Ripton imitated me. "Listen, Ripton—"

"It's not a joke."

"It's not a joke," Ripton said.

"YoMike, who be washin dishes in restaurants, you see Puerto Ricans or Dominicans doin that work? We won't work for nothin, nigga. It's Mexicans," Carlos said.

The boys laughed, Ripton as loudly as Phil. "Never gonna catch me washin dishes," Phil said.

"I used to wash dishes—" I started.

"Here we go, a lecture," Ripton smiled to his friends.

"I washed dishes in two restaurants. I used to get up in the dark, get to work and run the dishwasher. That was the first place. Then I ran the dishwasher in a dinner restaurant"—I heard myself, a guy in a suit with money to spend—"It gave me money in high school, which let me get to college, which let me get jobs after college that pay for what you eat here, the beds you sleep in. I didn't have problems washing dishes—I hope you don't. I don't want to hear that. It's not who you are, it's what you do."

"It's who you know, Mike, who you kiddin?" Carlos said.

"It's what you do, Carlos. How smart you are, how hard you work."

"I see how it is, it's who you know," Carlos said. "You White, you work in a corporation. You work wif Leslie's father. You Mexican, you wash dishes."

"That's not the way it is. I took over a failing business—"

"Mike's tight," Phil laughed.

"Cut the onions smaller," I said to him and walked into the living room. I calmed down, then came back to sauté the onions, garlic and peppers in olive oil, to add the spices and follow the recipes their mothers had given. We baked chicken with adobo, sautéed the ham and put aside some of the rice and beans for Leslie. I grilled the hamburgers and hotdogs, salmon and shrimp on the terrace.

"This is food," Carlos said when we came to the table beneath the mezzanine, the first meal we'd all sat for together in our apartment. We cleaned up and sent the bigger boys home at eight o'clock, the first night they'd not slept over since camp ended. Ripton and Morgan took separate baths and Leslie read *Frog and Toad* adventures in their sofa bed on the second floor, Toad looking for spring around the corner.

Leslie picked Morgan and Ripton up from Heschel the next afternoon. They wanted pizza, their regular after-school snack around the corner from school, before hailing a cab to come home. But they also wanted to hurry to Tompkins Square—the regular kids had agreed to meet for baseball.

The house was empty when I arrived home at seven. I changed out of my suit and went to the park, where children seemed to have survived their first school day. The bigger boys came for dinner and to watch the beginning of the Yankees playing the Red Sox. The Yankees were so far ahead in the standings that the Red Sox couldn't catch up, but the division rivalry and loyalties remained intense, in our house most between Phil and the rest of the boys. I turned on the TV in the kitchen and pulled my exercise bike near it; I'd been riding for an hour most days.

The bigger boys came each day after school. "Carlos is here, is Ripton home?" the doorman would announce. Or he'd hand the house phone to one of the visiting boys. "Is Ripton home? Can we come up and play?" We sent the bigger boys home by eight o'clock on school nights, got our boys bathed and into bed with books.

The last day of the regular Major League Baseball season was the last Sunday in September, nearly three weeks after the start of school. The Yankees played Tampa Bay, a game with no meaning in the standings, but if the Yankees won they'd set a record for the most regular season victories in the history of the American League. The boys wanted to watch, but wanted more to be in Tompkins Square.

I got on the exercise bike when we came back, and Leslie went down to the corner grocer because we didn't have enough milk. "House phone," I yelled to the boys in the TV room when it began to ring—they weren't going to hear it over the whirl of my bike and the noise of the game.

Ripton ran to answer it. "Hello? Who?" he asked and then shouted, "Will, do you know Kindu?"

"What?" Will yelled back.

"Kindu, a kid," Ripton hollered. "You wanna let him up?"

Will walked towards Ripton. "Sure," he said softly. "He goes to school wif us."

"Who's coming up?" I asked Will, sweat dripping off me, pooling on both sides of the bike. I would have gotten up for a tee shirt if an adult were coming, but kept riding.

Leslie came in with a boy behind her, Philippe's size, the tallest of our bigger boys, darker with short nappy hair, his face rectangular and strong. He reminded me of a photograph from grad school, a Nuer tribesman sitting on another man's shoulders; this boy had the same face—regal. Will and the boy touched hands and shoulders. "This is Kindu, Will's friend," Leslie introduced Ripton, me and the boy. "We met in the elevator."

"Hello, Ripken." Kindu shook Ripton's hand. "Hello, Sir," he said and walked the few steps up to my bike. I dried my hand.

# CHAPTER FIVE

# SPLIVY

*December 1998*

"Ripton," Will corrected.

"Ripton," Kindu repeated. "Sorry."

"Yo, Kindu!" Carlos bounded in from the TV room, wiggled and hugged with Kindu.

"*Do ya smell—*" Phil hurried in.

"*. . . what The Rock is cookin?*" Kindu smiled.

"*What do you think . . . ?*" Phil started.

"*. . . It doesn't matter what you think,*" Kindu, Will, Carlos and Ripton finished The Rock's line.

"Corlears," Will said to me—Junior High School 56 Corlears. "We all together."

"I went ta your house," Kindu said to Will. "Your sister knew where you at, she tookt me here."

"I met Kindu in the elevator," Leslie said.

"Mrs. Rosen askt where I was goin cause I pressed Penthouse. I said, 'to visit Ripken.'"

"*Ripton,*" Will corrected.

"Sorry—Ripton."

"Call me Leslie."

"My mom's '*Gruss*,'" Ripton said.

"What?" Kindu asked.

"My last name's *Gruss*," Leslie explained.

"Mrs. Gruss," Kindu said.

"Leslie."

The boy smiled again, brightly as Phil, exactly the same, without a trace of ridicule.

---

Summer then autumn had gone and with them our first magical season of baseball in Tompkins Square. The Christmas to New Year season was here, the city sometimes frozen but then only for hours or a day. New York was more often overcast. The initial nervousness of our home filled with strange boys had given way to that being normal life, and an unusual quiet came with winter. We no longer ordered Chinese as often and as much, we no longer stocked milk and orange juice for a dozen other kids.

Ricky and Dakota, both Ripton's age, kept coming two or three times a week. The bigger boys—Carlos, Will, Phil, Juan and suddenly Kindu—came every day. They were five and six years older than Ripton, yet he and Will sat and played video games together, the others sometimes joining in. Leslie and I knew the bigger boys came for our home as much or more than anything else, but they seemed like good children, the older ones friends from school.

Carlos, in the seventh grade, had met the other bigger boys in Tompkins Square only a month before Ripton took us to the field. He'd been at the same school with them for a year, starting there in an honors program for gifted students.

Will, Juan and Philippe told me they'd been best friends since second grade at an elementary school on Avenue B. They began seventh grade at Junior High School 56 Corlears Junior High School (an inexplicably official name) the year before we met them. So did Kindu Dupree Jones, who lived in the Seward Park public housing projects south of Delancey, on the southern border of the Lower East Side, nearly a neighborhood away. But Kindu was in a different section and didn't get to know them till he was transferred into class with Will and Juan. Philippe was transferred to the section Kindu had been in.

I asked the boys how they all became friends. Kindu said he spent lunch periods visiting with his old classmates, but they were smoking weed: "All they would talk about was what it felt like to be high," Kindu said. He didn't want to hear that; he knew too much. He watched Will, Juan, Philippe and Carlos doing The Rock impersonations, cocking their eyebrows, furling their brows.

A few weeks after the school year ended Kindu had gone looking for Will in our apartment.

---

In winter, when they were toddlers, Leslie and I dressed Ripton and Morgan in Dr. Denton's, those furry pajamas with feet and plasticized soles. My parents had dressed me the same. But when Ripton started at Heschel, and Morgan in his toddler program, Leslie decided to save time by dressing them each evening in their next day's school clothes—underpants, socks, tees or button-down shirts, blue jeans or chinos for Ripton, Morgan in his gray Lands' End sweatpants.

I didn't complain. Leslie put more time into the boys. She normally took them to school four mornings each week to my one. And she took them every day when I traveled. She was also a partner in an OB-GYN practice, and if it was easier for her to dress our boys to sleep in street clothes I felt I had no right to object.

"Brilliant!" her father once said, impressed at the efficiency of street clothes for sleep.

---

I threaded the faucet end of the Python onto the spout and unlooped hose through the kitchen and short hall into the living room where Kindu was shrouded in a plump comforter, asleep across the love seat and ottoman, feet escaping in white socks, the ebony of his shins in bands between whites. Carlos and Phil were whispering, awake beneath their comforters in early-morning voices near noon on the pullout sofa. I stretched hose to the aquarium in the corner between Kindu's chair and the bed, sunk the Python into the gravel, left to turn on the water and returned. "YoMike, we wanna aks you something," Carlos smiled, sweetly conspiratorial.

"For sure," Philippe flapped his eyebrows. "We wanna know why your home clothes are so old school?"

"What do you mean?" I pushed the Python into more gravel-sucking mulm.

"We know why," Phil traded glances with Carlos.

Kindu rolled on his side, watched me at the aquarium and pulled his du-rag back down to his ears and lower on his forehead. "What time is it?" he asked.

"YoKindu, we aksin Mike," Carlos started, keeping his eyes on me, "why his home clothes are old school?" grinning in a singsong voice.

Ripton, Will and Leslie walked in from the kitchen, the chorus from off stage, and sat themselves around the edges of the sofa bed, watching.

"Why you think, Kindu?" Carlos persisted.

Kindu, too kind to answer, pulled the comforter over his head and curled tight.

I hadn't thought of my home clothes—they were what I put on at home. I did pay attention to my suits, with vanity; Armani, and once I could afford more, a tailor near Avenue A whose shop was a shrine to Frank Sinatra. He wore pants waisted high above his hips, thin leather bracers, and in summer, no shirt over his fully tattooed torso. He kept bolts of beautiful fabric. Leslie's mother kept me in a supply of French cuff shirts. I collected antique cuff links. I was particular about ties, socks and shoes. I was particular about everything. Except my home clothes.

"Money," Phil coughed.

I hadn't realized what was obvious to them. Nearly all my home clothes, pleated pants, tees and button shirts, were older than the bigger boys. Some were from when I'd been in high school, the rest from college. I'd frozen my personal life then. I wore canvas sneakers. I didn't own a pair of jeans.

"Mike's *splivy*, dressin casual," Kindu sat up in the chair.

"It's true, Sweetie. You could use an update," Leslie was kind.

I kept cleaning my tanks.

The boys told Jonny about the prodding. "I'll outfit you, Mike. You'll be a new man," he told me a day or so later. "You'll have to change this retro thing," and he suggested options. "You'll super-like Prada," Jonny told me.

I hadn't heard of it. We took a cab that weekend to Madison and Seventieth Street. A swank salesman on the men's floor made eyes with Jonny. "Can I help you?" he asked our children's babysitter, considering me skeptically, arguably the sugar daddy.

"My friend needs clothes," Jonny answered.

The salesman sized me more. "What are you interested in?" he seemed skeptical.

"Shirts," but I wasn't sure, looking at broad collars flapping down to shirt shoulders. "And pants." The ones on display were impossibly narrow and glistening.

"Everything," Jonny interrupted. "Pants, shoes, short- and long-sleeve tees, button-down shirts, a vest, a jacket, a coat. We need a wardrobe."

I'd never shopped for a wardrobe. I cringed, calculating costs I didn't know but feared.

"I see," the salesman lilted. He and Jonny parked me in the changing room and walked the sales floor together, coming back with shining fabrics I never knew existed. I emerged to a mirror and their review at each ensemble. I bought a new wardrobe and Jonny a coat. I left wearing my old clothes.

The boys were looking for my shopping bags.

"Holla at your boy!" Kindu singsonged. "Prada? What you buyin? Mike goin splivy," he teased.

"YoMike, what you buy?" Carlos stood by Kindu.

"What you get?" Kindu started picking through the layers of tissue paper and Prada tags at the top of the bags.

"Shirts, pants."

"Good for you, Sweetie," Leslie came to my rescue. "What did you buy?"

"Shirts, tees, pants."

"Looks like Mike bought the store," Philippe said.

"You want to do a fashion show?" Leslie asked. She and her older sister put on fashion shows when they came back from shopping with Ria at Bloomingdale's.

"I don't think so," I wanted to hide.

"Come'on, Mike, do a fashion show!" Philippe teased.

"YoMike, you lecturin about money and goin ta Pradas? You gotta do a show," Carlos urged.

"I'm not doing that."

"You takin us to Pradas?" Kindu asked.

I grimaced, grinned and shook my head.

"We not good enough?" Carlos smiled.

"When you get older, get good jobs and work hard, you can go to Prada as often as you want." I was lecturing. Pushing back for my embarrassment. But I'd come to understand later that something else was also at play with the bigger boys; they cared. We'd learn that little else was more important to them than dressing well when they went out. It was wrong, disconcerting to them, for this man they cared about to be so disheveled. They were looking out for me.

---

Parent-teacher conferences at Heschel started halfway into the fall semester—fifteen-minute private meetings with each of our boys' teachers in their classrooms, sitting on children's chairs drawn up to a children's table. These meetings always began with the good, then segued to the bad. We'd gone through enough of them to know, particularly with Ripton, that the little good teachers could find was a preamble towards "Won't stay quiet"—"Won't stand in line"— "Won't sit up"—"Won't keep his hands to himself"—"Won't stop grabbing kids by the head."

The Heschel curriculum for preschoolers and kindergarten kids began in English. The youngest children were taught simple Hebrew prayers and Jewish customs surrounding the Sabbath and holidays, then the Hebrew alphabet, reading, speaking and writing, liturgy and theology until, by middle school, the children were intended to be bilingual and half the courses given in Hebrew.

Ripton, his teacher told us as we sat uncomfortably on tiny chairs, wasn't showing an interest in prayer, theology or Hebrew language. He was in danger of falling irreparably behind. Leslie and I agreed to put more emphasis on his homework and I suggested that we find a Hebrew-speaking babysitter. I thought the language might sink in from hearing; both of our boys would become more readily bilingual. Yuval Boim answered the advertisement we placed. He was born in Israel, raised as a teenager in Houston, studied acting and recently graduated from Boston College two years behind Jonny McGovern. They knew each other only in passing, Yuval was attracted to more conventional theater and Jonny to edgier performance. Each came to New York to make his career.

Yuval started picking our boys up from school, taking them for pizza nearby, speaking Hebrew and helping Ripton with his Hebrew homework. But once our boys were back on the Lower East Side they didn't want to be embarrassed by Hebrew, certainly not in front of their friends. Aside from an hour to ninety minutes two times a week, Yuval didn't have much opportunity to perfect our children's bilingualism.

It didn't take Yuval long to let us know he didn't like the other boys around, bigger or smaller. He didn't like the crassness of their speech or behavior. He didn't see good coming to our children from friendship with them.

---

One cool and drizzling afternoon in early November, within memory of the Yankees' run through the playoffs and World Series championship, before it was too cold for baseball, Jonny managed to get

Morgan, Ripton, Will, Kindu and himself into one cab to Paragon for baseballs and batting gloves and into another for their trip home. He sat in front both ways, separated from the boys by the clear safety divider.

"YoDavon!" Will screamed through the open window passing Union Square, recognizing their friend from Tompkins Square, the Tides and Jacob Riis housing.

Davon didn't hear.

"Faggot!" Will screamed louder.

Davon looked.

"You gay!" Kindu whooped.

Jonny paid the driver in front of the Christodora House. He made sure our children were safely across the street and into the building. He grabbed Will and Kindu when the elevator doors closed, shoving them against the back wall. "I'm a faggot, get it?" he screamed into their faces. "I'm a fuckin faggot, you got a problem with that?" He let go but kept the boys intimidated against the wall, his jaw clenched, poking a finger into each of their chests. "You got a problem with that?"

"No, Sir," Kindu answered. He was more or less telling the truth. He wasn't particularly biased.

"No, Sir," Will answered. But he did have a problem.

Ripton and Morgan were silent.

At home that night, no one told us about the trip home and the elevator ride. The main topic was a business trip I was taking the next day, not because I was leaving, but because Ripton told Leslie he wanted her to rent a stretch limousine to take our group to the airport and the rest of them around New York after I left. He'd gotten the idea from a local television commercial for a car service. The bigger boys were excited. Leslie had priced out stretch limos—we needed the large size because the next smaller fit six and we were more than that. The minimum rental was four hours. Bridge and tunnel tolls and drinks—sodas, beer and cocktails—were extra and the car came stocked. "It would be fun," Leslie encouraged me.

"It would be great," Philippe coaxed.

"YoMike, let's do it," Carlos recommended.

"How much is it?" I asked Leslie.

"Not too much," she answered. "Less than you think." She smiled, Sylvester hiding Tweety Bird in his throat.

I did but didn't want to know the cost—if it were expensive, I wouldn't be able to get the money out of my head. I tried to convince myself it wasn't really extravagant. Kids graduating high school managed to rent limousines, at least suburban and Uptown kids; there weren't many stretch limousines rolling around the projects with Black and Latino kids waving out the windows come June. I twisted myself up over fun, affordability, conveying appropriate messages of middle-class modesty and my northern New England prudence. "Please, Dad," Ripton implored.

"It'll be fun," Leslie said. "Everyone wants to go."

"When do we need to decide?" I asked.

"I reserved a car so they don't run out. We can cancel till noon tomorrow." Leslie was highly functional. She gave a bashful smile.

We planned to leave for the airport at six o'clock the next night. The boys woke slowly for baseball that morning. Carlos, in a bad mood, rooted around what we'd been calling the "*sports room,*" the long and narrow space behind the foyer designed as a study for Leslie and me. We'd used it to change our boys' diapers and store their clothes until Ripton became obsessed with fishing and its paraphernalia. It became his place for tens of rods and more reels, tackle boxes crammed with fresh and saltwater flies and lures appropriate for blue gill to blue marlin. Ripton needed to be prepared. When baseball began we put plastic tubs on the floor, one for balls and batting gloves, another for mitts, one for bats and one for the catcher's equipment—mask, chest protector and leg guards—Ripton insisted he'd probably require. The equipment rarely ended up in the right bins, or any bin at all, and then only when Elena, our main cleaning woman, did the rearranging. "*Coño,*" Carlos growled. "Fuck." He'd been miserable for days, avoiding explanation.

"What's up?" I surprised him.

"I'm lookin for the football. I seen it."

I'd owned a football since college, deflated, never particularly good.

"No, I mean the past few days. You've been in a lousy mood."

"Nothin. You seen the ball?"

"No, but it's lousy, if you find it."

"I wanna play."

"Why are you in a bad mood, Carlos?"

He stopped looking around the room and turned to me.

"My moms makin me go see my father, that's why. I hate it."

I didn't know about his father. "Where is he?"

"In the Bronx. Near where we was at."

"Who is he?"

"Some asshole my mom got wif—got pregnant, rah? He don't care about me."

"Who doesn't care about you?" Ripton stood beneath the doorway lintel.

"Nothin," Carlos said.

"Who?"

"Nothin."

"Scuuuse me"—Ripton sounded hurt.

"You seen that football?" Carlos asked him. Ripton thought he had, and they searched together but couldn't find it.

"Can we go to Paragon?" Ripton came to me.

"Now?" I asked because his face and tone said so.

"We wanna play."

"What about baseball?"

"We're gonna play baseball, but it's football season," Ripton answered.

The NFL season had begun in mid-September. Aside from Phil insisting he liked the Jets, the rest of the boys were Giants fans. The team was mediocre.

"Okay," I agreed and the boys threw the new ball around when we got back to the park. They did stop for a short baseball game, the bigger boys and Ripton trying left-handed swings for the home run fence. They switched to a game of touch and quit at three o'clock to crowd our two downstairs showers, a house full of boys with towels wrapped around their waists.

"Can we use your iron?" Kindu asked Leslie.

I'd never seen Leslie with an iron. I could never master anything other than the flat panels of shirts and pant legs. Angles, buttons, collars and sleeves were obstacles. Elena, who cooked a few dinners each week in addition to cleaning, also ironed the clothes we asked. My dress shirts were laundered, ironed, folded and boxed at the cleaners in Red Square. "Sure," Leslie answered. It was with the ironing board and household cleaning supplies in the closet next to our washer and dryer.

Standing in their boxers, Juan then Kindu ironed the blue jeans they'd been wearing around our home and their rumpled tees.

"Why are you doing that?" I asked.

"Ironing," Kindu answered.

"I know, but why?"

"Goin in a limo, Mike, gotta look splivy."

"But it's us. Nobody's gonna see you." I knew better, but tried.

"It's a limo," Juan said.

"Big money, dogs, for a stretch limo. Derek Jeter be in a stretch limo, rich niggas in stretch limos," Carlos smiled.

"We goin in style," Philippe said. "Big style . . . Kindu, dogs, will you do these?" Philippe held out his blue jeans. "And this?" Philippe draped a blue and red polo over the narrower end of the ironing board. Kindu started to press his friend's clothes.

"I want you guys to read, I want you to think. It's not how you look." I turned around for Leslie, who wasn't there. "That's not why we rented a limo. Money doesn't mean who you are."

"Look at you, wearin Pradas and Armanis, what you talkin about?" Carlos reprimanded, half jokingly.

"I do, and I make my money, and I studied and went to college and graduate school and work hard. I want you guys to study. That's all. I don't want this ghetto bullshit of bling bling. Like money comes."

"It does, work the government," Phil said, "government give you money, gotta outsmart the man."

"Bling bling, dogs," Carlos smiled. "Mike, you somethin special."

"Cash Money Millionaires," Kindu teased, still at his ironing. "I'm gonna make my own money too, down on the street corner I know that," and handed the newly pressed jeans to Phil. He fitted the front of the polo onto the top of the ironing board.

"Kindu, dogs," Phil smiled with admiration, pulling on his pants.

"That's not funny," I said.

"I be on my grind, don't you worry," Kindu grinned. "Broome Street."

"*I got ten around my neck*, Lil Wayne, dogs, *Bling!*" Phil quoted.

"*Bling!*" Ripton repeated. "*Ten around my neck.*"

"Riding in a limousine doesn't say a damn thing about who you are, except maybe you have bad taste," I answered.

"Oh, Dad's gonna ruin it," Ripton said. "Here it comes."

"Don't Oh-Dee, Mike," Will said.

"I want you guys to read, I don't want you to fall into this bullshit of limousines."

"Mike's tight," Phil jabbed a little.

"I don't like limousines, it's not what I wanna be teaching you guys."

"So forget it," Carlos said.

"No, I don't mean that." It was more complicated. I didn't want to rent the limousine but I did because I didn't want to break the fun. I wanted the adventure. I didn't want them to want it. "I'm ambivalent."

"Dad killed it," Ripton said.

"I think it could be fun," I said, feeling I'd mishandled the whole topic.

"Work hard, play hard, that's what Michael means," Leslie said.

Her answer satisfied the boys. Kindu handed Philippe his pressed polo shirt. Will ironed his clothes, then Carlos ironed the Mecca tee and black jeans he'd been wearing the last few weeks, matched to a pair of black lace boots and a black denim jacket he kept in the house. Ripton picked a pair of Mecca jeans and an Ecko tee from the armoire in the TV room where we kept his clothes. Morgan wore his Lands' End gray sweatpants and a blue tee. Leslie dressed in Eileen Fisher—she always dressed in Eileen Fisher pants and tops, the clothing designer who kept an original store across Tompkins Square on Ninth Street even as she grew far beyond our neighborhood. Leslie was a regular at the twice-a-year Ninth Street store sales. She liked Eileen Fisher's soft fabrics and clean lines—cotton twill, stretch cotton, silk. She chose cotton jerseys and cropped stretch crepe pants for home, more formal tops, jackets and pants for work. She favored softly scooped and sometimes a modestly split neck. Leslie was slender, five foot seven, blue eyed, light skinned and lightly freckled in the way red-haired people often are, though she preferred to think of herself as blond. I'd called her *"Blondie"* for the few years in college when we were friends before lovers. Her hair was an opalescent shade between the two. She'd kept it long through her medical internship and residency, cutting it to above the shoulder when she joined the Downtown gynecology practice she'd become a partner in. That's also when she started wearing Eileen Fisher.

"Your limousine is here," the doorman called up from the lobby.

A late-middle-aged man, tall and strong in a black suit and five-panel chauffeur hat, waited for us in the lobby. "Mr. Rosen?" he looked at me.

"Yes, Sir," I said, surrounded by Ripton and the bigger boys.

"I'm Mr. Crawford," he told us in a Jamaican accent, "I'll be driving you this evening." The other elevator car arrived and Leslie, Morgan, Ricky and Dakota came out. Mr. Crawford opened the lobby doors for us and hurried to his car, taking one lane of traffic in our two-way street because it was too long to fit into the parking spot beside the fire hydrant. He opened its curbside rear door.

"Damn!" Will said. "We be stylin!"

"Damn, dogs," Philippe rested his hand against the black shine, glided it across the car, across the hood and the other boys followed.

"Right," Juan lilted, and the nine boys stepped back onto the sidewalk, admiring their limousine.

An early twentyish man in a pinstripe Yankees hat at a kilter to his thin, brown face, its brim flat with the manufacturer's sticker shining from the white bottom, in a navy blue Yankees hoodie and a fire engine red tee hanging below, close to his knees, came around the Ninth Street corner pulled by a brindled pit bull in a barbed steel collar. Two others came around a few steps behind, dressed as the first young man, who stopped with his dog and friends, taking in the limousine, Leslie and me. "That yours?" the young man asked.

"For now," I answered.

The dog wagged its tail and tugged at its leash towards me. "Is it good here?" the man nodded backwards, towards our lobby.

"What do you mean?" I asked.

"My moms used to swim here, back in the day."

"When it was a settlement house?" I asked, because the building had a pool then.

"Yeah, a community center. Somethin. Then it became *Con-Do-Min-Ee-Ums*," he rolled the last slowly, like a sickness. "That's what my moms says."

Leslie and I were silent, the boys on the sidewalk listening. "There used to be a pool," I answered.

"The Panthers used to give free breakfast here, and teach kids to read. I remember that. Before the rich folk moved in. You have a good night," the man was friendly. He, the dog and others walked on.

Mr. Crawford shut the rear door and the boys rolled down the windows on both sides of the car. "Can we go to Avenue Deez?" Carlos asked.

"I really have to get to the airport," I said.

"We can on the way home," Leslie offered.

"Dennis!" Ripton shouted to a neighbor who'd come out to smoke.

"YoDennis," the other boys rushed to the window, shouted and waved.

"Whereyagoin?" Dennis smiled then sucked at his cigarette. He was in his after-work parachute pants and tee. The gray tuft of hair on his chin and three-day beard suggested a musician or sculptor, but Dennis was a broker on the floor of the New York Stock Exchange.

"The airport, taking Dad," Ripton answered. The boys liked Dennis, approachable early evenings into the night and through the weekend on our stoop at his cigarette breaks.

"Whatswiththelimo?" Dennis exhaled.

"We stylin," Philippe answered.

"Chinaorisrael?" Dennis asked.

"China," Carlos answered too loudly.

"Haveagoodtrip," Dennis waved to me.

"Don't yell when we're goin down the street, okay?" I said to the boys as the limousine started, slowed at the stoplight and carved a long arch west on Tenth Street. Leslie and the boys dropped me at the airport and rode back into the city. They toured Midtown, past St. Patrick's Cathedral and Rockefeller Center, Grand Central Station and the Chrysler Building, through the bling of Times Square with our boys hanging out and waving wildly at the WWF theme restaurant, past Madison Square Garden where Patrick Ewing held a waning court then down the West Side Highway beside the World Trade Towers in white light, around the tip of the island, up through the South Street Seaport and around Corlears Hook to the Houston Street exit of the expressway, up the length of Avenue D, down the entirety of Avenue C then up Avenue B till the limousine stopped again in front of our apartment building, Mr. Crawford opened the back door, the boys got out and Leslie signed the payment voucher.

"Howwasit?" Dennis was still outside smoking.

"You have to stop," Leslie pointed to his cigarette.

"IknowIknow, Imtryin, I stopped drinking, I stopped drugs, Igotta-havesomethin," he inhaled but turned the cigarette into his palm and slid his hand behind his back. He and Leslie frequently had the same conversation.

---

New York was much colder when I came home. Snow banks piled at the side of the highway, and from the black crust I knew the storm had come a couple of days earlier. The snow was white on unmoved cars through the Lower East Side, parking regulations suspended for the late-December blizzard.

It stayed cold over the next days and deepened into Christmas. We took Ripton and Morgan skiing in Montana, then to visit my parents in Florida. They'd moved a few years earlier, my father's arthritis grown too severe for Vermont winters at the end of a dirt road. Heating with wood and other country virtues had lost their allure and my parents retired to a golf course community on the Gulf Coast surrounded by dear cousins I'd hardly heard of.

The visit with my parents wasn't salutary. My father hadn't been physically abusive in decades. His temper had mellowed to a general curmudgeonliness fertilized by pain and expressed in growls at my mother and apoplexy at the driver of a car in front of him, but Leslie had never forgiven him for kickboxing me, for throwing my head into walls, for the unpredictable and terrorizing anger she knew through my remembrance. I'd explained the abuse away to myself as I fell asleep night after night in earliest consciousness, carving my hand around the dent made in the wall from my head, across crushed plaster and cracked paint, understanding over the years that he was terrified when he returned from Korea unprepared to earn a living or be a father to a fifteen-month-old he'd never seen and a husband to a wife he'd been long and far from and who'd grown to be a mother. I eventually partnered with my father developing real estate and experienced his lack of tolerance for anxiety, the paralysis pressure brought him, and came to forgiveness. Leslie felt nothing of that—she wouldn't allow our boys to be alone with him.

My father found Leslie aloof. She didn't cook. She didn't want family dinners. She refused to eat many if not most foods. Sat silent and seemingly elsewhere while conversation went on around her. She went to sleep early. Our children could do no wrong in her eyes and anyone who thought so, anyone who expressed doubt, was subject to her fierceness. My father asked our boys to be careful running around my parents' newest Judith Brown sculpture; Leslie told them they could run as they wanted. I asked our children not to eat crackers covered with peanut butter and jam while sitting on my parents' sofa; Leslie told them to sit as they wanted—leaving Skippy peanut butter fingerprints on ivory-colored cushions.

We returned home the day after New Year, the day before school began. Ripton telephoned Will and the bigger boys came to our house within fifteen minutes. "How was it?" Will asked.

"Mad good, my grandparents are cool," Ripton answered while he and Will sat playing Mario.

Days returned to as they'd been. It took me too long to notice that Carlos had been shivering when he came to our apartment. The other boys wore black North Face *puff jackets* bursting in patches of goose down, an inner-city uniform, but Carlos was in his black denim jacket, the same one he'd worn through autumn. "Do you have a winter coat?" I asked him.

"YoMike, I never get cold," he answered, awkward at his shivering.

"Do you have a winter jacket?"

"Not yet," he looked at the ground.

"Are you getting one?"

"Later," he trailed the words softly, looking still at the ground.

"When later?"

"I don't know. I don't want to talk about it."

"When are you getting a jacket?"

"I don't know, I told you, I don't know."

"This winter?"

"My moms can't afford it now."

"Next month?"

"She gave me money for school. That was all I could get, rah?— she got all of us. She sent me to my dad, I tolt you that. I hate goin up there, and he said he can't give me shit. 'I can't afford nothing.' Bullshit! So I got me some sets, that black jacket and jeans, those boots you seen. It all kinda matches. I just gotta get through the winter, but it's mad brick, I give you that."

I finally understood his black denim jacket was meant to match, to be lost in the black nylon ocean of North Face puff jackets the others wore. In earliest autumn, shopping himself for school clothes, Carlos calculated his best way to be the poorer kid among poor kids.

I'd known cold, shivering through the night but aware I'd be warm sometime the next day. My cold didn't come walking to school and returning home, going to the grocery store and hanging out with friends. "Let's go to Paragon tomorrow," I said.

"I'm fine, Mike."

"In the morning."

"I'm fine."

"Of course you are. You'll be better with a North Face."

It was colder the next morning than it had been so far that winter, a cold I saw looking down on Avenue B from our bedroom because the sun hitting blacktop didn't melt the thinnest lip of gutter ice and the macadam was laced white in frozen salt spray. No one braved the weather, not even the dog walkers. Leslie and I took breakfast orders when the boys woke. "Let's go," I said to Carlos midmorning.

"We don't have to," he answered.

"Ask Kindu if you can borrow his North Face."

"Mine's good." The black denim.

"It's freezing."

"I'll be good."

"We're walking."

"Can we take a cab?"

"Ask Kindu for his coat, and I'll give you a hat and gloves."

Paragon devoted an entire floor to winter wear, the largest space given to North Face for hats, mittens, gloves and style after style of parkas and anoraks. "Where can I get me a puff jacket?" Carlos asked the young Latina saleswoman.

She escorted us to rows of Nuptses, built for and named after the mountain in the Khumbu region of the Nepalese Himalayas two kilometers from Everest. There was no such thing as a *"puff jacket"* according to North Face. "Puff jackets," the floor woman smiled and waved her hand as if a wand across two rows of multicolored parkas.

We paid at the front counter. Carlos ripped out the tags and put on his new trophy. The cold was still crisp; it had settled into the lowest places, too heavy to leave and sunlight did nothing but illuminate. We walked for a while. "Where did you live, before the Lower East Side?" I asked him when it seemed okay.

"The Bronx, you know that," Carlos answered.

"I know, but, where?"

"The projects. Not like Jacob Riis. I love the El-Ee-Es." Carlos clapped his gloves together. "Yes!" he said loudly, his full breath bursting white. "It was bad. I mean, shootings every night, you lie in bed and people get kilt."

"Is that where you always lived?"

"I been born there."

"What happened, afterwards?"

Carlos didn't answer.

I watched his breath hiss in the cold. "You don't have to say."

"When my father was kilt, we moved in with Pichon, my moms' friend. That's '*bird*,' in Spanish. But he went into the hospital, like, a momf after we got there—he smoked, like my moms, and he was sick. He never got out. We couldn't stay so my moms tookt us to the shelter."

We slowed behind a woman walking two standard poodles, one white in a black coat, booties, harness and leash, the other black in a white coat, booties, harness and leash. The woman, tall in black stretch ski pants, blond hair straight beneath a black fur-covered hat, wore a white Obermeyer parka with black stylings and black Regina fox-fur boots with white calfskin lowers. Her dogs, white pantings to the cold, pranced away from her on both sides of the path, their leashes cutting off our way.

"What the fuck?" Carlos whispered.

"Excuse me," I said to the woman.

She pulled in her black dog enough for us to pass. I looked sideways. She was young, thin, stunning—a model living nearby. "White people are crazy," Carlos said after we stepped ahead. "YoMike?"

"Yeah?"

"That glove you got me?"—and stopped.

"Yeah?"

"You heard, rah? About Will's moms?"

"No."

"I thought you heard."

"What?"

"Before Christmas, rah? The bitch asked me if I wanted my glove. 'Course!' I told her, course I want it. It's my baby."

"What do you mean?"

"She wanted to send it to her family in the Dominican. Niggas there needs Christmas gifts, but I need my glove, rah? Then it's gone. Bitch sent it away, I know she did."

"You left it at Will's, after she asked about it?"

"Lots of my stuff's there. I don't leave stuff at home, wif my moms, nigga, she's bad. I can't leave my wallet out or nothin. But that glove you got me, you believe that? I loved that glove."

I hadn't known. Nor about their mothers. "We'll deal with it in the spring," I said. He and Will would have gloves.

---

Dakota, Ricky and the other younger boys rarely came to our house as winter wore on. Besides Phil, the rest of us followed Yankee trades, read about pitchers reporting to Tampa for spring training the first week of February and other players over the following week. We half paid attention to preseason games until April came with the Yankees home and the boys, through a flurry of calls, going to Tompkins Square for opening day. Morgan remained the youngest and Ripton's captain the oldest. The boys we hadn't seen since autumn were taller and stronger, more of themselves. The Black captain had slipped into manhood and Ripton's captain looked to me even more inappropriately aged to be with children in Tompkins Square, yet he was part of them because it was their neighborhood. Ricky, like the others, was a larger version of himself. Dakota, too, was taller, but weight overshadowed his height. Routine returned, our farrago of peacocks and trudgers, happy, melancholy and tetchy kids, a houseful coming back for video games and food after baseball.

"Mike," Kindu came over and whispered while I was writing at the kitchen table. He and I were alone in the room, his face concerned.

"What?" I asked.

"Morgan and Dakota, in the little room, you gotta stop it," he urged.

The bottom half of the Dutch door was closed and the top half ajar, the sofa bed pulled out, Dakota shirtless on his back with Morgan shirtless lying on top. "What are you doing?" I asked. They looked at me through the backlit crack in the doorway. Morgan slid off of Dakota. I walked into the room, shut the door and turned on the light. The two, sitting on the bed, squinted. "What were you guys doing?" I asked.

"Nothing," Dakota said.

"You're in here doing something," I said.

"Dakota told me to," Morgan looked at me, then away.

"What?"

The boys glanced at each other. Morgan didn't answer. They pulled their tee shirts back on.

"Dakota told you to what?" I asked. The other boys were loud on the living room side of the Mr. Ed door.

"To lie on him," Morgan said.

"Without shirts?"

Morgan nodded.

"I don't want the two of you alone. I don't want doors closed, do you understand?"

They did, they said.

"Morgie, stay here a minute," I told my son.

Dakota left.

"What happened?" I asked.

"He told me to."

"Did he threaten you? Or scare you?"

Morgan shook his head.

"You sure?"

Morgan nodded.

"Did he tell you to do anything else?"

Morgan shook his head, his eyes to the ground.

"Are you sure?"

He nodded. I wasn't sure, but thought he was telling the truth.

I kissed Morgan's cheek and told Leslie. She wasn't concerned except we both didn't understand Dakota and were uncomfortable. Dakota focused something on Morgan beyond our awareness, seeming nascently sexual. We didn't want to kick Dakota out of our house—we didn't want to kick any boy out. But we'd brought a trouble in, and needed to care for Morgan. I called Dakota's mother. She didn't yell, scream or curse. She was perfectly wise, it seemed, about children.

"Keep an eye on things," I said to Kindu. "Morgan shouldn't be alone with Dakota."

"Sure, Mike."

"We don't want to make a big deal out of it."

"Sure."

---

Kindu joked as much as any of the boys, but not often at someone's expense, the incident with Jonny withstanding. He didn't curse. "My moms don't allow it," he answered when I asked. "She slapped us, and whacked us with the belt. You ever get whipped wif a big leather belt?"

I shook my head.

"It hurts. You don't go messin wif Elaine," he smiled.

Elaine was raising ten brothers and sisters in the Seward Park Extension public housing projects. Kindu's father, Johnny, had worked for the Transport Authority, but it seemed he was retired and couldn't endure the commotion of all the kids. He stayed Upstate in his house, rocking on his big porch in a small town outside Albany.

Kindu's eldest brothers made a living selling drugs.

"What do they sell?" I asked.

"Everything."

"Like?"

"Weed, coke, crack."

"Heroin?"

"Yeah." An older cousin started the business, the oldest brother, Jamar, then Fuquan went to work with him. They did business on Broome Street beside their apartment building, across the street and catty-corner to a police precinct. They sold to people they knew in the apartment building and nearby.

"Does your mom know?"

"Sure. Elaine don't like it but there's nothin she can do. They got to earn a livin. She don't allow it in the house. She found a bag of Jamar's stuff in the toilet once, in the tank, rolled in plastic. He said it wasn't him, but she knows. She slapped him and flushed it down. That's his product, see, so he was angry. He owed for that, but it was Elaine so there's nothin he can do. Now they keep their stuff outside."

"She knows you're here, right? She's okay with that?"

"She's okay."

"And your brothers?" Kindu spoke like a youngest brother—with a sense of awe about Jamar and Fuquan. Our other older boys were different. Will, Philippe and Juan were the oldest siblings in their families. Carlos was the third child, with three younger brothers, but he spoke about himself as older than Jesus and he almost never mentioned his older sister, as if she were a stranger.

"Jamar and Fuquan tolt me, 'Go to those white people.'"

"No kidding."

"Bein' on the grind's hard, Mike. No matter what, you gotta be out there for your customer or someone else'll take 'em cause a junkie needs to buy. A van come down the street you don't know if it's cops, some guy walk up to you, you don't know if it's under-cover. Niggas fight'en for the street and you gotta protect it, that's your business. Niggas stabbed, shot. My brothers tolt me to come here."

Ripton launched a campaign for us to buy a new bat when we came home after the first game that spring, insisting that he, the bigger boys and their friends in the park had outgrown the TPX we'd bought to replace the one destroyed throwing it against the concrete.

We went to Paragon for a heavier bat the next morning. It was busy when we got to the park—Robinson, Davon, Jesus and others who came once in a while were excited by spring. There were enough boys for full teams. "Let's get the catcher's stuff," Carlos said to Ripton and they ran home. We left our apartment unlocked during the day. Except for computers and some jewelry, we didn't own many money things.

Ripton strapped and buckled on the catcher's equipment and played for his side, another younger boy strapping on the equipment for the other.

"But you gonna fail, dogs," I overheard Kindu saying to Carlos when their team came to bat. His voice carried concern.

"I don't gotta choice," Carlos answered, swinging the bat, paying attention to the pitches the older captain was throwing. I stood behind them, near the dugout.

"But nigga, you got-ta go." Kindu shook his head slowly.

"I can't," Carlos said.

"Can't what?" I interrupted.

"Oh no," Kindu said.

Carlos looked at the ground and swung the bat with wrist flicks. Neither boy answered. "Can't what?" I repeated.

"Nothin, Mike," Carlos mumbled.

"Can't what?"

"I don't want to talk about it," he barely breathed.

"I'm gonna stay here till you tell me," I said.

"This is between you twos," Kindu said and walked away.

"What are you going to fail?" I asked.

"Nothin."

"What were you talking about?"

"School," Carlos whispered.

"Why?"

"I can't go too much." He stopped swinging, held his arms down, the bat cocked slightly, ready to putt.

"What do you mean?"

"I can't go, 'sept once in a while."

"Why?"

"Ain't got enough sets."

"What?"

Carlos looked up at the paucity of my English. "Clothes, Mike. I got me two sets, you know, matching."

"And?"

How could he explain any better? "I borrow from the guys, but that's a day or two. Two, three days I can go to school, rah?"

"You're skipping two or three days a week?"

"I ain't got sets."

"Nothing's more important than school, Carlos, clothes don't matter. What you wear, nobody's gonna remember in five years. You're not gonna remember your classmates in twenty years. But if you do well, that will change your life." That's the line my father gave, what I bought into, nothing more important than doing well in school. It wasn't the bigger boys' way nor, to my stifled concern, how we'd been raising Ripton and Morgan.

Carlos didn't respond. I remembered the bigger boys ironing their clothes. I thought of Abe Lincoln walking a path through the woods to a one-room school, Rabbi Hillel as a young woodcutter with no money for classes, lying on the roof of a school in winter to steal lessons until it caved in.

"I can't be lookin poor," Carlos finally said.

Maybe Abe Lincoln hadn't worried about looking poor. "Where should we go?" I asked.

He studied me. "For sets?"

"Yeah," I nodded.

"Transit," he answered, "that's where I like. And Jimmy Jazz."

The baseball game and another continued. Leslie and I brought food and drink as before. "Where's my bat?" Ripton asked after we'd gathered our things to go home.

"Jesus had it, when the game ended," Juan remembered.

"Yeah, dogs, he did," Will said. "But Jesus wouldn'ta took it."

"Sure he would'a, what you think? That nigga's different?" Carlos asked.

"We known him," Will argued.

"He figures Ripton's rich, what the hell," Carlos insisted.

Will shook his head.

"We gonna go ta his house," Carlos said to Will. "You'll see."

"You sure?" Leslie asked. "It's okay?"

"Nigga ain't gonna mess wif me. Not *Car-Lo Suar-Aiz*," Carlos stressed the syllables, flexed his right bicep and smiled to Leslie.

Who smiled back.

"I wanna go," Ripton said.

"No, dogs," Will answered.

"I wanna," Ripton said.

"You too small, son, wait till you get bigger, in a few years," Carlos answered.

"No-no-no-no," Leslie was loud. "I don't want Ripton or Morgan learning—"

"Has to, Leslie, what you think? This is the El-Ee-Es. Gotta take care hisself."

"I don't like it," Leslie said.

Carlos looked to me, frustrated. Leslie was condescending, but she didn't mean to be. Of course Carlos was right. We'd placed our sons in the middle of an intersection of conflicting cultures, and dream as we did that our choices would be benign, it was apparent again that they couldn't always be. If our sons remained in private school, traveled by car service and taxi, kept middle-class company, they'd probably fend for themselves fine in a privileged world. But if they grew deeper into this world in the park, what we'd allowed into our home, added to the mix that they were White, of course

Carlos was right. Leslie and I hadn't thought that part out when Ripton wanted to play baseball.

Carlos and Will left by the gate along the third base line. The rest of us walked home across the Ninth Street pathway.

The doorman rang up half an hour later. Could Carlos and Will come up? They swaggered in, shoulders stiff and undulating side to side, hands down to the waist, grinning, Carlos stopping to swing Ripton's bat in entrance.

"Jesus had it?" I turned to the door, sweating on my exercise bike.

"Course nigga had it, what you think?" Carlos puffed his shoulders further back.

"Did he say?" Ripton asked.

"What you mean?" Carlos asked.

"Jesus," Ripton answered.

"He was whack," Will said, "he didn't want ta give it."

"Nigga don't lie, didn't say he didn't have it," Carlos was bemused.

"Carlos was right. Nigga said, 'What you care? Ripken's rich,'" Will explained.

"I told 'im, 'You don't go stealin from my brother,'" Carlos said.

"Nigga said, 'The White nigga?' You believe that?" Will reveled in the telling.

"Crazy," Carlos said.

Leslie came from the living room. "Oh my," she said.

"You see, Leslie, you see?" Carlos held out the trophy. He and she locked in a smile.

Carlos and I went to Transit, a store I'd passed countless times because it was on Broadway, two blocks from where my real estate office had been for half a decade, but I'd never paid attention. We clicked through two art deco–era subway turnstiles, a gate inside the doorway. Aluminum subway car sheathing lined the walls, the steel poles riders held when trains moved anchored shelving that urban clothes were displayed on, subway maps and station signs were pasted and hung everywhere. Sports star faces were ubiquitous, encouraging kids to "*Just Do It.*" "What do you need?" I asked Carlos.

"Three sets, I think."

"You sure?"

Carlos thought. "Yeah," he answered.

"What do you like?"

He took me to oversized tees and polos, to baggy and less baggy jeans. Carlos put together five sets—Mecca, Ecko, Enyce. He promised to go to school.

---

Will said his mom would repay me if I charged a pair of sneakers he'd found to my credit card. He showed me the website offering Jordan knockoffs.

I tried to convince him that he was wasting $120. He tried to impress me with fashion savvy. I argued for books and school. He and the other boys argued for splivy sneakers to match splivy outfits. I stalled and Will persisted. I lectured about the sadness of linking self-esteem to footwear and the wrong of charging inner city kids so much for something that wouldn't change their lives. Will, Philippe and Carlos were courteous while I spoke, then crowded around the computer cooing through the brightly colored offerings.

Days later I acquiesced to his sloe-eyed supplications. Will handed me the cash from his mother as we sat at the computer.

An express package arrived from Hong Kong a few days later.

Will was overjoyed and wanted another pair of sneakers the next month. He said his mother could pay me twenty dollars a week till we were even.

Phil asked for the same terms.

We kept track of boys' debts on slips of paper clipped to the refrigerator door.

---

I was riding the exercise bike and Carlos was in my seat at the kitchen table a few nights later. The Yankees were losing on TV.

"Checkmate," I reached down and teetered towards the board to move a bishop.

"It's not," Carlos argued. He'd had me teach him the rules a couple months before, we played most days, he practiced alone on the computer and improved constantly.

"Yes it is."

"I can go here," he moved his king to a space he didn't yet realize I controlled.

"Gotcha," Ripton taunted me. "Dad's wrong." Ripton had learned chess a short while after Carlos and didn't take as keen an interest— he was five years younger.

We played with the nicely weighted wooden pieces I'd bought on Thompson Street and the Vermont maple and cherry board my parents had given me as a birthday present in college. The phone rang and Ripton answered. "It's for you," he said to Carlos.

"Hello? . . . *Bendición*," Carlos started. "*Tabien, tabien, Mami*," he said. Then, "YoMike, my moms wants to talk wif you," he handed me the phone and stayed nearby.

I stopped pedaling. "Hello . . ." I answered, breathless.

"Hi, this is Carlos' mommy, Evelyn Velez," a woman's voice was unsure.

"Nice to talk with you, this is Michael."

"Hi, Mr. Rosen, I want to thank you for taking Carlos for clothes. That was so nice. I can't afford it, not wif my kids. You and Mrs. Rosen are so nice to him."

"He's a good kid."

Carlos watched me.

"I keep telling him to be nice to you and Mrs. Rosen. We're so grateful. I hope he's good because he's awful lucky to meet you."

"We like him," I answered, uncomfortable that she seemed cloying.

"I keep tellin him ta be good."

"He's great."

"Mr. Rosen, see, I can't handle Carlos. I was hopin you and Mrs. Rosen could take him in. He don't listen to me. If you can't take him, I'm gonna have ta put him in a group home."

"What do you mean?"

"Carlito, he's a good kid, but he's angry all the time. He's hittin people, he's screamin at everyone and I can't take care of him."

"I'm sorry."

Carlos' face twitched.

"I don't know what to do." She started crying. "Carlito's good, see, but I can't handle him," between sobs. "If you can't take him, I'm gonna have ta send him away."

Carlos might have heard her sobs. His face stayed taut.

"Let me talk with Leslie, I'll call you back," I said.

"What did my moms want?" Carlos asked when I hung up.

"She . . . She says she's having a hard time with you."

"Yeah, what else she say?"

"She says you're angry."

"Damn right I'm angry. She's a bitch."

"Carlos, she's your mother."

"I know she's my mother. She tells me I have a bad attitude. She and her boyfriend get drunk, he hits her, I can't stand that. I beat the shit out of him last week, nobody gonna hit her. That a bad attitude?"

"You beat up an adult?" Carlos was thirteen.

"He was drunk, I smacked that nigga, boom!" Carlos punched a fist into his palm.

"What about Jesus, how old is he?"

"Jesus ain't shit. He's eighteen but he can't do nothin. Nothin against him, but that's how he is. I gotta take care of my moms, I gotta take care of my little brothers. Nobody gonna hit her. Jose gotta understand that, I'll beat the shit out of him again that nigga touches my moms. I don't care she sends me to a home—that's what she threatens. My father told me to take care of her and my little brothers. I gotta do that," Carlos was defiant yet crossing the edge to tears, where he wouldn't let himself go. "You know about my father, rah?"

"Sort of. Not really. You never told me."

Carlos held his right thumb in his left hand and started picking at the skin around its nail with his pointer finger. "We was havin a picnic on Good Friday, like we always done. My father was wif us—my stepfather but I call him my father. He and my moms split up, but they was friends. It was hot, like, and the ice cream truck was goin around, you know, wif that song. My father got in a fight and he won, but the guy used a screwdriver and kilt him. That's how come we went into the shelters."

"Did they put the guy in jail?"

"A'course. I had to testify. He got ten years. I could kill anybody, I'd kill that nigga."

I didn't know what to say. "Are you going to go to school?" I asked eventually.

"I'm goin."

"Is it safe at home?"

"It's okay. I'm sleepin across the hall, wif my mom's friend."

"Who's that?"

"Brenda. She has a couple kids. I stay at Will's, weekends here, but at home I sleep across the way."

"Who is she?"

"Some lady. She and my moms been friends."

"She doesn't have a husband, or boyfriend?"

"Nah, not now. She did, her kids are babies."

"You're okay there?"

"Yeah, sure. She got a good couch."

I told Leslie about the phone call and talking with Carlos. She and I didn't want him to be sent to a group home, though we weren't certain what such a place was, if it existed; "*group home*" sounded like a threat from an earlier era.

We weren't sure what the bigger boys had become to us at that point. We hadn't had reason to consider how committed we were to them, nor would we ever have expected to. They were kids visiting our home. We didn't know if they were true friends to Ripton, or to our family. But they'd become more than that already, regardless the contradiction; we wouldn't let Carlos be hurt. Yet we weren't ready, weren't prepared, to take him into our home, into our family. We did decide, if his mother pushed to have him taken away, that we'd have Carlos move in. And at that point, we'd do the same for each of the bigger boys. Our family boundary was becoming muddled. All the more because Leslie and I, forever friends from the day we met her first moment at college, were in a hard place. I'd become more aware, more vocal, about unhappinesses in our marriage, particularly over differences raising children. We didn't know how to reconcile what I was, after these years, finally airing. It wasn't a good time to bring another boy into our home. If we had a choice.

# CHAPTER SIX

# LOVE

*August 1999*

On a Wednesday in late August when the Yankees clinched their division, looked strong for the playoffs and perhaps a repeat as world champions, Ripton suggested, "Hey, let's have a World Series!"

The boys froze their teams. They committed to Thursday and Friday as playoff games and the coming weekend as a best of seven World Series. Carlos, Will, Kindu, Ripton, Dakota and Morgan were with the older captain. "We the Yankees," Carlos shouted.

"We the Yankees," Ricky disagreed. He, Philippe, Juan and Ricky were with the Black captain.

"I ain't a Yankee," Philippe was adamant. "We the Mets, yous the Yankees, beat yo ass in the playoffs and the World Series," he bragged and pointed at Carlos. "It gonna happen."

"That's stuuupid, nigga, you can't have a American and National League team playin each other in the playoffs," Will said.

"I'm stuuupid? You stuuupid! You can't lose in the playoffs and go to the World Series, what the fuck? It's just pretend," Phil reasoned.

"I ain't no Met," another boy complained.

"Who you wanna be?" Philippe asked him.

"The Yankees," the kid shrugged—the obvious.

"We called it first," Ripton argued.

"It's all good. We be the Mets. It don't matter," Ricky suggested in compromise.

The Yankees won the first playoff game too decisively and the boys decided they should trade Kindu and another boy to even the sides. The Yankees still won.

Philippe called Robinson to come to Tompkins the next day, a new Met, and the playoffs leveled before the Yankees won two more games and finally the World Series.

———

Carlos and I planned to go clothes shopping on the Sunday after the World Series. We didn't so much talk as know school was here, and agreed on a time. We went to Transit and Jimmy Jazz, buying enough jeans, polos and tees to get through every week of eighth grade—I hoped. We started walking home, splitting the shopping bags between us.

"YoMike," Carlos gave his surprised voice as we turned away from Delancey Street.

I knew we'd forgotten something at a store. "Yeah?"

"YoMike," he smiled. "Ya ever notice that I always say '*YoMike*' together like. Not '*Mike*' or '*Yo, Mike*' but '*YoMike*'?"

"Yeah, I noticed."

"Why you think that is? Isn't it weird?"

He was reaching. We both knew it. "What are you thinking about, Carlos?"

"Well . . . You think you can help me? I need a job. My moms not givin me money."

"You're thirteen. I don't think that's legal. To work."

"I'm almost fourteen."

"But you're not. That's, like, February, right?"

Carlos nodded.

"And it's sixteen. When you're sixteen we can talk about work."

"My moms'll sign my working papers. I can do that now."

I'd thought sixteen was the legal working age. "Working papers?"

"Yeah, when you're thirteen, if your moms signs papers."

"She doesn't give you anything?"

He looked at the ground. "Nothin."

"Where do you get money?"

"Brenda."

"The woman across the hall?"

"Yeah."

"You're still sleeping there?"

"Sometimes, mostly at Will's and Phil's, but she gives me money when I'm there. I gotta see me brothers, rah?, and I can't stay wif my moms."

"Brenda has her own kids? I remember."

"Yeah, two."

"And she gives you money?"

"Not lots, but she cares about me, we're close."

"What do you mean?" "*Close*" was wrong.

"You know."

"I don't."

"You know I don't lie, I never lie."

"What does '*close*' mean?"

"Like, sleepin together. I ain't stayin on the couch no more."

"She's . . . fucking you?"

He nodded and his braids flew. He strutted his shoulders with arms straight and jigged like a basketball star side to side after a winning game. A moustache was beginning to fuzz above his top lip. "Women loves me."

"You're thirteen. It's not legal. For her to touch you."

"She takes care of me."

"Does your mom know?"

"Hell no!"

"I'll call Peter, at Red Square, the guy who manages our buildings. I'll see what we can get. You should sleep at Will and Phil's when you can, and in our house on weekends. She's too old for you, Carlos, it's gonna mess up your head, no joke. You get working papers and I'll work on a job. And don't sleep with her."

"You get me a job, I won't hafta go around the same. Ta see my brothers, and my moms in my moms', but me and Brenda's friends, no joke."

I didn't push. He'd been talking about a girl named Jasmine.

Peter Marciano hired Carlos as a janitor at Red Square for two hours after school each weekday and full time on Sundays. He vacuumed hallways, mopped the lobby, worked the trash compactor and hauled garbage to the sidewalk Sunday afternoons. Carlos was paid eight dollars an hour. Minimum wage was a bit above five.

---

Transitions in general and particularly for Ripton from summer vacation to school to summer vacation were hard. He became more brusque during those times than his already impatient self, less tolerant, criticized Morgan and the bigger boys, claimed bats, gloves, video games, the TV and the computer as his alone. Sometimes he wouldn't want the bigger boys around until they didn't come, and then he was lonely, especially for Will.

Beginning third grade was hard on him. Ripton hadn't been in touch with classmates over the summer and hadn't looked forward to seeing anyone again. His new teachers at Heschel, one for secular and the other for Jewish studies, began the year having a hard time with him.

Leslie and I didn't have an easy time with each other. She didn't like my business travel and I felt remote from our marriage.

Tuesday mornings stayed mine to take Ripton and Morgan to school. Leslie and I agreed that I'd pick them up on Tuesday afternoons and take them on Thursday mornings as well—to be more involved with our sons.

We agreed to see a marriage counselor, which we'd done once before, four years after we were married. Leslie had finished a hellish internship and residency in obstetrics and gynecology then. Sigmund Freud was our counselor. Not the Austrian, but his New York doppelgänger, a thin-faced man with brushed-back white hair above a high forehead, a neatly trimmed beard, thick and black round glasses, a precise three-piece suit and tie. I don't know how tall he was, or his build exactly, because he never stood. He sat, instead, with an unlit pipe and listened to Leslie and me talk with each other—never venturing a thought.

The new counselor Leslie and I went to see this second time, younger than us and relentlessly effervescent, worked in an office one floor above Leslie's in a parenting center we'd occasionally visited to gain guidance on issues regarding our children. Leslie particularly liked the head parenting expert there, sufficiently qualified beyond my standing. She had recommended the new counselor.

I arrived early for our first session. The waiting room might have been a pediatrician's office, a showroom for Little Tikes, the toy maker of Fold-up-n-Go Train, Handle Haulers Haul & Ride, Discover-Sounds Hammer and Electronic Home Kitchen. It was a place of primary colors and one iridescent sea turtle swimming across the floor, an extraordinary piece, worn to transcendence as children clamored over the hardwood protuberance of bony scutes across shell.

"If you decide to leave," Leslie said during one of our Wednesday afternoon sessions, "I want you to tell me here. I don't want to worry outside."

"Okay," I answered, then added, "but if we break up, I want us to tell our boys together."

Leslie flashed to anger in an instant. Perhaps because I acknowledged the possibility of our marriage ending. "Okay," she said coldly.

Her anger wasn't misplaced. I'd broken the boundaries of our marriage. Leslie and I decided to speak to try to repair that breach. Our friendship had always been strong; relying on that, we struggled through what had to be discussed. Nothing was easy about our conversations.

---

Christmas 2000 we decided to take Ripton and Morgan skiing in Colorado and then to Florida, close to but not with my parents. We found an island an hour away where Ripton could indulge his passion for fishing.

When we walked into our condominium at the foot of the Colorado ski area, Ripton demanded the larger of the two bedrooms for himself and his brother. It had a king-sized bed and the bigger television. The boys started watching TV as Leslie and I unpacked their belongings. Then we went to our room. Exposed to each other without the distraction of a filled home, in quiet, the awkwardness was too palpable between us. Leslie suspected something more askew. "Are you moving out?" she asked.

"I . . ." She saw I meant *yes.*

I had rented a one-bedroom apartment in a building across Tompkins Square, within sight of our home. It was small for the boys and me, but then again, I didn't have clear plans. I knew that I'd never find a woman as strong, as honest and dependable as my wife, someone to rely on as much. I dreamed I could be a good father to Ripton and Morgan as my marriage eroded, a good friend to the bigger boys. It was a dream. I knew I'd hurt everyone.

"You prick," she exploded. Our door was shut but it and the wall were thin. "You were supposed to tell me in counseling." I'd never heard Leslie louder. I told her I wasn't certain. She shouted. I shouted. We realized we had to talk with our boys, still on the bed in front of the TV. It wasn't the best way to break such news to our children.

"Mommy and I need to talk with you guys," I said.

"We love you," Leslie started.

They ignored us.

"We need to talk with you guys," I said again. They were laughing to a *South Park* rerun; Kenny had just been killed, blood everywhere. I turned down the TV but our sons wouldn't acknowledge Leslie or me. "We love you both, very much, but—"

"They killed Kenny!" Cartman cried in low volume.

Morgan turned to me, holding Monkey. "Are you divorcing?" he asked.

Ripton crawled his way to the foot of the bed farthest from us, drew his knees to his chest, wrapped his arms around them and started rocking back and forth, back and forth. I'd done the worst thing. "I don't know," I said. Ripton kept rocking.

"Mommies and daddies don't always get along, but they love their children. We'll always love you. We'll always take care of you," Leslie was calm.

"Both of us," I said.

Ripton kept rocking, partially watching *South Park* with barely any sound. Or not watching TV—somewhere else.

The first night after we returned home, Leslie and I agreed that we'd both put our boys to bed. We bathed and dressed them in their clothes for the first school day of the next millennium. They climbed into bed, Leslie between them, and asked for a Berenstain Bears book. I pulled a chair close and Leslie read. Mama Bear redeemed Papa Bear from another stupidity.

"Remember guys, like we spoke about, I'm sleeping in my new apartment tonight—" I started after Mama Bear's rescue.

"You're leaving?" Ripton was stunned.

Morgan held Monkey.

"Yes, but—"

Ripton's face disintegrated. He burst into tears, jumped from the bed and rushed to the stairs.

"Ripton, stop," I pleaded, hurrying around the bed to catch him.

He started running down the stairs. "Go away!" he sobbed.

"Ripton!" I reached for his shoulder.

"Let me go!" he screamed.

I slowed him down, stepped in front and hugged him.

"Let me go," he pushed away then collapsed, sobbing, into my chest.

"I love you, Ripton. Mommy loves you, we'll always love you," I said softly and held him. "I'm always your dad, Mom's always your mom. We're your parents, we'll always take care of you."

He sobbed more quietly in longer breaths, relaxed into me, spread his arms and we hugged. We stood like that, hugging, then I lifted and carried him back to bed, tucking him beside Morgan. Leslie stood at the side and glared. I kissed both boys and left, avoiding her eyes.

The silence of an empty apartment was more painful than I'd expected, not hearing my boys' breath at night, not being able to look
at them on my way to bed and again when I went downstairs in the
morning. I knew the pain I was creating for Leslie. She and I kept
meeting by the sea turtle on Wednesday afternoons, sitting in silence
until we were inside the counselor's office. We talked about working
things out. I went to the house at six-thirty on Tuesday and Thursday mornings to wake and get our boys ready, to take them to
school. Leslie stayed upstairs till we were gone. I put the boys to bed
those same nights. She went to the gym after work, to dinner or the
movies with friends those evenings and came into the apartment
from the second level while we were still downstairs, so she
wouldn't see me. I could hear her filling the greenhouse tub and her
splashes later on while we read books in the boys' bed and I waited
for them to fall asleep.

I stopped seeing the bigger boys except on the Tuesday and
Thursday evenings I was at Leslie's. They left on their own at 8:00
p.m. those nights, no longer needing a reminder that it was time to
go, sensitive to our separation.

I don't know what would have happened but for my knees. A
month after we separated I told Leslie in couple's counseling that I
was having surgery; the doctor had been Leslie's housemate in medical school. We agreed that I'd move back to the Christodora, into
the small room with the Mr. Ed door behind the living room, where
Morgan had been on top of Dakota. Leslie was waiting in the recov-
ery room when I woke up from anesthesia. She drove me to the office when I was ready to leave the day-surgery clinic. Leslie put our
boys to bed that week, woke and took them to school. When I could
make it up the stairs, I started putting the boys to sleep. I climbed
back up a half hour later, resting at the foot of their bed to listen to
them breathe, watching them in the never-quite-dark of New York.

The bigger boys stopped automatically leaving at eight o'clock on
school nights and stayed over on weekends.

I wrote at the kitchen table, the same spot that had been mine.
Leslie sat across and we talked a little before she went to bed. Mor-

gan came hungry into the kitchen one Friday night. I helped him at the refrigerator. Leslie kissed him goodnight and started to bed. She was two or three steps up when Morgan pushed me towards her. "Go with Mommy," he said. Leslie stopped. I didn't move. She and I looked at each other. Morgan pushed me harder. "If you're in love, you sleep in the same bed," he said. Perhaps Leslie expected me to start up the stairs. I knew I should. But the break needed longer to repair. I made food for Morgan.

Leslie and I continued a not-unfamiliar housemate normalcy. "Celibacy isn't so bad, better than I thought," she said to our counselor two months after I moved home. She was right. Ripton, Morgan and the bigger boys seemed fine. Our home life seemed fine. I was fine. Nothing was right, though. I spoke with my father. He and my mother started dating when they were sixteen and fourteen. They'd been together since, surviving my father's service in Korea, his temper, early economic hardship, my mother's breast cancer spread to seven nodes and needing a double radical mastectomy, then aggressive treatment and a pessimistic diagnosis. They'd survived all sorts of things long relationships do. "When you see her from behind in the kitchen, and go up to hug her, do you get a hard-on?" my father asked me over the phone.

I hesitated, not sure I needed the question.

"Oh," he answered my quiet.

Our separation lasted thirty months. There were many times one or both of us expected to divorce. We told the boys that we would; it seemed inevitable. Leslie was at the kitchen table clutching a box of Kleenex, the trash basket overflowing and handfuls of tissues at her feet, rocking back and forth, sobbing. "Who's going to take care of me?" The bigger boys, Ripton and Morgan were sitting in dusk on the sofa and floor of the TV room, the volume turned low. Morgan held Monkey. The boys made room for me. "Your mom, Leslie and I, are going to separate," I told them softly.

"We know," Ripton mumbled, mostly elsewhere.

"Leslie tolt us," Carlos said, "cause she just cryin."

"Is that divorce?" Morgan asked.

I kissed him and Ripton. "Yes, but I'm always your dad," I said, "forever and ever."

Will told me the bigger boys left at eight o'clock and walked into the park. "I think we caused it," Will said to the others.

"What you mean?" Philippe asked.

"We always there, dogs, they got no time. Not wif Ripon and Morgan, not wif each other. Think about it," Will said.

"But they're a perfect family," Kindu said. "A mom, a dad, two kids. They never fight, no one hardly yells."

"I don't know, dogs. I think we done it. Will's right, we musta kept 'em apart, rah?" Carlos said.

I let myself back into our apartment the next morning. Ripton and Morgan were asleep, wearing the same clothes from the day before. We got ready and were downstairs when the car service came. I picked them up at school that afternoon. We went for pizza and started to the subway home. The boys wanted a cab, how they usually traveled, but I insisted. We crowded into the train, rode it to the Fourteenth Street station and walked underground to catch the L crosstown. "Can we give money?" Ripton asked when we passed a musician. He put a dollar into the man's empty case. We passed another man, unconscious on the tile floor, his head on an outstretched arm, his hand wrapping an *I ♥ NY* coffee cup. He was bloated, in crusted clothes. Ripton saw and kept seeing, unable to do otherwise. "Can we give money?" he asked, and put another dollar into the man's cup. We rode the next train to First Avenue and caught the bus from there to the Christodora. We sat at the kitchen table and did homework. Will called up from the lobby. I ordered food from the Chinese restaurant in Red Square. The door shut upstairs—Leslie coming home—and I heard splashing in the greenhouse bathtub while the boys and I read *Love That Dog*. I stayed at the foot of their bed till they were asleep, Ripton breathing loudly, the way he had off my side of the bed beneath a dishtowel the first night we brought him home.

One night, still not able to sit in a restaurant alone, I brought home a falafel from St. Marks, left the brown bag on the living room windowsill of my small apartment, took off my suit and put my business clothes away for the weekend. I carried a Chinese stool to the window. My view was a bit above the tops of the maples outside, beside the street, a clear line through Tompkins Square Park above century-and-a-half-old American elms twisting towards the Christodora. The living room light was on in our apartment. The boys could have been wrestling or getting ready for the gun game; some of them might have been on the computer. I unwrapped my falafel and watched, tears coming down my face. I was newly forty-four, owned a Wall Street firm, had done much of what I'd dreamed and was sitting alone with a sandwich, without my family, hurting the woman who'd counted on me, without my sons and the bigger boys.

My phone rang as I sat by the living room window the next morning, holding a paper cup of coffee from downstairs. "YoMike? You okay, you need help?" It was Carlos.

I did, unpacking, but his company was worth more than that. Carlos glanced into the bedroom and kitchen when he came, and we sat on my ceramic stools in the living room. He wanted to play chess, but the set was in my old apartment. I'd tried to convince Leslie that I'd bought the pieces and my parents had given me the board, but she insisted Ripton wanted to play—I couldn't hurt our son by taking them. Carlos and I went out to the Thompson Street chess clubs. We watched old and young players in crowded rooms, hands flashing to the clocks, picked what we wanted and went back to my home with a good-feeling set and board. We played day after day, taking care of each other. Evelyn called my home after a while. "Carlito's getting worse. He listens to you, can't you be his dad?" she asked. I wanted to help, needed to, but I wasn't capable of being his father. "Checkmate," Carlos beamed, and it was—the first time he beat me. Which kept happening.

Kindu too started coming around and in February also asked for a job at Red Square. Peter Marciano hired him for two hours after school each day, like Carlos, plus a full day on Saturday.

Peter called me at the office late one Monday afternoon not long afterwards. He'd caught Carlos sneaking back in the day before, pretending to start his work as if he hadn't stolen away. But the doorman had seen him walking down Houston Street hours earlier. "He's a good kid," Peter said. "How do you want to handle it?" We agreed to both speak with Carlos. I was most concerned with the odds of racism. Carlos and the other bigger boys were coming to that midteen time when brown-colored boys lose their cuteness. Much of America remains afraid of dark, virile and not-middle-class men. I was afraid of the cycle of incarceration that too often starts then.

Carlos told me he went to play baseball for the Tides. He was afraid Peter wouldn't have allowed him. Carlos dreamed of becoming a major league player, not a janitor; he wanted to keep his priorities straight. "If you'd planned it beforehand, I'm sure Peter would have let you go." But I wasn't completely certain—Carlos was a worker to Peter, a slot to be filled in a job that needed to get done. I hadn't thought of baseball season when I'd helped arrange this job.

Peter Marciano called again a few weeks later. The building superintendent had caught Kindu sneaking out. Peter fired both boys. I reached the two of them and we agreed on dinner. "What did you do with your money?" I asked as we sat at the table.

Carlos gave me the same look as when I hadn't understood about sets. He kept at his chicken wings and shrimp fried rice.

"I gave my moms money. I went shopping, for clothes, and I tried to make sure I kept some money in my pocket," Kindu answered.

"Peter says you were sneaking out of the building."

"We was goin to play baseball," Carlos was dismissive.

"You and I spoke about that," I told him. "You were supposed to work it out with him."

Neither boy responded.

"You were stealing, no different than any other thief."

"I'm no thief," Carlos was indignant.

"It's not like that," Kindu hurried.

"Yes it is. You sneak off for three hours each, that's forty-eight dollars. You're taking that money from Leslie and me, because we're owners here. It's no different than taking forty-eight dollars out of our wallets. How can I recommend you for jobs again?"

Carlos picked at his rice.

"You're killin me, Mike," Kindu stared at the table.

"That's twenty-four dollars out of my wallet. Me alone. That's what this dinner cost," I swung my hand above the table.

"We was wrong," Carlos kept picking at his rice. "I know we was."

"Me, too," Kindu said. "I'm sorry, Mike."

---

The assistant principal from the Heschel School called at work. She'd spoken with Leslie, and wanted me to know that Ripton was angry at our separation and was beginning to act out. The school suggested counseling. I'd noticed his anger and knew it came with fear. I didn't know how best to help. I thought counseling made sense and was simultaneously afraid of a slippery slope, our son beginning to see a therapist and never stopping. Leslie wouldn't hear of it. "He's angry, Michael. You left us. He deserves to be angry, we deserve to be angry. You're a prick."

I wanted to explain that I didn't leave our sons. I'd always be their father. But I stayed quiet. I'd always stayed too quiet. I told Leslie again that I'd like the boys to see my apartment. I wanted them to stay overnight. She still wouldn't hear of it. I didn't push. I was looking for a larger apartment where I could make a bedroom the boys would like.

---

A couple months later I rented a larger apartment in Red Square. The movers were efficient, and by midafternoon I was alone with my belongings in a two-bedroom apartment with a small terrace and a view of Wall Street's skyscrapers, the World Trade Towers rising above everything. My cell phone rang. "YoMike, you need help?" Carlos asked. He and Kindu came over. We unpacked the rest of the day, ate Chinese takeout from Red Square and played chess.

---

I saw Ripton and Morgan each Tuesday and Thursday, taking them back and forth from school, ordering dinner or making it at Leslie's, putting my sons to sleep. Carlos came to my house often and Kindu sometimes with him. I only saw the other bigger boys at Leslie's. They were back to leaving at eight o'clock on the nights I was there.

I wanted Ripton and Morgan to see my home and start sleeping over, I wanted them to understand that I lived somewhere, that I wasn't a father who appeared twice a week then disappeared. I wanted to hear them breathe while they slept, to feel the peaceful energy of their lives.

Leslie eventually agreed. "Make sure they have Monkey and Puppy," she instructed. I'd not known of Puppy, Ripton's first stuffed animal, matching Monkey for security once Dad left home.

I packed their animals, other belongings and we walked to Red Square, turning the corner on Houston Street to the Chinese restaurant, pizza shop, Subway sandwich franchise, Dunkin' Donuts and Blockbuster Video on the ground floor. Though Ripton and Morgan went to these places and knew I lived in the building, I don't think they connected the stores to my home till we passed by and they realized they could shop and order in, watch movies and rent new Nintendo games with ultra-ease if Dad agreed.

I showed them their bedroom first, the bunk bed with WWF sheets, pillowcases and blankets, two pairs of pajamas folded on the bottom bed, their computer, TV and Nintendo. I showed them their bathroom, the living room, kitchen and my bedroom.

"It's one floor?" Ripton tried to figure this new place out.

"Yup."

"It's smaller than our house, a lot," Ripton turned his head around the place.

"This sort of is your house, too."

"Yeah, I know," Ripton wanted to be kind.

Morgan nodded his head, agreeing, both boys not knowing where to go and what to do next. "It's nice," Morgan said.

"Thank you."

"No, it really is. I really like it," he insisted.

"Let's take a walk, I'll show you around." I meant south of Houston Street, where stores were small, local and eccentric. We walked, took Chinese back to the apartment for supper, the boys played Nintendo and decided to watch TV from my bed because the screen was bigger. Ripton called the bath first. He dried off and I handed him his baby blue baseball-bat-and-glove decorated pajamas. Morgan's were of soccer balls and shoes on grass green cotton. The boys went back to TV as if they'd always worn pajamas and lain in my bed. When it was bedtime I showed them their new kids' books, more fishing and baseball, *Love That Dog*, than at Leslie's and no Berenstain Bears. They both lay down in the bottom bed with Monkey and Puppy. I pulled the computer chair close and we read. I finished a Shoeless Joe Jackson tale. Both boys claimed the top bunk then argued over it. Ripton won by size and Morgan was angry. I tried to make peace, achieved a begrudging one of "*wwhhhhs*" from the younger, tucked them in, kissed them goodnight and turned off their light.

"Dad?" Ripton called on my way out.

"Yes, Sweetie?"

"Leave the door open, okay?"

I did and practiced Chinese characters on the sofa, rote work, anxious around the wall from their bedroom, wondering what the rest of their childhoods would be for us together.

"Mor'n," Ripton called down to his brother a few minutes later. Who ignored him, unlikely asleep. "Mor'n," Ripton called louder.

"What?" Morgan was still annoyed.

"Let me sleep with you."

"You wanted to be there."

"Let's share.

"It's too small, Ripton."

"Then come up here."

"No."

"Come'on, Mor'n."

"No."

"I can't sleep."

Time went by, then I heard shuffling and weight shifting the ladder. "Get out," Morgan was angry.

"Come'on, Mor'n. Move over."

"Dad!" Morgan called.

I went into their room. They were crowded into the lower bunk, Morgan against the wall keeping the blanket tucked around him so Ripton couldn't get underneath, both of them clutching their animals.

"Dad, tell him it's not fair," Morgan pleaded.

"Ripton, you wanted the top," I said.

"I want to sleep with Mor'n."

"I'll sleep on top," Morgan said.

"I want to sleep with you."

"It's too small."

I didn't know what to say. Ripton was frightened. He'd never been able to sleep alone, while Morgan wanted independence.

"Come'on, Mor'n," Ripton insisted.

"Dad?" Morgan pleaded again.

"Just tonight," Ripton argued.

"Okaayy," Morgan sighed.

"Dad, you sleep on top," Ripton told me. I agreed, listening to them breathe as I fell asleep. I ended up staying in the top bed each night they came to my home.

I started dating a woman while Leslie and I were separated. Some months on I asked her to stay—for the first time on a night when the boys would be in the apartment. Testing her forbearance, the expectation of romance, though I hadn't understood. She'd met Ripton and Morgan, earning a measure of their approval when she'd presented them with a set of hand-carved, painted and signed matryoshka dolls. Ripton's were of Babe Ruth, Mickey Mantle, Lou Gehrig, Joe DiMaggio and Yogi Berra, one inside the other. Morgan's were of the current team. The smallest was his favorite player, Chuck Knoblauch.

The dolls looked like Slavic weight lifters. They were thoughtful in a curious way, but not for seven- and nine-year-old boys. Near bedtime I explained to my sons that the woman was staying overnight. I read them a story about Babe Ruth, tucked Ripton in on top and Morgan on the bottom. I left the door open, as Ripton asked.

Ripton climbed down to Morgan. "Dad," Morgan called.

"Stay here," Ripton said when I walked in.

"She's sleeping over"—the woman.

"She can stay in your room," Ripton suggested.

"But I want to stay there too."

"Oh," Ripton answered.

Morgan was concerned for his brother. "You can sleep here, Ripton," he offered, lying down beside him and opening his blanket over the two of them. I kissed them both again.

She was there the next Friday when I brought Ripton and Morgan from school. Will, Carlos and Kindu rang up from the lobby. *Street kids*, I somehow thought when the video picture popped into focus. *My kids*, I realized. Philippe and Juan came soon after.

The noise of Nintendo contests from the boys' room, calls for Mario to jump and spin, whoops for hits and fly-ball outs in Backyard Baseball, "*nigga*" this and "*my son*" that, hadn't till then seemed overwhelming in years. I asked the boys to be quieter and they didn't know how. I asked again. "*Coño!*" Carlos' voice erupted through the wall. The woman walked to my bedroom and shut the door.

"Can the guys sleep over?" Ripton came into the living room and asked me near bedtime.

He and Morgan took baths, put on their pajamas and shared the lower bed. Carlos took the upper. Juan used the fold-out chair on the floor. I gave the others sleeping bags, sheets and pillows.

The next morning, Philippe was snoring on the sofa in the living room. Will and Kindu were woven on the floor between chairs and the coffee table. The woman took the morning paper and left.

The boys and I went to an old Ukrainian diner down Avenue A. We filled two booths and ate greasy eggs with greasier hash browns, rye toast and orange juice in tiny glasses. I poured milk from one of those small metal pitchers into thin coffee. We talked and laughed and made plans for a trip to Shelter Island the next Friday night. I hugged Ripton and Morgan when I brought them to the Christodora lobby, started *"I love you"* but the words caught. I wiped tears and waved as the elevator door closed.

It was Ripton's idea to go to Shelter Island, where we'd almost finished building a vacation home before Leslie and I split up. We'd gone there on weekends since before the boys were born and had purchased land on a pond that felt like Vermont.

Ripton and Morgan wanted to stay in New York on weekends once they started playing baseball in Tompkins Square. But Ripton remembered the grass baseball field behind the public school near our weekend house, beside the jungle gym he and Morgan had played on since they were toddlers, and enticed the bigger boys with it. Most of them had never been on a grass field. Baseball was the dirt, rock and shattered glass of the East River fields or the blacktop of Tompkins Square.

The woman I was dating said she wanted to come.

That Friday I had trouble finding our new, almost completed house, remembering which dirt driveway was ours. We pitched a tent beneath the overhang of the back deck and four boys crowded inside. The other three slept around it. We woke early and drove to the soda fountain restaurant across from the public school, a place with spin-around seats and an open griddle. But the boys ignored breakfast and ran across the street, past the old cemetery onto left field. Carlos threw himself into the air and back splashed onto the grass, rolled and squirmed with his arms and feet in the air, sprung up and dove again singing. The others flipped onto their backs and squirmed in the grass like puppies.

Phil ran to the pitcher's spot, a fawn-colored crust of drying mud giving up the last morning dew. City kids don't think about dew. They don't come out of their apartments and look up for sun and clouds.

Our sidewalks and streets are wet when it rains, when snow melts, when a hydrant is running because the Fire Department is checking things out or a guy on the block had opened it so kids could spray themselves on the hottest days. Dew doesn't fall in the city. I remembered to look up on the field, the sun framed by popcorn clouds.

Carlos stood in the batter's box, his hands clasping a pretend bat, tapping his front foot timing Phil's windup and delivery of an imaginary ball. He swung, hit on the sweet spot and flipped the bat to summersaults, "Delgado hits a towering home run!" he shouted for TV fans, Carlos Delgado his favorite player, Puerto Rican and his namesake, and started a home run trot around the bases. Kindu took one swing and hit a home run, "And Griffey hits a monster!" he shouted, Ken Griffey Jr. his favorite player, African American and albeit hobbled, on his way to the Baseball Hall of Fame. Ripton hit a home run. "Jason Giambi!" he shouted and started around the bases. "Chuck Knoblauch!" Morgan shouted after he swung. The others took a pitch each from Phil and hit the ball out of the park, shouted a player's name, tossed the bat and home run trotted around the clean dirt path of the bases cut into mowed grass. Carlos pitched to Philippe. "Pedro Martinez hits another!" Philippe shouted and started his trot.

"He's a pitcher, Stuuupid!" Will rebuked his buddy. Pitchers didn't bat in the American League.

"I don't care!" Phil pumped his fist. "It's make-believe. Pedro Martinez!" he shouted again, grinned, and kept on around the bases.

"NiggaPhil," Carlos smiled to the others. The boys started an authentic half-field game when Phil finished. I gave Ripton money for drinks, told the boys that my friend and I would bring back lunch and drove off to see the island. The clouds grew dark and it started to drizzle. I bought sandwiches, coffee for us and drove back to the boys. They didn't care about the rain. The woman and I sat in the van, the windshield wipers on, watching them play. Tears ran down her face. She kept silent, not drying her eyes or cheeks, tears falling into her lap.

"What's wrong?" I asked.

She didn't answer, staring through the wet windshield and sometimes sipping her coffee. Her tears ran faster. Morgan was pitching to Carlos. She started, "I'm sorry. I want to be anywhere but here. Drinking a cappuccino, anywhere. The bigger boys, they're not Ripton's friends. They're taking advantage of him. They're using you. This isn't how I want to be" and she swept her hand across the boys outside. I looked. Carlos hit a pitch down the left field line, deep into the outfield. The boys watched, I watched. Friends and family had also said we were being used. I loved my sons, and I loved these boys. Carlos' hit cleared the fence of the school parking lot and thudded on the trunk of a car. He whooped and slowed into his own home run trot. The others joined him, all of them running. I'd never seen anyone hit a home run on Shelter Island.

# CHAPTER SEVEN

# ONIONS | *Autumn 2000*

The summer of 2000 ended. Roanna, the Heschel School principal, had her assistant call me at work the first morning of school. Ripton had kicked a globe in class. She'd told Leslie. Roanna expected to meet us the next morning before class began.

Leslie wanted to meet outside the school building, to make sure we seemed united. Yuval would take the boys to school.

We walked into a conference room and saw the head of the lower school, its psychologist and assistant psychologist, Ripton's two teachers and Roanna facing us around a table.

"Ripton needs to see a psychiatrist," Roanna started. "He can't stay here unless he starts seeing someone."

"If this were public school, they would have called the police and taken him to a psychiatric ward," the school psychologist continued. He was avuncular, bearish, a footballer's body topped off with a full white beard, broad black-knit yarmulke and chalk white face.

*For kicking a globe?* I wondered. The bigger boys had told us of beatings and knifings, of gang enforcement in their schools. I nodded in sardonic appreciation that Heschel had the tolerance to invite us to a meeting rather than call the police and haul our newly ten-year-old off to a psychiatric ward of the nearest hospital.

They recommended he see a psychiatrist on the Upper West Side near school. Leslie took Ripton for a Wednesday afternoon appointment and we agreed that I'd go with him the next week. She and our son both disliked the man, call him Dr. S——. He wasn't sympathetic to Ripton. He only seemed to hear the school's side. Ripton stayed beside me on the man's couch when we were there the following week. Dr. S—— was middle aged, tall and thin with a trimmed beard and the same black-knit yarmulke as the school psychologist. His office was made in autumn earth tones, tolerable colors, his upper shelves filled with child psychiatry and psychology books and the shelves near the floor stacked with building blocks, dolls, tractors, trucks and board games. Dr. S—— tried to find a rapport with Ripton, who was having none of it. Dr. S—— told Ripton he'd like to speak alone with him, for me to sit in the waiting room. Ripton refused. A few weeks later Leslie refused to take Ripton anymore—he detested and mistrusted the man and told me it was my job from now on.

After several more visits, Ripton said it was okay to leave him alone on the couch. I started down the hall and heard the door close. "Dad! Dad!" Ripton screamed a moment later, beating on the door. "Let me out!"

I ran to the office and tried the knob. It was locked. "Ripton, I'm here," I shouted.

"Calm down, Ripton," Dr. S—— was stern.

"Let me out!" Ripton pounded.

"Let him out," I hollered.

The door opened and my ten-year-old escaped beneath Dr. S——'s arm. Ripton hugged me and cried. Dr. S—— looked down on us. I held Ripton till he calmed, then we left.

Roanna called Leslie and sang Dr. S——'s praises; he'd helped other Heschel families. She also wanted to tell us that the school had decided to make Ripton's day less stressful by giving him a respite from morning prayer and studying Hebrew. He liked the school nurse, so he could visit her during these periods. It would be more calming.

Leslie and I were back in Roanna's office a few weeks later with the same six Heschel people. "You have to hire a shadow," Roanna told us, someone to stay near Ripton, help keep him focused and monitor him in the hallway when his teachers sent him there—which was more and more. The psychologist recommended we hire a student from a teachers college. I watched the man's beard rise and fall as his lips moved. He reached up with a big hand to keep his yarmulke from falling. I said that I was worried that Ripton would be stigmatized; I remembered being his age. He'd be "*stupid*" to "*retarded*." He'd be other things and none of them good.

"Oh no," the psychologist assured us, "the other students won't know. The shadow would be an *assistant teacher*."

Leslie and I spoke on the sidewalk afterwards. We didn't think a shadow was right, but Heschel wasn't giving us a choice. She was growing to detest the school. Though her parents were its first large benefactors and her mother served on the board, I was the one who had wanted our sons to go there. And now that Ripton most needed the compassion of his teachers and the administrators, this school, founded on the aura of an accepting man, was abandoning him. We searched, we advertised. Of course we couldn't find a student attending a teachers college to be a shadow. They were in school all day.

We told the school, which still insisted on a shadow. As a last resort, Yuval agreed to stay with Ripton. He was known at Heschel as our children's babysitter. He wasn't an assistant teacher. No one needed to be told he was in school all day because the school said Ripton was a mess.

Yuval told us that Ripton was in the hallway most of the time, more than we'd realized. He was afraid and angry, Yuval said. When he acted up in class, even to the smallest degree, the teachers didn't try to work with him but sent him to sit out the period. Yuval thought Ripton was trying to find boundaries, to feel supported and not abandoned. I didn't think that I, Leslie or his school were doing good jobs of it. "Why did you adopt me, if you were going to divorce?" Ripton asked one day as the two of us were crossing a street.

"We're always your mom and dad, whether we stay married or not. We always love you, and we'll always take care of you."

"Yeah. Whatever." Ripton didn't seem assured.

"Mom, I want eggs," Ripton would shout from the TV room to Leslie across from me at our kitchen table—before I left home.

"Ask for it nicely, and say '*please*,'" I said to him.

"With cheese?" Leslie shouted back from the stove.

"Mom, I want milk," Ripton would shout.

I walked down the hall. "You can get your own milk, Sweetie. You're old enough. Or ask nicely."

"You want the large glass?" Leslie shouted.

"What the fuck is that?" Ripton demanded when he saw grains of coffee floating in the milk Leslie handed him.

"Don't swear at your mother," I said.

"Don't tell him how to talk with me, that's my business," Leslie told me.

"You're teaching him how to treat women. His girlfriend or wife," I said when she and I were alone.

"That's ridiculous. If it doesn't bother me, it's not your business," she answered.

"It is. We're teaching him how to treat people. He'll treat his wife the way he learns to treat you."

"That's ridiculous," she repeated. She had a point. It wasn't the best moment for me to be giving advice on how a man might treat his wife.

The wooden crosspiece beneath the lintel of the doorway into the TV room was shattered and the double doors exposed to rip away their hinges when I went into that room one afternoon to pack the boys' clothes, Monkey and Puppy. Another time I saw a shoulder-high gash in our hand-trawled foyer wall. I looked at the wound. Its entry was clean through the first pigment and plaster. The bottom of the gash was pummeled at an acute angle, the top and longer exit line was obtuse. Its deepest point, the crux of the cut, was compactly pressed. I took a hockey stick from the sports room, lifted it to hit the wall and the heel fit precisely into the slash. I saw Ripton's anger. The door of the armoire where we kept Ripton's clothes was split in half. The bigger boys told me Ripton was breaking things. He and Morgan were screaming at Leslie. She allowed what they did.

"Don't talk like that to your mother," Carlos reprimanded Ripton.

"It's my business, not yours," Leslie scolded Carlos.

---

The next time I went to Shelter Island was to close the house for the winter and the boys wanted another adventure. We left on a Friday night, pitched tents, spread blankets on the living room floor and went to the baseball field the next morning.

We listened to music on the radio during our ride home.

"Turn the station," Will said when the news started. Ripton reached for the button but I wanted to hear about the presidential race.

"Why you care?" Carlos asked from the back.

I explained that I thought it mattered who was president.

"Kids said Lieberman would be the first Jewish president, if Gore died," Morgan said.

"Dah . . ." Ripton derided his brother.

Joseph Lieberman was Al Gore's vice-presidential running mate.

"What you mean?" Carlos asked.

"Vice president becomes president," Ripton explained.

"There's never been a Jewish president," I said.

"What you mean? All them White niggas ain't Jews?" Carlos was shocked.

I'd never thought of Washington, Lincoln, FDR, JFK and all the others as Jews.

---

In my Red Square apartment, I'd created a different life with my boys than we'd had at home before. I'd bought furniture that wasn't indestructible. I'd hung paintings on the walls. Morgan was in on one of the new chairs with his leg draped over a not particularly secure arm when I asked him to sit up straight. Which I never would have in the Christodora.

He exhaled in impatience and did.

"What would happen if you broke the arm?" I asked.

"You'd buy a new one."

Which was a fair response. I was upset, but he was telling a child's truth.

The boys went to the table when we first came home from school, sat and did their homework. I ordered in or cooked and we ate dinners together. I started taking them to synagogue on Saturday mornings. Ripton would be bar mitzvahed in a few years and then Morgan; I wanted them to know Judaism as more than a school topic. I started putting on my tallit and tefillin and saying morning prayers in their bedroom before waking them up on Wednesday mornings, that they should see and internalize more of the rituals. I'd been wrong not to do these things.

I realized there was no reason for Ripton to be ostracized at Heschel, no cause for a child to be excommunicated in a hallway.

As the school year was ending, Roanna called Leslie, insisting Ripton be tested for learning style and comprehension. She recommended a psychiatrist on the Upper East Side. Leslie had spoken with the woman and set up the two days of testing by the time she told me. A week later I took two subways and was standing on the sidewalk in front of the psychiatrist's office when a black car-service limousine pulled to the curb and Leslie, then Ripton, stepped out.

Ripton and I walked to each other and hugged. "Good morning, Sweetie," I said.

"Good morning, Dad."

He didn't want to be left in a room alone with the testing psychiatrist, but agreed to sit with her if she kept the door open to the tiny waiting room where Leslie and I were pushed close and silent for hours. On the second day the psychiatrist insisted that the door be shut and Ripton refused. She had no choice but to continue with it open. Her test results came two weeks later. Ripton needed to attend a school for emotionally and behaviorally troubled children—the psychiatrist recommended nearly a dozen.

Her results didn't feel true, but we were in the system. I dreamed that we could leave New York for somewhere else with a good public school that took any kid in the town, and ignore the test results. But I was slow to think of reality; our children's lives, my business and Leslie's, were tied to this place.

Another private school wouldn't take Ripton; they'd require Heschel's recommendations and a school report, which were both debilitating. Any of the better public schools, those that could select their students, would require the same. The neighborhood public schools, the ones accepting all children, were warehouses. Their budgets were small and shrinking, the classrooms were crowded, resources were scarce, school libraries were shut, sports programs and other after-school programs had either been discontinued or were endangered. Leslie and I didn't see a way other than to pursue a spot for Ripton at one of the schools the psychiatrist recommended. I sent for the brochures and applications. Leslie said she'd look at places after I applied, went on tours and made recommendations.

I went to Wall Street each morning but spent my days applying to the specialized schools. My mother also knew someone who knew someone who worked at another school she thought sounded like the sort of place Ripton might fit, so I needed to speak with that person. Leslie was told of another school we needed to look into. Ripton and I started with interviews. The school buildings seemed dark to me, and quiet. I felt sadnesses and fears in the hallways. People didn't laugh. These were hard resorts of hope for parents to help their children. I was sure my perception would change once Ripton was at home in one of these schools, but I wasn't at ease. These were places for children with Asperger's syndrome and other diagnoses along the autism range.

Ripton had been at Heschel for seven of his ten years, from prekindergarten through fourth grade. His classmates were what he knew. He wanted to stay and didn't understand about Yuval or the hallway, didn't understand about schools for emotionally and behaviorally troubled children, didn't understand about being abandoned by the only community he knew. Leslie and I saw him trying to be what he thought the school wanted. "I had a really good day," he said as the three of us sat at our homework table. "We learned about Tu B'Shvat—I did the best. Rivka said so." We went for a walk around the neighborhood then I served the boys chicken pot pie I'd made. "I traded Pokémon with my friends," Ripton said. "David and I traded Chikorita and Celebi, I had two Celebi. We're best friends again."

My eyes teared. The school reports continued the same or worse. Roanna told us that Ripton's classmates were afraid of him. Parents were afraid for their children to be near our son. None of his classmates visited. He wasn't invited to other kids' homes. "That's really good, Sweetie," I answered. "You have to keep doing good."

"If I do good, I can stay, can't I?" Ripton looked into my face.

I took a breath, speaking on the smooth exhale, making sure not to lie, "I hope so."

"Can't I?"

Morgan stopped chewing and watched me, his hazel eyes wide. He knew we'd been looking at schools for Ripton but hadn't put our interviews together with what would happen to him. "Am *I* staying, for sure?" he asked.

"Yes." I believed I was telling the truth.

"Can't Ripton?"

"I hope so."

Neither boy found solace in my answer. They were wise not to. Ripton and I toured a school deep in Brooklyn, an hour away without traffic. We parked on the street and walked towards the low-slung building set back in a manicured lawn. An administrator stood waiting, ushering us through silent hallways, past quiet classrooms. There were nearly as many adults in each room as students, the school overflowing with shadows. The administrator told me that some of their students were able to mainstream in middle school and still others in high school.

She finished her tour and dropped us with the assistant principal. Our application and supporting material from Heschel was spread on his desk. He shook Ripton's hand first.

"Nice to meet you," my son said. He'd stayed not more than an arm's length from me since we'd gotten out of our car.

"So, Ripton, what's your favorite subject?" the assistant principal was jovial. He seemed kind.

"Math," Ripton didn't have to think.

"Good! You do really well," the assistant principal said, his finger tracing through the school reports. "What else do you like?"

"Baseball."

"Great! What do you play?"

"First base."

"Do you play a lot?"

"Yeah, with JCC and Joe Espinosa."

"What's Joe Espinosa? That sounds interesting."

"It's a team with my Heschel friends. Do you have a team?"

"No, but kids play on summer teams. You know, *Ripton*'s a great name for a ball player, *Rip Rosen*."

Ripton smiled.

"Is it a family name?"

"It's Vermont. My mom and dad named me and my brother for Vermont."

"Robert Frost lived in Ripton," I said.

"Oh, really? My wife would appreciate that. She's a poet," the man looked to me. "Do you like poetry?" he asked.

"I do. I write."

"That's great. What style do you write?"

I had no idea. I'd tried to find a connection so this man's school might accept Ripton and now I didn't know how to answer him without looking ignorant. "I like Mark Doty. And James Galvin, I've been reading him lately."

"My wife runs a poetry group. Her work isn't contemporary, like theirs. She's a naturalist, but maybe you'd be interested?"

I said of course how much I would be—in reading her work. While finding a new school for Ripton and worrying about his future, making sure he survived in his old school, as my relationship with my business partner was falling apart and my family was battered by the effects of separation, *yes yes* I said how excited I was about the possibility of reading new poetry.

The assistant principal wrote down his wife's name and her book titles. I said I'd buy her poetry. He accompanied us to the principal, who smiled and shook our hands. Ripton looked into her eyes and said, "Nice to meet you," again. The principal told us how unique her school was, how children did so well. I kept nodding my head, *yes yes*.

The assistant principal called a few days later. I told him I'd been reading his wife's poetry. And how much I liked it. He told me how much he liked Ripton and that we needed to complete some parts of his file. He called again the next week. They'd accepted our son.

Bless them. They were the only school. Leslie and I had finally realized that Heschel had no intention to keep him. Roanna was erasing Ripton from the moment he was allowed to skip morning prayer and Hebrew. Roanna and the others were peeling him away from the Jewish aspects of a Jewish community. *Keriah.* Jews tear their clothes when they hear of the death of close family, the same when a son or daughter marries outside the faith. Roanna started making sure months earlier that Ripton would become outside the community. Leslie and I were too slow to understand. We were too distracted.

"It's not Ripton," I said to Leslie when we spoke about his acceptance.

"What's not?" she asked.

Our son was a difficult boy having a hard time, sensitive and fragile inside his outside of loud and large. He wasn't Asperger's or otherwise autistic—though I know these aren't solid lines. He wasn't ADD or ADHD. He had mild sensory issues. The experts couldn't fit him into an easy box of "*normal*" and were putting him where he'd be long or forever outside—they'd measured, poked and shoved him that way. Once the door closed behind, he would be what these people called him. "They're wrong. He should be at a regular school."

"You think so?"

"Yes."

"Me too. I've been thinking the same."

Leslie knew of a Brooklyn school supposedly like Heschel, combining Jewish and secular studies, but with a culture of compassion. I called the principal and told her about our son, including the psychological testing and the diagnosis prescribing a school for emotionally and behaviorally troubled children. She told me that she was a Heschel refugee. She wanted Ripton's school records and the Upper East Side psychiatrist's study. Her assistant called some days later, asking that I come for an interview. The principal told me, as we sat, that she didn't see anything in Ripton's capabilities, personality and behavior she felt was inappropriate. She wanted him to attend a day of class.

"He's great!" the principal said when I picked our son up at the end of that day. "He fits right in." Ripton's general knowledge was good, but his Hebrew and prayers were weak and would take work. I should call the next morning.

When I did, she said we should apply. The weightlessness I felt, the possibility, made me aware how heavy it had been. I asked the principal about Morgan—we hoped our sons might go to the same school. More than the travel in opposite directions, we had no respect for Heschel. The principal asked to see Morgan's records, then for him to spend a day, and then for us to apply for both boys.

Morgan blamed his day at Hannah Senesh and the terror of leaving his Heschel friends on his older brother. If Ripton was bad, why did he have to be punished? Why was all this happening? Why couldn't his brother be normal? Ripton, for his part, didn't want to leave Heschel. He blamed us. He said the people in Brooklyn were nice, but he didn't want to go to a Jewish school anyways. If he had to leave Heschel, he wanted to go to a *"regular"* school.

My divorce lawyer knew the principal of the Earth School, a public grade school on Avenue B almost equidistant between Leslie and

me, not more than a few minutes' walk from either. The school tried
for small classes and encouraged parent participation. The principal
agreed to meet, telling me to bring Ripton's school records and test
results. She reviewed these as we sat, closed the file and asked me to
explain our son. When I finished, she said Ripton might fit. She
wanted to sit with him and then with Leslie. I explained that we
hoped to find a school for both sons. She said how hard it would be
to find openings in two grades, but to bring Morgan's records as well.

Hannah Senesh accepted Ripton and Morgan. They were upset.
They didn't want to lose their friends. Morgan blamed Ripton, Ripton blamed Leslie and me, Leslie blamed me. The Earth School
wouldn't have its lottery results until late July or early August. Hannah Senesh required substantial deposits to hold the two spots. We
paid them, thankful that its principal had the wisdom and courage
to see Ripton for the loud, socially awkward but intelligent and well-
intentioned boy that he was.

Come late July, the Earth School accepted both boys. They were
going to walk to school.

---

A man was standing inside the window of the Duane Reade drugstore across from my office. He looked in his midthirties, thin, with
carefully combed brown hair. He was facing the street, leaning from
behind into a display of shining Colgate toothpaste boxes, Irish
Spring soap, Herbal Essence shampoo, Tampax and Always Maxi
Pads stacked and arched around primary-colored return-to-school
spiral notebooks, three-ring binders, pencils, Day-Glo highlighters,
pencils and pens. With his midnight blue workman's coveralls, I figured he was arranging more soap or pencils into the display. But he
was standing like a mannequin, smiling, holding a square of hand-
lettered cardboard to his chest: LOVE IS ALL WE HAVE. This is New
York—he had to have been insane. Customers were hurrying in and
out, a few inches away, ignoring him. I stood transfixed, confused,
wondering where his scam was, if he were part of the display or dis-

turbed. He turned to me, smiled and jibed his head to the words. *Love is all we have.*

I'd been in the office for almost forty-five minutes and was trying to get off a phone call to talk with my chief operating officer, standing impatiently in the doorway. The room shifted, the fluorescent lights lacerated and the phone line scratched. "Oh-my-God," Jonah shouted, staring into the next-door office and through its windows at what I'd in moments see to be torrents of paper, flame and smoke flowing from the top of the North Tower. "A plane," Jonah said, "has to be."

That corner office filled with all the people at work. Soon after, a commercial jet flew between us and the buildings across Trinity Place, slicing a hole with a diagonal wingspan across more floors and disintegrating into the South Tower. The people in our corner office shrieked and groaned.

My cell phone rang; Leslie knew about the planes. She saw the Towers burning and wanted to make sure I was alive—I was often at the Trade Center. "I'll get the boys," she offered. "Come when you can."

The top floors of the South Tower collapsed onto themselves, churning until the sky was gray cloud rushing towards us. The others hurried from the corner room. Palms flat against the glass, I waited as the plume came but realized the windows might burst and I shouldn't be there. I stepped halfway back. The room went dark. Unharmed, wishing I hadn't moved, I hurried to the window and pressed my face to the other side, into dust and what I hadn't yet come to realize was human debris. I watched until it slowly lightened. People on the street were dust. Four firemen walked at the back of the small crowd, their coats and helmets gray, spread in a loose line from sidewalk nearly to sidewalk, three facing the way they were going and one turned backward toward the destruction. The North Tower crushed in on itself, boiling dust down Rector Street. The firemen bent and disappeared. The others, a few steps from the corner, rushed to duck beside the two-story building there, turning into what they might have thought was safety. But at the confluence of Rector with Greenwich Street they found the same cloud rolling. Our office went dark a second time. I didn't move from the windows.

The air conditioners, computers, printers and photocopy machines went silent and cell phone service stopped. Then the regular phones stopped working. Three of our staff, coated in dust and terrified, came up the stairs. From Shanghai and Beijing, they were computer programmers who'd immigrated for what they hoped were better opportunities. They were caught below when the South Tower started to fall. They'd seen people jump holding hands.

We counted ourselves, spoke about how we'd get home, made plans if we couldn't and talked about the meeting we had that Friday with a Connecticut group we hoped would be an important client. The others packed and left. I fed my fish, walked around the office to check on things and locked the door on my way out.

The phones were working at the Wall Street firm, farther away from what would become *Ground Zero*. Leslie said she'd gone to school soon after we last spoke. Ripton was hiding beneath his desk. Both our sons heard the Towers collapse. "When can you come?" she asked.

I walked to Broadway and north, past rubble and fires, beside rescue workers, police and firemen, ambulances, police cars and fire trucks. Dust was covering cars, mailboxes, the streetlights and electric wires overhead like an autumn snowfall. Some around me were breathing through scarves and dust masks. I picked up a few pages from the countless on the ground, a ticker-tape parade up the Canyon of Heroes made by a great suck of documents. I chose pieces burnt around their edges, dry to the touch: a Japanese newspaper, a *From the Desk of Casey* C—— piece of notepad with a baby blue insurance company logo printed beside the woman's name, the sort given in corporate life. I read the woman's obituary in the *New York Times* a few weeks later. She'd started at the insurance company two months before.

I met a young couple weighted beneath large backpacks, the man cradling a thin white cat with black-tipped ears. They lived in an apartment south of the Towers, were at home for the destruction and waited for quiet before carrying out what they could. We walked past emergency nurses and physicians lined up beside white-sheeted gurneys on the street at Downtown Hospital, the closest to the Trade Towers; but there were few injured and no ambulances came. The dust covering the ground ended when we walked beneath the Manhattan Bridge. The sidewalks and streets afterwards were as if nothing happened. The couple and I parted. I walked to my apartment, changed from my dust-covered clothes and shoes, picked up the puppy I'd recently gotten for the boys and went to Leslie's.

"CutedogMike," Dennis sat on the stoop, already in his paratrooper pants, a tee and sneakers. "Whatshisname?" His hand was shaking. He held a cigarette to his lips long enough to suck twice.

"Mr. Jenkins. How ya doing, Dennis?"

"IcantIcant . . ." and he took another drag.

"I know. I just came from there."

"Igotthefuckout, whentheyfell, Iaintgoinback, nofuckinway."

I went into the building.

"What's his name? He's cute," Leslie bent and petted the pug, who pushed against her.

"Mr. Jenkins," Ripton announced because he was the one who wanted a dog and named the puppy. He pursued me. Leslie was allergic, scratched her eyes, sneezed and took antihistamines on our way to a pet owner's home. I didn't know how to care for a dog but Ripton was relentless.

"That's a good name," Leslie said. The dog wagged its tail, squirmed and licked her hands. I thought she'd pull back, sneeze or scratch her eyes.

"His middle name is MooShoo. I named him that," Morgan said. "Pugs are Chinese."

"He's so cute," Leslie kept petting the dog.

"Hug him," Morgan told her. "He loves it, see?" and he held the dog by his ribcage, lifted him facing out, the dog and our son resting body to chest and nestled face against face. Morgan held the dog out to Leslie.

She hugged Mr. Jenkins fur to face.

The bigger boys came soon afterwards.

"We heard it fall," Ripton told them.

"Couldn'ta," Will answered.

I had been the closest and had no recollection of sound.

"We did," Morgan backed up his brother. "It was like, *bbughhhhh-hhhh* a long time."

I could always smell the deep acid of burning. The flames and falling came back. But try as I might, over the weeks, I could never recall any sound.

At Leslie's, we walked between the news on TV in Ripton's room and the terrace to watch smoke billow from downtown. Neighbors came. Our parents, relatives and friends called our cell phones.

"Who done it?" Will demanded.

"Gotta kill them niggas," Phil was indignant.

"Who?" Ripton asked.

"Thems who done it, them gotta pay."

By nighttime the correspondents were talking about Osama bin Laden and al-Qaeda.

"Mike, where them peoples at?" Juan asked.

"Afghanistan."

"Them gotta pay," Phil offered again.

"Wasn't there a war there?" Juan was trying to place things.

"Suckup!" Carlos slapped Juan on the shoulder, but a bit hard. "Juan goes"—flattening his voice—'*Wasn't there a war there?*' all White like."

"*Wasn't there a war there?*" Phil pushed the impersonation, like the TV newscasters we'd been watching.

"We backed the Taliban against the Russians. We sent them weapons and they won. They took control of Afghanistan, insisted on an Islamic regime and invited al-Qaeda. We became their definition of evil."

"That's whack?" Carlos complained—"That's not right," Will was angry—"But what's al-Qaeda?" Juan asked—the three boys at once.

"We sent weapons, and in a way, they're using them against us," I said.

"I say nuke 'em, they A-rabs, rah?" Phil asked.

"The Afghanis, the Taliban, they're mostly Turkman. Al-Qaeda, most are probably Arab."

"But they Islam, rah?" Juan asked.

I agreed.

"Same thing. They A-rab," Phil reasoned. "Like them peoples on the sidewalk." He meant the Muslim couple who'd opened a pet supply shop two doors from the Christodora. The man was my age, no longer young. He was brave or pushed to open a new business, a cigarette always in or near his mouth. He wore a button-down shirt open at the collar, pressed black pants and black tie shoes. His wife, stout and younger by a decade and a half or more, was black in hi-jabs wrapping all but her face and intricately embroidered abayas draped to the ground. She wore black pumps and sometimes high heels. They had one young son and a baby cradled in her arms even as she worked the cash register. The four were at their store seven days a week from early to late. There were no other workers.

"I don't think they're Arab. They're Pakistani or Afghani. They're Iranic peoples, probably, but I don't remember."

"FuckinMike, man," Carlos was smiling.

"I don't care, I ain't trustin them niggas, I say ship 'em back."

"Phil—" I started.

"I ain't jokin. I ain't walkin by that store, they probably figurin how ta kill us."

"They're probably American, you idiot," I said.

"Watch your language," Leslie admonished me.

"Not real American," Phil answered.

"You born in the Dominican, dumb ass," Carlos reminded him.

"But I'm not A-rab," Phil insisted. "No Spanish crazy ta be blowin up America."

Will and Juan laughed at the idea. Kindu smiled. Carlos whooped, "YoMike, that true. Spanish ain't be blowin up no buildings and doin suicide," and he moved into a tango.

I avoided what little I knew about Puerto Rican drives for inde-pendence, Pedro Albizu Campos, the Nationalist Party, revolution, pain and death. "I'm disappointed in you guys. This country was built on acceptance. More than some White kid in a suburb, you gotta know racism is wrong."

"I ain't racist," Phil pursed his lips.

"No, of course not. What do you call it?"

"Them peoples kilt us," Phil explained.

"What's 'Iranic peoples'?" Juan asked, a student in the first row with his hand up.

"Suckup!" Carlos slapped Juan far harder than before.

Juan cradled a bicep. "Fuck, Carlos!" he cried.

"Man up, pussy. Ya wanna hit me? I stand here, hit me!" Carlos' smile was sinister.

Juan reached to the kitchen table and hurled a cobalt blue bottle of my fountain-pen ink at Carlos, shattering against the stainless-steel kitchen sink, glass and ink flying in a fantail across the sink and tile backsplash, running cobalt to azure to turquoise. "Fuck you!" he seethed.

"Stop!" Leslie screamed.

Carlos was at Juan, his right hand fisted and cocked.

"Stop!" she screamed again.

Carlos grabbed Juan and bearhugged him, the smaller boy kicking while the larger swung him as a rag doll. Juan was already sixteen, Carlos a half year younger. We'd met them nearly three and a half years earlier. They got along least well of all the boys, at opposite ends of the five. At best, they tolerated each other with little in common except strikingly similar lives.

Juan's mother moved from Puerto Rico and gave birth to him when she was sixteen. She told her son he was conceived in date rape. Juan didn't know how old his father was, or much else about the man except that he was Black, became a cop, Esther married him and they were together for three years until James did something to Juan—Esther refuses to say what—and she took Juan away.

Esther gave birth to a daughter by another man a year later. "I remember him a little bit," Juan said of his sister's father. "He was a nice guy. He was living with us." Until he was knifed to death when Juan was nine. "I was too young to know how much I cared about him." Juan's mother shipped him off for the first time then, to his maternal grandmother in Brooklyn. He hated going, except to get away from Esther's beatings. She was twenty-five, a mother by one man she left and another who was murdered.

Esther eventually started with another man and two years after the murder gave birth to a younger brother. "But that guy's not wif us no more," Juan said. Juan's mother told the man to leave; he'd been beating her. By this time Juan lived full time with his grandmother.

He lived with his grandmother through elementary school, which ended in fifth grade. His family felt that the junior high school there was bad and his godparents, in the Jacob Riis projects a few blocks from where Carlos would move, agreed Juan should live with them. His godfather had fought with James Robinson in Vietnam.

Juan took refuge in TV; the monsters and good guys in *Power Rangers* became his world. Justin, the Blue Turbo Ranger, was his favorite—it was a color thing.

Carlos also took refuge in TV, especially once his mother started kicking him out, after his father left. *Popeye* was his favorite. "All's I need is a TV and food." He inherited a small portable from Jesus, who'd inherited it from his father's mother. Carlos said his mother also only needed a TV and food. She's never worked since he's been alive and he doubts before that. "She never liked me, maybe cause I'm too much like her, or cause my dad raped her—not who I say's my dad, that's Carmello Ayala, Carmello, Ricky and Baby's dad, but Carlos Suarez, my biological dad, who had me."

Carmello Ayala came into Evelyn and her first three children's lives—Tita, Jesus, Carlos—soon after Carlos was born. He was two and a half when his mom and new dad had their first child together, Carmello Jr.

Carmello bought Carlos his first baseball glove, taught him to throw, catch and bat. They watched Yankee games together. Carlos remembers Evelyn and Carmello drinking beer, rum and coke and dancing in the kitchen close at night with the radio on. His dad taught Carlos to salsa. He remembers his dad hitting his mom "when she got out of hand." The man was bigger than life to him.

Carlos was eight when Carmello left, for another woman. That's when Evelyn first called her mother about Carlos, saying she didn't want him in her home.

His grandmother said she'd have him.

Carlos packed his TV and other belongings into a shopping cart and pushed it the dozen blocks to his grandmother's. He did that whenever his mother kicked him out, then pushed it a dozen blocks home when she decided he should come back. He remembers the turn of the wheels on concrete and blacktop, the shimmy against acceleration when he was caught by a changing light, the glint of chrome in sunlight, taking refuge in *Popeye* when he arrived either way.

Evelyn got with another man soon after Carmello Ayala left, then Johnny after that, and both of them hit the children. "You don't hit another man's children, I blame my mother. She knew it, so she let him. My grandmother said I should tell my father. I didn't do it, I known how he'd be, but someone else tolt him. That's why my father hated Johnny. It wasn't that he was wif my mother. My father didn't give a fuck about that. It was that he was hittin us. You don't do that, you don't hit another man's children, that's like spitting at him." Carmello told Johnny he'd mess him up if Johnny ever touched his children again.

Carlos was nearly home from school in the spring of fifth grade, a few days before Good Friday, when he saw his dad. "*Papi,*" he yelled over the basketball courts and courtyard that separated their apartment buildings and ran to him.

"Carlito," his dad waved a thick arm high above his head and his hand broad then scooped to hug his son.

"Can I have an ice cream, *Papi?*"

The two started off together to buy a treat then realized Johnny was across the way, about to walk into Evelyn's building. "See that piece of shit?" Carmello boomed so Johnny would hear, in Spanish as he always did. "He's nothing. You understand me? And you can't be afraid of nothing. That piece of shit won't touch you, or I'll kill him. You understand me, Carlito?"

Good Friday, a day off from school, was warm. Evelyn brought Carlos, Carmelo, Ricky and Baby down to the courtyard in front of their building to enjoy the weather. Other families were barbequing, but they couldn't afford to. Carlos heard the Mister Softee ice cream truck jingle at the same moment he saw his dad. "*Papi*, buy me an ice cream," he ran to Carmelo, who gave his son ten dollars, enough for all four boys, and waited for the change.

Carlos hurried to the ice cream truck with Carmelo Jr. and came back in time to watch Johnny throwing a glass of rum in his dad's face. From upstairs, Johnny had seen Carlos asking Carmelo for money.

Carmelo rubbed the sting from his eyes. Johnny stabbed him with a screwdriver and stabbed him again. Carmelo, eyes open, punched Johnny then punched him again. Johnny, surprised Carmelo was fighting, ran to the street. Carmelo followed. Johnny hid in the back of an empty van. Carmelo wasn't fooled. Carlos ran to a phone booth and called 911. He came back and saw his dad walking out of the van, but with blood on his shirt. "I'm okay, Carlito," Carmelo assured his oldest son. "I told you don't worry about that piece of shit. But I'm going to rest," he said in Spanish, waving with an arm high above his head, his hand broad as he walked up the steps to the concrete platform before the portico of his public housing high-rise. He searched for his key, turned and assured his son, "Don't worry, Carlito."

The police came and Carlos took them to Carmelo's apartment. The front door was open, his girlfriend and some others frantic. Carmelo was on the ground. "*Papi*," Carlos cried. Carmelo was dead.

The police found Johnny a block away, his eyes swollen too shut to see.

"YoMike, I gotta aks ya a question," Carlos said when he told me this story, "but ya gotta promise to tell me the truf, rah?"

I promised.

"If I hadn'ta aksed my dad for money, he woulda been alive, cause he wouldn'ta gotten into a fight. So it's my fault he's dead, rah? It is. Rah?"

"No, it's not."

"It is, cause he'da been alive. You promised to tell me the truf."

"You were eleven years old, asking for an ice cream. That's what a kid's supposed to do."

"Yeah, but if I hadn'ta aksed for that ice cream, he'da been alive. So I kilt him."

"You didn't." And I explained again.

"You just bein nice. I aksed ya to tell me the truf."

"It is the truth."

---

"Stop!" Leslie yelled a third time.

Carlos put Juan down, who swatted at him and huffed into the living room. Will followed.

Leslie and I cleaned up the broken glass and ink. Kindu came and helped. Carlos, tense, walked to the TV room. "Crazy nigga," Philippe smiled and followed him. The announcer was talking about death toll estimates when I walked in a few minutes later. "I still say, we gotta fuck them peoples. We gotta blow up their country," Philippe insisted.

"Which country, Phil?" I asked. "All of them in the Middle East? In Central Asia?"

"Whatever, it don't matter. All of it. You know I'm gonna join the marines. See what them peoples have done ta us?"

I shrugged. The guardians of our nation would seek retribution with or without Phil.

"Dad's gonna turn all peace, you watch," Ripton warned.

"YoMike, you knows we gotta fuck up them peoples, you seen what they done," Carlos explained.

"Giuliani's the man!" Philippe said with our mayor telling us on TV that the National Guard had moved in, below Fourteenth Street was cordoned off, below Canal Street was a second and stricter boundary and the New York Stock Exchange would open within days. Our city would be put back together better than before and anyone with a business or job destroyed would be taken care of.

"You joinin, I joinin too," Will came from the fringe of the hallway into Ripton's room.

Carlos and Kindu stayed quiet.

"I'm mad hungry," Ripton told us. He wanted Chinese and we phoned the restaurant at Red Square but they didn't answer. Leslie and I made eggs and toast for everyone except Kindu, who didn't eat eggs, and toasted waffles for him. I watched Kindu bathe them in maple syrup near to the rim of his plate and he rinsed much of it down the drain later. A Vermonter wouldn't pour out maple syrup. That was sacrilegious.

We watched CNN, Carlos and I tried to play chess, he and Juan made a rough peace and the wind shifted, blowing that smoke and stink into the neighborhood. I started coughing and closed the terrace door and windows on the south side of the apartment. The bigger boys decided it was time to get to their families or to each other's homes; they'd come back in the morning.

Leslie and I both remembered that it was my night to have our sons and it was nearly their bedtime. "If you want help packing Ripton and Morgan's things . . ." she started.

I didn't want them to have to leave. "I'll come back in the morning," I said. Leslie and I put them to bed at nine o'clock.

The dog and I walked out onto a silent street—to no cars or trucks, and it took a few moments for the softer canopy of sound to filter through; people walking, passing on bicycles and kick scooters.

I started to the park, then remembered the couple from the pet supply shop and Mr. Jenkins was happy to turn that way. The owners sat outside, the baby asleep in the woman's arms and the boy collapsed into his father's. The man and I nodded as we normally did. I wanted to ask why they hadn't gone home. Were they anxious? Did they sense the fear that would fan across the country? "Hi," I said beyond my nod and Mr. Jenkins pulled to press against the hem of the woman's abaya.

"Hello," the man answered, what I guessed a Pakistani accent coated in tar and nicotine. He and his wife had a too-concerned look. Or perhaps it was exhaustion.

It was too early to go back to my apartment. I thought of friends to call but my cell phone wasn't working. I turned back to the park, passed the couple at their store and Dennis came out of the Christodora, a cigarette between his lips, flicking his lighter. I said hello.

"Hey. WhenIwasoutbefore," and he took a long drag, "theywerelightincandlesinthepark. Yawannasee?"

We walked into Tompkins Square. Light danced along the underside of the Hare Krishna Tree, the American elm spreading its enormous canopy over an area where young children and their parents usually played kickball or soccer, where people sat on benches, played their guitars and read the newspaper. Srila Prabhupada and his followers had sat beside this tree in the autumn of 1966, chanting

*Hare Krishna, Hare Krishna, Krishna Krishna, Hare Hare*
*Hare Rama, Hare Rama, Rama Rama, Hare Hare*

for the first time outside India while others danced, played cymbals and tambourines. Allen Ginsberg was with them. The undulating trunk of the Hare Krishna Tree was garlanded in pressed flowers the saffron and crimson colors of Hare Krishna robes much of the time and petals were strewn on the ground. Tens of candles burned as a shrine at its base now, left in shock and grief, hope and desperation beside papers and poster board with notes and pictures of loved ones, which business in the Trade Towers the person worked for, where he was last known to be, hopes she was wandering confused, a phone number. "*Marie, if you see this . . . Call home . . . We love you . . .*" Candles and shadow played in an almost imperceptible breeze. Dennis and I watched. The dog watched. People came with fresh flowers and more candles, said their hopes and left. The dog pulled at his leash, struggling for the tree, climbed between its thick roots hugging the ground and lifted his leg to pee nearly hidden within.

"Michael," Dennis called softly, the hand of a lit cigarette waving into the tree, tobacco glowing as it was fanned. "Anowl, see?" And I did; an eastern screech owl, *Megascops asio*, what I'd grown up with in Vermont, no more than six or eight inches tall, gray, waiting motionless with mirror eyes on a lower branch for a mouse or baby rat. The bagpiper who sometimes played at night in the park, a large and solid man in a Davidson-plaid kilt, started up a mournful calling. I nodded to Dennis, who stayed with the shrine, owl and pipes.

Mr. Jenkins followed me when I went upstairs after I let myself into the apartment in the morning. I sat on a side of the sofa bed watching our sons cuddled into each other. I missed that the most. The dog jumped onto the mattress and nestled between them. I listened to them breathe.

Mr. Jenkins heard her first and hurled himself over Ripton for the stairs. The boys woke, saw me and put their heads down again.

"Mr. Jenkins!" Leslie came down in her light gray and blue flannel nightgown, the dog snuffling at her feet. Leslie rested her hand on the back of my head, her skin warm. The boys watched us there.

The *New York Times* wasn't at the front door and the television announcer said school was cancelled. The bigger boys came and we fed everyone except Kindu eggs and toast, waffles and maple syrup, pizza pockets, Stouffer's macaroni and cheese, milk, bowls of cereal, Gatorade in various colors but mostly red and more. By lunchtime the Chinese restaurant was delivering. "Mike, not bein Juan, but who is that bin Laden dude?" Phil asked from the other end of the dining room table, his mouth full of fried chicken wings and fried rice, looking at Juan next to him, who seemed amused and annoyed.

Neither Leslie nor I knew much.

"Why do they hate us?" Juan dared to ask. He and Carlos were at opposite ends of the table and didn't look at each other.

"The Crusades . . . cultural imperialism . . ." I went into too long an explanation and the boys, except for Juan, faded to their food.

"We gotsta kill that dude." Phil looked up when I finished.

"Can I ride my bike?" Morgan asked.

"I'll take you out," I said, wanting to flee the intended destruction.

"Phil's right," Ripton tried to keep the conversation in place.

"We'll get 'em, we rule," Will bit into a Hot Pocket, grease, tomato sauce and melted cheese coating his lips.

"You think we're the best?" I asked, apparently not able to control myself.

"YoMike, we wons everything, rah? We gots them Hummers and missiles," Carlos explained.

"No doubt bout that, nigga. We the best," Phil boasted. "Any duck sauce over there?" he asked our end of the table.

The boys, save Morgan, were smitten with Hummers. They were drawn to big and shiny, sleek and electronic things. Our nation's volunteer military was filled with boys exactly like our bigger ones. I imagined them some years older, weighed down with heavy backpacks, sweltering beneath battle gear in an Afghanistan summer, angry, listless, hungering for Hot Pockets and shrimp fried rice on the Lower East Side.

Morgan rode his bike while Mr. Jenkins and I walked close to him around Tompkins Square. We went to the baseball field, past the primary-colored jungle gyms where a few parents pushed their children on swings and guarded them on the slides, past the neoclassical Temperance Fountain where Mr. Jenkins marked territory and to the Hare Krishna Tree, where he worked into the deep roots again and did the same. A few candles inside glass holders were burning, the others empty or blown out. Morgan looked at the shrine, the photographs and messages. "Dad, what is it?" he asked.

"For the Trade Towers."

"I know, but what?"

I explained as best I could.

"Were you inside?"

I thought he'd known, and described being close.

"Did you see people die?" The dog sniffed around the photographs, shied from the burning candles.

"I saw the second plane crash." I left out the rest.

"We heard the buildings fall."

"That must have been scary."

"Ripton was hiding under his desk." Morgan started pedaling away then turned to circle slowly around the dog and me. "Dad, are you and mom getting married?"

"We're separated, Morgy. We're not divorced."

"I know, but are you?" he completed a circle.

"We're getting along better."

"I don't want you to be home. I like your apartment."

"Nothing's happening now. But it's important Mom and I get along. Sweetie, at school yesterday, were you okay?"

"Yeah, sure. Dad—" and he circled more, "but because Ripton's messed up, it's not fair I can't be at Heschel." He kept riding.

"He's not messed up. He had a hard year. Heschel wasn't a good place for us."

"For me it was."

"They didn't treat us well, Morgie. You must have seen that."

"Yuval sat in the hall with Ripton. Kids were afraid of him."

"Yeah?"

"Some, they said he was a freak, being there like when there was assembly and stuff, or he was in the nurse's office."

"What did you think?"

Morgan thought a moment. "He's unhappy," he answered plainly, "about you and Mom. He's real sensitive."

"When we go fishing, he makes us throw everything back, right? He cries if a fish dies. He gives money to every poor person we go by. There's no way he's hurting anyone, but people don't understand him. Heschel didn't care about him. Morgie, are you making friends?"

"Yeah, DJ's my best friend, but I like lots of kids."

"I'd like to meet him—DJ."

"His dad's a marine. He's gonna be one."

The world was filled with military things. "What's his last name?" I wondered whether Morgan's best friend was Spanish, White, Jewish, Black, whatever.

"DJ."

"But his family name?"

Morgan shrugged, my question odd. "Dad? It's not fair you take us skiing, Ripton gets to go fishing in Florida, but you never take me to Dallas."

Where he was born. I'd never thought of it. He'd not mentioned his birth mother in years. He'd not called himself *Morgan Brock*.

"It's not fair."

I told Leslie later. We didn't know when or how, but agreed Morgan deserved his homecoming.

———————

Yuval called late morning, then Jonny McGovern, checking if we were okay. They came up to Leslie's apartment within minutes of each other, allowed beneath the police cordon with a childcare excuse. I hadn't seen them in a month or more, happenstance of schedules. Jonny wore aviator glasses, a black muscle shirt with "GAY PIMP" in silver rhinestone letters and equally tight jeans. He was more muscled again. He threw Morgan into the air. "Me, too," Ripton demanded, howling each time Jonny let go and caught him again. I hadn't seen our older son give himself to such joy in so long. "More," Ripton shouted when Jonny stopped from exhaustion.

"You're too big, Ripperman," Jonny put him down, out of breath and sweating. "You're growing up."

Ripton looked around the living room, as if for something to hold on to. "Let's play baseball. You, too," he said to Jonny and Yuval.

Jonny slipped his aviator glasses back on. "The Gay Pimp doesn't do baseball," his stage voice declared.

"I'll play, but I didn't come here till middle school, you know," Yuval warned. He wore Docker chinos, a Ralph Lauren cotton polo and prep school glasses.

"So?" Ripton asked.

"So I—"

"*You play ball like a girl!*" Ripton exploded in his laughter, quoting one of our favorite movies.

"Yuval, dogs, is that how you throw?" Philippe taunted with his smile.

"Like this?" Will asked, putting the wrong foot forward, his elbow too far back, his body rigid when he threw and the others laughed. Yuval's face flushed red. Ripton copied Will more spastically.

"You gay," Philippe chastised Ripton, then the recognition of faux pas settled in. "Like, happy," he deadpanned, lifting his palms up, shrugging in supplication to our sons' caregivers.

"Nigga Phil," Carlos mumbled and frowned in amusement.

"Ain't ya gonna whack 'im?" Will demanded of Jonny.

"Tell the truf, ain't nothin everyone done say. What you smilin at?" Philippe focused on Kindu.

"My million-dollar smile," Kindu answered.

"Ain't ya gonna shove 'im against the wall?" Will demanded of Jonny.

"Ya gives us a lecture 'bout this, that and the third," Kindu concurred, focusing on Jonny.

"This, that and the third, nigga." Carlos took a few happy salsa steps.

Jonny only feinted a step towards Philippe.

"Nigga gonna kill ya, son!" Carlos swiveled his hips and mimed a dance partner in his open hands.

Jonny patted Phil on the shoulder.

We played a short-handed game in Tompkins Square. Yuval threw perfectly well.

---

"Imnotgoin," Dennis said when I walked into the Christodora a couple mornings later.

"What are you talking about?"

"Bastardsopeningthemarket," he waved his cigarette in short, angry sweeps. I was lost for a moment. The bottom of Manhattan had become, save for the few official vehicles, a pedestrian and bicycle village. Newspapers weren't delivered. Restaurants and groceries walked and rolled their goods from Fourteenth Street. The boys played baseball in Tompkins Square. The trees seemed larger and more important. Without my business or the Yankees on TV, I'd lost track of the days and had forgotten it was Sunday.

"Ifwedon'tgo, werefired," he took another smoke. "Youknowwha-tImdoin?"—and another.

I was silent.

"I'm-not-goin-back, thatswhat. I'm-burning-my-suits, youwanna-come?"

A few of us stood in a vacant lot as Dennis burned ten suits in an oil drum that night. He was on the stoop when the dog and I came to the Christodora the next morning.

Two weeks later, the morning we were able to go back to work, I called half my employees into our conference room and fired them. We'd lost our major client. I'd fire everyone else the week between Christmas and New Year's.

---

Ripton was old enough, per Earth School rules, to be dismissed on his own from school. Morgan had to be picked up from his classroom.

Leslie waited with him for Ripton outside school one afternoon. The front door burst open and Ripton rushed down the steps. Another boy hurried through the closing door, bounded down the seven steps in two jumps and slugged Ripton in the face. Who punched him back. Leslie pushed the two apart. Michelle, the Earth School principal, came and took each boy aside.

Leslie called me in panic. Michelle had given detention to Ripton and his classmate. Leslie was terrified that our Heschel experience was repeating itself; Ripton would be ostracized, and then worse. The other boy, dreadlocks to his waist and a Rasta name like his father's, a sweet reggae musician from Brooklyn, had thrown the first punch. But something happened in the classroom for which Michelle held each boy responsible. Ripton protested that she was picking on him. Leslie insisted the line was crossed when the Brooklyn boy slugged our son in the face. Only he should be given detention. "It's a good place for Ripton," Leslie said of the Earth School. He had been doing well. But what if the experts had been right? "My stomach hurts," Leslie said.

I was relieved that Ripton had learned to stand his own.

Leslie wanted me to meet with Michelle and speak with Ripton. But Michelle said she had no concern, other than for Ripton to learn that he couldn't fight in or near school.

"Dad, can I go back to Heschel? I hate it here," Ripton said when we started talking.

I explained that he couldn't because Heschel didn't want us. If he got kicked out of the Earth School, for fighting or anything else, we had nowhere else for him to go.

"You and Mom messed it up for me and Morgan."

"It didn't work, Sweetie. And remember, you didn't like the Hebrew and prayers."

"I miss my best friends."

"You'll make friends, I know you will."

"I hate the kids. They're stupid." And he wasn't making friends. Ripton played with the bigger boys, with Morgan and the friends his younger brother made, and alone with his video games. He still wasn't invited to anyone's home after school.

---

Ernesto Ferran, the counselor who eventually helped Ripton and us, said that Leslie and I solved problems together better than most married couples. We did work well together. Ripton would have otherwise been catalogued, filed, boxed and sent off to storage in a way his life didn't demand. Leslie, our sons, the bigger boys and I had grown back together. I became obsessed with a Claude Lévi-Strauss quote I partially remembered from graduate school, something about the size of groups we lead our caring lives with. I hunted through boxes of my books displaced from when I left home. I'd come across this idea on the right-side page of a book—that Parisian sophisticates and Amazon rainforest villagers led their most intimate lives with the same number of people, regardless of the populations of Paris and an Amazon village, regardless of the vastly expanded quantity of acquaintances those in modernity encountered. I remembered

Levi-Strauss saying the number was nine or a dozen people and we were that, with our sons and the bigger boys. I rode my bike to a local college library and pulled Lévi-Strauss from the open stacks and couldn't find the passage. I contacted two of the anthropologist's biographers but the idea didn't sound familiar to them. I reached out to my graduate school advisor, who didn't remember any such idea but suggested a title I found at the original Barnes & Noble bookstore, on East Eighteenth and Fifth. A woman in the reference department agreed to hold the one remaining copy for me till the evening.

I'd arranged with Leslie to use our hatchback that day. Its lease and parking space payments had always been paid through her office and she treated the car as hers. Phil and Carlos agreed to help me move boxes out of my Wall Street office and I planned to stop at Eighteenth and Fifth before unloading for the last time. It was almost seven when we got the last belongings of my finance career into the car.

"Mike," Phil began when I started the motor.

"Yeah?"

"Can you take me and Carlos shopping before we gets home?"

"Sure," I said. "What do you need?"

"Clothes for school, on Fourteenth, it's close."

"I need to stop for a book on Eighteenth Street. They're holding it."

"Holding a book?"

"White people," Carlos jibed from the backseat.

I hurried to Barnes & Noble but couldn't find a parking space. I left the car in front of a hydrant and the keys in the ignition so Carlos and Phil could listen to the radio. I ran across the street, picked up my book and found one reference to *Paris* in the index. I congratulated myself for perseverance, until I found that it had nothing to do with social groups and friendship. I abandoned the book and slid past the cashier.

The car wasn't outside. I looked again, making sure I had the right fire hydrant. The spot was empty. I searched up and down on each side of the street. It wasn't likely that the cops had towed the car away, not with the boys inside. I started north and there it was, a block away and perfectly parked. The legal driving age was eighteen. Phil, fifteen and sitting in the front seat, had driven around the block or backed the car up a block and through an intersection. The music was loud, both boys rapping, and they smiled when I knocked on the window.

"YoMike, where your book?" Carlos asked after Phil gave me my seat and I turned down the radio.

"It was thirty bucks. And it was the wrong book. I left it."

"Damn," he said, sounding more like "*Deaaam*," "White people. Thirty dollas for a book? I never pay thirty dollas for no book."

"You know Mike, son," Phil said.

"I left it on a table, I feel bad about that."

"What you mean?" Phil asked.

"I left it there. Someone's gonna have to pick it up and put it back on the shelves."

"That just dumb. That what some nigga paid for, that his job," Carlos explained.

I started for their store on Fourteenth Street.

"What are you getting?" I asked.

"Tees, you know, the white ones. I ain't got a tee for tomorrow," Phil said.

"YoMike, you ain't sccn, we wearin white tees?" Carlos explained.

I hadn't. They wore these shirts once, and only to school, while the cotton was "*crispy.*" "But that's crazy!" I said, angry at the waste.

"Three dollas, Mike, three dollas," Phil singsongcd and his face was ecstasy.

"Once?" I demanded.

"YoMike—" Carlos started.

"Three dollas, three dollas," Phil kept cantillating. "Right here," he told me where to stop.

I went with them. They walked to no more than a stall inside what had been a store before the neighborhood collapsed in the early seventies, now carved into small spaces for plain merchants selling common wares. Nothing was displayed. "Gimme two," Phil said to a man behind a rough plywood counter, who seemed acquainted with my boys. He reached into a cardboard box stacked on top of others and slid out two tees folded inside clear plastic bags. "Six dolla," the man said in an East Asian voice. He wore black pants and a white button-down shirt.

Phil handed him six crumpled dollar bills.

"Gimme two," Carlos echoed.

---

In midwinter Ripton's teacher sent notes to Leslie and me, asking to meet. "Nothing's wrong," she assured when I called, "but it's important we talk."

We gathered at a kids' table on short chairs, knees to our chests. The teacher said she was speaking privately, trusting our confidence. She adored Ripton. Our son was smart, unconventional and doing extremely well. He had great potential and we should get him out of the Earth School now, get him out of our school district and into an excellent middle school in another district that automatically fed into a good high school.

Leslie and I hadn't considered middle school. It felt like we'd just arrived at the Earth School, the road of Ripton's struggle a moment behind. He'd received one report card, and regardless of what they said to us, both our boys seemed happy. Being close to their school was a pleasure. Learning about new places, filling out applications, explaining to Ripton that he'd be leaving and taking him to interviews—the waiting and anxiety felt intolerable. We knew nothing about one public school district versus another—and I felt guilt that perhaps we should have.

It turned out that we were in District 1 of the New York City Department of Education, though a search of "*Earth School*" on the department's website gave no indication. Nor did it hint at why we should care. Talking with other parents, we learned that District 2 was south, west and north of us—covering what were well-known, monied and predominantly White communities. Our neighborhood included 137 public housing buildings, quite a number of them high-rises. According to census information, nearly 72 percent of the people in our community weren't White and a bit over 45 percent of the population received some sort of governmental income support.* The East River was to our east. We were a dark and poorer neighborhood cut off from White and richer ones.

District 2 had five or six competitive middle schools continuing into high schools and a few other good ones that didn't. Our district had Tompkins Square Middle School, two or three years old, in the same building with the Earth School, and not a single high school we'd be comfortable for our children's safety in, to say nothing of education.

In addition, the two districts had a complicated lack of symmetry; their elementary schools ended in fifth grade and fed to middle schools beginning in sixth grade, while our elementary schools finished and middle schools began one grade later. Asking our teachers and administrators for help with a transfer for our son would be a burden on them; teachers had their classes and administrators had their hands full with sixth graders needing schools. And we couldn't imagine telling Michelle that we wanted Ripton to leave early.

We decided to tour Tompkins Square middle school. Their teachers and founding principal were young, energetic and untested. It was Mark Pingatore's dream to create the first innovative, progressive, student-parent-centric middle school in our community and he'd eventually open a similar high school his students could continue into. But without a graduating class, and before the dreamed-for high school, it was guesswork as to where middle school students might afterwards go. We knew that Tompkins Square shared a library with the Earth School and PS 64, an older and much larger public elementary school in the same building. The library was understocked and open only part of the school week. The computer

---

* Manhattan Community Board Profile, 2007.

room had few computers. There were no sports teams and very few other after-school activities. The classes were crowded and noisy—we thought too many students for one teacher. We'd seen the middle-school students crowding the front steps and sidewalk at dismissal, shouting and laughing, filling the space too tightly for others to get through. "Go home!" Mark Pingatore stood on the top step yelling. "You have to leave!" The early-teenage students, overwhelmingly Black and Spanish, benignly ignored him as long as possible while his voice escalated. There were almost no White kids. The scene wasn't encouraging.

We started looking at District 2 middle schools. Ripton and I went to pep rallies in their auditoriums, the principal cheerleading for the glory and heritage of his school, charismatic teachers rising to shine, students delivering earnest soliloquies on their initial awk-wardnesses transcending to happy community in those places. One school specialized in theater, another in journalism, another in science and a fourth in cooperative education. Each choice was allur-ing, if they'd have our boy. Seats were open for children from our community only after all the District 2 children were placed.

---

I called Leslie and asked to meet.

"Why?" she wanted to know, anxiousness on the surface of her voice. We'd been solving problems, getting along better and some-times well, but rage had been her most consistent response for most of the time since I left home.

"I want to talk about a few things," I said, because it sounded less threatening than saying I wanted to talk about one thing.

She paused. "I can meet for fifteen minutes, at noon next Tuesday, at the café downstairs." She meant a cafeteria near her office. She'd given herself five days.

I went early, bought a cup of tea in a to-go cup and sat waiting at a table for two. It was crowded. Leslie walked in looking like she al-ways did at her office, carrying a calm elegance.

"Do you want anything?" I asked.

"No," she answered. "What do you want?"

I'd practiced my words. They were awkward, but sounded the most honest. "I want to ask you to consider regrowing our marriage."

She was silent. What had she expected? Her face stayed set. "I'll call you in a week," she answered and left.

I walked to work down Broadway, avoiding the darkness and dirt of the subway. I recognized the man from the drugstore at Bowling Green, the miniature park at the bottom of the island famous for the wrought-iron fence surrounding the small field patricians bowled on before the revolution. The man stood now beside the steps to the subway, still in workman blue coveralls holding another hand-lettered to his chest: *LOVE IS RESPONSIBILITY*.

Leslie called a week later. "I'll consider what you said," she told me, "but we'll need to work with a marriage counselor, and take our time."

———

Leslie and I didn't tell our children, but started counseling together. She walked back to my apartment with us on a Friday night and others. We sometimes sat in the afternoon and early evenings when I took the boys home to the Christodora. I felt warmth return. The prospect of spring, more optimistic days. Baseball, too, was arriving, inevitably. It was four years since we had first met the bigger boys.

———

"Do you know where Monkey is?" Leslie called on a Wednesday near our boys' bedtime. Late spring snow was falling.

I didn't know. I'd packed the boys' things and dropped them in the Christodora lobby after dropping Ripton and Morgan off.

I found Monkey tucked beneath the blanket of Morgan's bunk bed. Leslie didn't accuse me and I hurried the stuffed toy to Morgan. Ripton and he were in tomorrow's clothes when I walked in, Carlos,

Kindu, Juan and Will getting ready to leave. I gave Monkey and went down the elevator with them.

"Mike, a nigga is hungry." Kindu began a smile growing large as we started down Avenue B. He tried to speak again, started to giggle, struggled to push himself into character and repeated, "A nigga is hungry. Steak sandwich five dolla."

"NiggaKindu," Carlos laughed.

"What are you smiling about?" I asked Kindu.

"My million-dolla smile, Mike. Niggas is hungry," and he smiled the more.

I checked the number of us and figured we'd need twenty-five dollars plus more for their sodas to eat steak sandwiches from the place on Avenue D.

"Ya know ya be lovin it," Kindu saw me counting.

I had the money.

Snow was staying on the exposed parts of the wrought-iron fence around Tompkins Square, the half-inch widths of rail between posts and as a carpet on the ground inside. I heard muffled sounds before realizing words, two young men on a lawn inside the park, hiking, sprinting, throwing and catching football routes. They were White and college age.

Carlos saw them too and jogged across Avenue B, vaulted the fence and continued to the men. They stopped in the midst and stood together when he came close. Carlos spoke then jogged back slowly, hopped the fence and walked to us, his shoulders down. The others stepped in around him and they kept along Avenue B and I followed.

"What did they say?" I asked.

"They finished."

I looked back and the two White boys were hiking, sprinting, and throwing a fly pattern. The others never turned around. "Oh—"

"They always finished," Carlos said, pain in his voice. "White peoples."

We turned east across Seventh Street. "Mike, Leslie's the best, you know that, rah?" Will said from nothing.

"We been talkin, we want ya ta know that's what we think," Carlos said.

Our tracks stayed in the snow.

---

I wanted to volunteer in our neighborhood, to give back, meet people outside the business world I was increasingly estranged from. Nothing had gone well since the destruction of September 11.

I started cutting onions in the soup kitchen at Trinity Lutheran Church a few mornings each week. I was the only White person there. The woman who ran it was Gullah from the Sea Islands of South Carolina. She had one son dead from crime and jail. Her other children and grandchildren seemed to be in profound trouble. She didn't think much of my problems and pointed towards fifty-pound bags of onions. Vidalia the size of oranges and small grapefruit were the easiest. The small onions were torture. I took to setting up a table outside on the kitchen patio facing the front garden, a space welcoming to the street and a breeze blew away the fumes. "Michael, Michael," someone startled me one morning from the other side of the iron fence. It was our local city councilmember, a Fiorello LaGuardia type in charisma, brilliance, build and locution. I was wearing my royal blue Brooklyn Dodgers baseball cap and a soup kitchen white plastic apron. I wiped off my cutting knife and was at the fence before realizing I still carried it. "An onion can save your soul," she said.

"What?" I wasn't sure I'd heard through her Puerto Rican accent.

"An onion can save your soul. Even one onion."

I wanted nothing more. I wiped tears and nodded.

"*Brothers Karamazov*," she said. "Do you believe in God?"

"No, I don't think so."

"An onion can save your soul, Brother."

CHAPTER EIGHT

# ISHMAEL | *Mid-2002*

Ripton received an invitation for an interview from Clinton School for Writers and Artists, whose mission was *"to ignite a child's mind by integrating the arts into the curriculum."* Leslie and I assembled a portfolio of his drawings and writings. While I hadn't thought of our children as artists or writers, I had taped their drawings to my living room wall and their poems to the door of my apartment; I'd wanted them to be proud. But once the invitation came, I realized their innate talent. Ripton, clutching his portfolio, waiting for his interview in a cafeteria full of other students, was an artist.

He wasn't accepted to Clinton, but was to Simon Baruch Middle School 104, though not into its top 20 percent tier, the elite school within the school. "I want to go," Ripton insisted.

"You're smart, Ripperman. Mommy and I want you to take the best classes," I tried to counsel him.

"I don't care. You can't stop me."

I was afraid the bigger boys' influence was affecting Ripton, that he was choosing for mediocrity in his education. "Ripton, it doesn't—"

"You can't say what I do," he looked at me. "You can't."

I kept hearing the boys talk about Jasmine, the most from Will and Carlos. "Who's that?" I eventually asked.

"Carlos' wifey," Philippe puffed his chest and patted Carlos' back.

"Wifey," Juan singsonged but I saw a sadness beneath his smile. He probably didn't have a Jasmine.

"Who is she?"

"My cousin, from the Bronx," Will answered.

Carlos was sixteen.

They were at the kitchen table late one night. "I hate that, nigga," Will complained to the other four, talking about an affront.

"Me too, nigga. Gotstabe wet n' warm," Philippe agreed, "that's, like, grabbin ya, all of ya."

No one had noticed I'd come downstairs and was watching from the foyer.

"That's the best," Will said and the others agreed.

"Rah? Gotstabe clean," Juan added.

"Juan," Phil punched his arm. "Like you get any?"

"Word? Juan? You not tellin us?" Carlos' voice danced.

"If nigga was in love, we'd be hearin everythin," Philippe chided.

"True, true," Carlos considered.

Kindu was listening but stayed away from digging.

"Who you wif, nigga?" Phil asked.

"Some ho?" Will laughed.

Juan made a furtive grimace to Kindu, for sympathy or rescue.

"I ain't usen um, not wif her. Outside, hell-yeah, but not wif her," Carlos said.

"What are you guys talking about?" I surprised them.

"Mike, man?" Will protested as the boys all turned.

"What you think, Mike?" Juan palmed the tabletop.

"Condoms," Kindu answered.

"I hope you're using them. Diseases. Babies."

"Hellll no—" Carlos started.

"Not with wifey," Phil said.

"You don't use condoms with wifey," Will explained.

"That's a rule," Phil danced.

I should have known sex was experienced and matter of fact. They were teenagers. "I hope you do. You don't need to be fathers." They looked unconcerned, facing another lecture.

"I'm gonna be a good father," Will herded teenage seriousness.

"I ain't bein no father," Carlos said. "I'm usin condoms."

"But not wif wifey, be honest, Carlos," Will said.

"I don't lie. I don't always tell the whole truf, but I never lie. I use condoms for fun girls, rah?, you know what I mean?, that the truf. Wif Jasmine, trust me, we ain't havin no kids."

"Listen guys, you don't want STDs—"

"What that?" Will asked.

"AIDS, nigga! You stuuupid, sex disease," Carlos answered.

"*Sexually transmitted diseases*, not just AIDS—chlamydia, genital warts, gonorrhea, syphilis—"

"You nasty," Phil shut me up.

"YoMike, my moms taught me, girls is sluts—" Carlos started.

"That's not true," I stopped him.

"Girls sleepin wif anyone," Phil said.

"You gotta look out for girls, not like in your day. No girls like Leslie, dogs. Nobody like Leslie," Carlos assured me.

"Not like Leslie," Will agreed, "you two old school."

"But if you guys like sex, why can't girls?"

"It different," Carlos said.

"Why?"

"Cause. It ain't right. Jasmine ain't sleepin wif other guys. I ain't gonna be wif no slut."

"But you are, right?—sleeping with other girls?"

"But we guys, Mike, it's different," Phil explained.

"You are sleeping with other girls—"

"You bein stuuupid," Carlos said, suddenly aggressive.

"You don't talk to me like that."

"You bein stuuupid now."

"Carlos—"

"You are."

"I'm gonna say something. Girls are no different than boys—it's not your right to have fun and not theirs. If they're sluts, you're sluts—"

"We different—" Phil said.

"My moms says girls wanna—" Will started.

"I'm talking. You guys have this *good girl/bad girl* thing. If a girl has sex with you she's a slut but you sleep with—"

"Ain't no *sleepin*, Mike," Phil corrected me.

"You have sex for fun but a girl can't, she's a slut. With *wifey* you don't use condoms because it doesn't feel good, but if wifey gets pregnant, what do you do then?"

"She ain't gonna," Carlos was curt.

"But if she do? That's what Mike means," Juan said.

"I know what he mean. She ain't gonna."

"She have the baby, that what," Will said.

"And you'll be a good father? You're ready to earn a living? What, at seven, eight dollars an hour, without a high school diploma, without college? You're ready to stay up feeding a baby, read to her, rent an apartment? Stay with a girl?—none of your fathers did that, right?"

"What the hell? And you did? You and Leslie divorced," Carlos said.

"We separated. And . . . I went to college, and I earn a living. And we read to Ripton and Morgan, and when we were separated, the boys spent time with me too."

"You a good father, Mike, I ain't doubt that," Carlos said.

"How are you gonna earn a living, to take care of a kid?" I asked.

"Cold-cold-crack," Kindu teased. "Big money."

"Kindu, nigga!" Carlos laughed and we found we were all smiling together.

"It ain't like that. I'm gonna be a good father," Will protested.

"How? Don't most guys walk away when a girl gets pregnant?"

"Or after she has a kid, tell the truf, nigga," Carlos turned to Will.

"What about abortion?" I asked.

"That wrong, that killin," Will said.

"Spanish don't get abortion," Carlos said.

"I don't get it. You're in no position to raise a child. Not until you finish high school, finish college, get a good job and are ready to stay with a woman and raise a family."

"I be forty, before that happen," Carlos had become playful, but serious.

"What about adoption?"

"I ain't givin away my baby," Phil said.

"No way," Juan agreed.

"We don't do that. That my baby, I love him, I ain't givin him away," Will said.

"But Ripton and Morgan's mothers' loved them. That's why they placed them for adoption." Leslie said the right word was "*place.*"

"What about adoption?" Ripton came from the TV room. He'd probably been listening for a while. "What are you talking about?"

"Mike says to give a baby for adoption, if wifey gets pregnant," Juan said.

"Hell no!" Ripton said. "I'm not giving a baby to adoption. I love my kids."

"But your mother loved you. They wanted you to be raised in a family they couldn't make then," I told Ripton.

"Bullshit. They didn't want me. That's all. I'm never giving a baby away."

"Your moms and dads loves you, Ripton. They loves Morgan. You livin in the penthouse, dogs, that's good," Kindu told him.

"I'm good. But I'm not giving my baby away."

"My moms'll help raise a baby. She wants that," Will said.

Leslie told me, afterwards, to relax. She explained that we should keep talking with the boys. She ordered condoms and put them in a bowl in the TV room. They disappeared, so she ordered more.

---

"Tell Jasmine '*Happy Birthday,*'" Will said to Carlos as he left the apartment.

"What are you doing for her birthday?" I asked.

"Nothin. Chillin."

"Why don't you do something nice?"

Carlos sat on my exercise bike. "Like what?"

"Dinner at La Isla?" A Puerto Rican restaurant he fancied on Fourteenth Street. "Or dessert somewhere?"

"I ain't got no money.

I gave him fifty dollars. Carlos told me that they enjoyed themselves.

---

Kindu and I watched and waited as John Howard shoehorned his lightning blue Mini Cooper into the ten feet no one else could use beside the fire hydrant in front of Casimir. John smiled and waved. A favorite of the boys, he was tall, coiffed, immaculately suited and an inordinately successful merchant banker. He'd taken to spending Monday nights at the same restaurant to eat, drink Ricard and talk. Gradually, the bigger boys had joined us. Kindu liked to order the grilled chicken with miniature baby carrots, a side of garlic mashed potatoes and the chocolate soufflé cake for dessert, the most curious and adventurous of the bigger boys. Carlos believed himself to be painfully shy and came for only short visits. He wouldn't eat anything, limiting himself to Spanish and preferably Puerto Rican food—besides fried chicken wings and pork fried rice from Chinese takeout, microwaved Hot Pockets and a few other well-chosen freezer foods. Juan and Will would half engage with our friends who visited, but they showed themselves reluctantly and quickly faded, wanting to be elsewhere. Philippe was the bon vivant; alluring, charming until the flush of new adventure began to fade and another gleam took him elsewhere. Kindu stayed, curious and warm with his million-dollar smile and kindness. I'd come to appreciate that Kindu had a resolve to push himself beyond what he'd been born to. Monday after Monday he came to the front room of Casimir and spoke with my friend Blue, with the musicians and composers Butch Morris, Henry Threadgill, Billy Bang, Juini Booth and Will Connell.

"Hello, Sir," Kindu smiled and shook hands with John, who sat down beside him.

"Ricard," John pointed to my glass. "Michael says fantastic things about you," he said to Kindu, *fan-Ta-STICK.*

Kindu's smile grew wider and his shoulders settled smoothly from his neck. "Thank you, Sir."

"Call me *John.*"

"Yes."

"You live nearby? Michael says you met playing baseball."

"Yes, Sir," and he caught himself. "We was in Tompkins and Ripton aksed if he could play wif us—," what had become Kindu's incomplete shorthand of our story.

"That's fantastic."

"I live in Seward Park, the projects, you know where that is?"

John didn't. "Where do you go to school?"

"Seward Park." A public high school at the bottom of the old Lower East Side and an expanding Chinatown, where earlier generations of Jewish students bragged they were accepted and newspapers now reported was dangerous and inadequate.

"Do you like it?" John asked. He had no idea. There's no reason he should have.

"It's okay. The other guys go to Norman Thomas." Kindu described the other bigger boys, being separated from them after Junior High School 56 Corlears Junior High School. He was assigned to Murray Bergstrom, said to be a good city high school. But he told the administrators he wanted to leave to join his friends. Public school transfers are only allowed for danger. Kindu put himself in the appearance of harm's way with the help of his brothers and was assigned not to Norman Thomas but to Seward Park, truly dangerous. "What do you do?" Kindu asked John.

"I work with companies," he answered.

"Would you like another drink?" the waitress was bubbly bringing John's meal.

He didn't. "When my mother moved to Cannes . . . Do you know where that is?" he looked at Kindu.

"No, Sir."

"On the French Riviera, the Mediterranean."

"Oh."

Kindu didn't know where the Riviera, France and the Mediterranean were. Only nowhere near the Lower East Side.

"Do you know the Cannes Film Festival?"

"No."

"Do you remember *Crouching Tiger, Hidden Dragon?*"

"That was phat, I mean, that was Oh-Dee!"

"I was a partner in the movie and we introduced it at a film festival in Cannes. A lot of movies are introduced there. Before it won Academy Awards. My mother moved to Cannes when I was your age."

Kindu raised his eyebrows.

"They built a *boulodrome*," and John stopped to spread egg yoke across his steak tartar, to mix in the anchovies, scallion and mustard.

"What that?" Kindu peered at John's plate.

"Raw steak, raw eggs. My mother built a bowling lane on their lawn. You use heavy metal balls, and people drink this"—holding up his near-empty glass—"pastis."

"You made that movie?"

"I was a partner."

"Dogs, like . . ." and Kindu was silent, awed. He started a chocolate soufflé cake with vanilla ice cream for dessert. "I gots ta go," he said when he finished.

I'd been at John's home the night *Crouching Tiger, Hidden Dragon* won its first Oscar, then a second and third. Then it won the Academy Award for Best Foreign Language film. "Will you be back next Monday?" John asked Kindu.

"Yes, Sir," Kindu flashed into his million-dollar smile.

---

Ripton wanted to go to Casimir. Kindu told him that John would be there. "When I grow up, I want to be like John Howard," Kindu said. My friend was always "*John Howard*" with the boys.

"He's mad cool," Ripton agreed, "not a nerd like Dad."

"He made *Crouching Tiger, Hidden Dragon*. He must be mad rich."

"He is. He lives in a Oh-Dee mansion, it's whack."

Ripton sat next to me the next Monday, across from John as I was from Kindu. He held out an Uno deck, the game of primary-colored cards patterned on the rules of crazy eights. "Who wants to play?"

John didn't know the game. Kindu and I were veterans of losing to Ripton, who explained the rules. We played and Ripton won.

"Do you play poker?" John asked. Both boys did.

"Texas hold 'em?" John asked. They didn't. "Bring a deck of cards, and I'll show you."

---

John cradled half a deck in each palm, pressuring fresh cards to convex between thumb and pinky with his middle fingers guiding, riffled his thumbs slowly up the edge of each stack and the cards slid ever so slightly into each other. He bent the deck to concave and cascaded the cards together, squared and swiftly shuffled them twice more, practiced, rested the full deck in his left hand and cut it alone there.

"Do that again," Ripton said.

John did.

"Again."

John's thumb and pinky grasped the bottom half of the deck, his ring and forefingers the top, sweeping the two parts away and the bottom replacing the top. "Pretty good, huh?" John asked. "And I'm right handed."

"Amazin," Kindu answered.

"Teach me," Ripton said.

"It takes about a year," John said as he did his one-handed split again, "to get good. You wanna try, or should we play?"

"Play," the boys answered. I watched. "Two cards down, boys," John reviewed the rules to Texas hold 'em in a casino voice as he dealt. "Those are your cards," and he took a disinterestedly careful look at his two. The boys practiced the same. "What do you bet?" he asked Kindu.

"Um . . . ?"

"No 'um.' Maybe you have a pair? Maybe the beginning of a straight? Up to fifty cents a hand, what do you say?"

"Real money?" Kindu was suddenly concerned.

"You're grown-up," Ripton protested.

John was delighted. "Pretend money, boys, whadaya bet?" he asked Kindu again.

"Ten cents."

"Ten cents. And fifteen more cents." Ripton showed he had learned poker.

"Big move. Ripton thinks he has a good hand. Perhaps he's deceiving us. Don't smile, Ripton"—my son's face spread into his widest smile, trying to squash the evidence of his happiness—"it gives too much away." Turning to Kindu: "Do you meet Ripton's raise?"

"What you mean?"

"Do you match Ripton's bet? If you do, you'll have to put in fifteen more cents."

"Sure," but Kindu didn't clearly follow.

"I meet Ripton's bet and raise ten. Thirty-five cents to stay in, big pot," John inhaled, leaned into the back of his chair and rocked onto its two rear legs. He seemed even larger.

Ripton met him and Kindu did after an explanation.

"I burn the top card," John said. "Then three community cards," dealing these onto the middle of the table. "They're in each of our hands, so it's strategic to determine what the others could have, not only you. Then I show one more card, after we bet. It's your bet, Ripton."

I could hear the boys breathe. Don Cherry was playing with Ornette Coleman, so I couldn't have heard them, but they looked like I did. Ripton passed. Kindu passed. John raised a nickel and the boys met him. John burned a second card, placed a fourth faceup and each of them left the pot as it was. Ripton had two pairs—kings and tens. John had two pairs—kings and fives. Kindu had a jack pair and nothing more. The three kept a tally; Ripton won a month of Mondays.

I hadn't focused on the bigger boys finding jobs the previous summer. Their mothers, as far as I knew, never advocated such a thing. Nor did Leslie. She'd been a hospital volunteer in high school one summer.

They shied away when I started hinting at work, but Leslie and I had become more responsible towards them and to my mind less able to allow them to run from the idea of work. They'd be finishing high school in the next years (at least we hoped). Kindu was already less than a year away from eighteen.

"I wanted a camera when I was twelve and my parents wouldn't buy it," I said to the bigger boys the next Saturday night. "So I went to the golf course and caddied."

"What's *caddy* do?" Carlos asked.

"Carry the clubs, nigga," Juan said.

"You dumb ass, don't know *caddy*?" Philippe goaded.

"I knows that, I just makin sure," Carlos said with a glimmer.

"Word! Spanish and Black don't golf," Will said.

"Tiger Woods?" Kindu reminded Will.

"He half Black, his mom's White or somethin," Carlos said.

"Thai," I corrected Kindu.

"What that?" Philippe asked.

"Regular Spanish and Black, ghetto, like us, not rich niggas," Will corrected himself.

"Michael Jordan do," Juan said.

"Michael ain't regular, he mad rich, you stuuupid?" Will demanded.

"Thailand, in Asia," I said. Not that they knew where Asia was, except perhaps Juan. "I caddied because I wanted an Instamatic camera. I can show you the pictures I took."

"I ain't carryin no golfin clubs for no White niggas," Philippe said.

"Word, I ain't carryin no golfin clubs for no nigga," Carlos said.

"I worked as a camp counselor after that, and when I was sixteen, I got regular jobs."

"What you do?" Kindu asked.

"I started as a busboy."

No one said anything.

"It's time you guys got summer jobs."

No one responded.

"We'd like you to look for work," Leslie supported me.

"Did you get summer jobs, Leslie?" Will asked.

"No." She looked sheepish.

"Then why we gotta?" he asked.

"Leslie's parents looked at it differently," I answered.

"Mom was rich," Ripton said.

"Word, that right Leslie? Rich people ain't gotta work?" Carlos asked.

"Michael worked, and we want you guys to. It would be good for you to make money," Leslie kept going.

"Who gonna hire us?" Will asked. "We Spanish, Kindu Black, rah?, no one gonna hire us."

"I can help you look," and I named neighborhood restaurants and cafés.

"What we gonna do?" Carlos asked.

"Busboy, like me, and I washed dishes after that. It paid more." I was walking barefoot to school in the snow.

"I ain't washin dishes," Carlos was indignant.

"I did," I repeated.

"Good for you. I ain't."

"That Mexican work," Philippe explained as he had before.

"I'm-gonna-sell-me-drugs, work-the-street, crack-cocaine," Kindu went singsong and danced his shoulders side to side. "Work wif my brothers, Mike want me earn a livin," and he broke into laughter.

Ripton, Morgan and the others laughed with him. Leslie and I looked on helpless. "It's not funny," I tried unsuccessfully to sound somber. Being with Kindu made me happy.

"I ain't washin dishes, nigga, I don't care," Carlos wasn't swayed. "Phil tolt you, I ain't doin Mexican work."

"It's Mexican," Ripton agreed.

Now our son. "I earned money for college—"

"*I earned money for college,*" Ripton spoke with marbles in his mouth.

"—and because of college I could get work that pays for—"

"*—and because of college I could get work that pays for YOU!*" Ripton cut me off, laughing.

"You tolt us," Juan said.

"I ain't washin dishes," Carlos wouldn't stop.

"I want you to make a resume," I said to Carlos. I imagined him beside an industrial dishwasher, throwing the door open and steam swirled. My hands remembered the heat.

The boys had no idea of what a resume should look like. Leslie found a website on how to make them and I helped edit until each boy had a passable one. I insisted they look for work every day. I also searched for them. The restaurant owners I knew hired Central and South American immigrant adults in their kitchens. They didn't trust the work ethic of local public housing boys. I wasn't convinced they were wrong. I remembered Carlos and Kindu at Red Square and decided I better not think too objectively. I told the man at my local coffee shop about the bigger boys because he hired new baristas from time to time. "Do they have experience?" he asked. I assured him they were good kids and increasingly my family. "I need people with years of experience," he insisted. Remarkable coffee reviews hung on his walls. A few days later I saw him training young people without experience. We were half a block from Avenue D, and his trainees were White.

I contacted the Boys Club and other community groups I thought might suggest or help with jobs. It seemed our kids were late for the programs these charities ran. Leslie and I encouraged more shoe leather. I wanted the boys to walk the streets for a couple of hours each morning handing out resumes. The boys promised they would.

I was typically poor at administration and though supportive, the bigger boys' job search wasn't Leslie's highest priority. As I'd feared, finding five jobs seemed itself a full-time job. I wasn't willing, yet, to ask friends for favors.

After a week I walked Mr. Jenkins to Tompkins Square and watched the boys play baseball. I was near Will and asked about work.

"We lookin," he assured me.

"Where did you go today?"

"Me and Juan walked 'cross Rivington."

Rivington Street wasn't long, it couldn't take two hours. "You *and* Juan?"

"We doin that."

"You walk into stores together?"

"'Course."

"How do you expect someone to figure out which of you to hire?"

Will insisted, improbably, that a local store would have two jobs. But the bigger boys didn't like to walk outside alone. They wouldn't go beyond the neighborhood without company. They hardly knew where the city's richer, Whiter and more conventionally known neighborhoods were. Will started taking practice swings. As if my question meant nothing.

Mr. Jenkins and I went to Leslie's that night. I cooked dinner for her and the boys ordered Chinese—they didn't want my grilled salmon. Will was playing video games alone in the TV room while I was cleaning up. "I have an idea," I told him.

"We's lookin for jobs, Mike. It ain't easy."

"Not that. I want you to pick a topic you'd like to learn about, anything that attracts you."

"Okay," Will squinted at the TV and shimmied the controller.

I realized that he'd been squinting at the TV for perhaps as long as I'd known him. I'd seen but not seen. "Do you need glasses?"

"What you mean?"

"You're squinting."

He pursed his lips. "I don't see good sometimes."

"What about the blackboard?"

"Ollrrot. Not so good. Sometimes."

"You gotta get your eyes checked."

"Ollrrot, Mike. What you mean, 'bout learnin somethin?"

"Will, I'm serious about your eyes. What do your teachers say?" I naïvely clung to the idea that the bigger boys went to classes regularly, and that a teacher might notice or care. Will asked again what I meant about learning.

"Something that you want to learn more about."

"Bodybuilding."

I'd hoped he'd pick Dominican poetry, Lower East Side history. "Great! I want you to study bodybuilding this summer."

"Just me?"

"I'm gonna ask everyone to pick a topic. We'll get library books and study for half an hour a day. Really learn something and write a paper at the end of summer. If we can't get jobs, it makes sense."

"Ripton and Morgan, them too?"

"We'll see."

"Them gotta write papers?"

They wouldn't. Our sons went to perfectly decent schools, did acceptably well, were young and it was summertime.

"That not fair. Why you pickin on us?"

"I'm not." Of course I was, but decided "*caring about*" was a nicer phrase. Whatever Leslie and I were doing, alone and together, informed or ridiculous, the bigger boys knew we were trying because we cared about them. Kindu selected baseball and Carlos chose crime stories—he wanted to see if he liked criminal justice. Phil decided on rap music and Juan picked sports coaching, he wanted to learn about taking care of kids. The six of us went to Tompkins Square library. We filled out applications for cards, all of us listing the Christodora as home. The librarian was quizzical and kind when I explained a bit. We walked the open stacks and picked out books. I gave each of them a notebook when we were back at Leslie's and picked a shelf to store them. I asked the boys to write a short summary of what they read each day. At worst, to note the pages they finished. They promised to return their books to the library on time.

Leslie agreed to remind them to do their work, but thought my plan was too grand. Of course it was. I couldn't manage and the boys wouldn't read. Their half hours slipped. Their books didn't get back to the library and I knew they wouldn't pay their late fees.

I was lamenting the failure of my efforts with the poet John Yau, who was filling me with stories from his lunch that afternoon with an even more famous poet, lauding his Black Square Editions imprint and trying to warm me to the idea of paying the printing costs for the next book in its library. "*Moby Dick*. It's a guy's story," John said.

I didn't understand.

"Men go off to sea. It's about camaraderie, love, ego, vengeance, the giant whale. Men risk their lives hunting the impossible. Have your boys read it aloud, they'll love it."

John Yau was brilliant. I agreed to fund the book he wanted and hurried to Barnes & Noble for enough soft-cover copies of *Moby Dick*.

---

"*Call me Ishmael. Some years ago—never mind how long . . .*" Juan read the first and went on to the second sentence. He needed help with the protagonist's name but settled into a certain smoothness. The five bigger boys and I sat at the dining room table, beneath the mezzanine they launched themselves off not many years earlier. The stuffed dogs were near our feet. We'd agreed to read on Tuesday and Fridays at six-thirty, during my time with Ripton and Morgan. I looked at the boys in a way I hadn't seen them for a time. They'd grown; Philippe, Juan and Kindu were tight, wearing polos that fit closer to their bodies, jeans that didn't settle over their rumps and Diesel shoes, dressier than Jordans. Will and Carlos stayed baggy. Carlos' braids were below his shoulders. They weren't quite children anymore. "*It is a way I have of driving off the spleen, and regulating the circulation,*" Juan read.

"What that mean?" Philippe asked, "'*drivin off the spleen*'?"

"I don't know. It's in your body, it excretes something."

"What?" Juan asked.

"Where it at?" Will asked.

"I don't know. Inside your stomach."

"*Inside* my stomach?" Carlos was shocked.

"Your gut, attached to everything in there."

"It's in the upper left of the abdomen, behind the stomach," Leslie said from the kitchen and came to point at her back.

"YoLes, what it do?" Carlos asked.

"It guards against infection, and destroys old red blood cells."

That seemed to satisfy all of us. "Keep going, Juan," I said.

"*Whenever I find myself growing grim about the mouth—*"

"What the fuck?" Philippe asked.

"Tense. Grim is not happy, like the Grim Reaper, the Angel of Death, the guy in a black cape and scythe?"

"YoMike, you weird," Carlos said. "*Scythe*, dogs?" None of the boys seemed to know the Angel of Death.

"Set your mouth, like you're angry," and I showed them.

"That my subway face, nigga." Carlos grew grim about his mouth, pinched the space between his eyes and furrowed his forehead. Then he relaxed and smiled. "No one gonna fuck wif me."

He was right.

Juan read: "... *With a philosophical flourish Cato throws himself upon his sword—*"

"What the fuck?" Phil stopped us again. We hadn't made it through the first paragraph.

"He was Roman. We can look it up." I had holes in my education.

"*There now is your insular city of the Mahhattoes, belted round by wharves as Indian isles by coral reefs—*"

I wanted the boys to care about this book, or some things in it. "What does that mean?" I imagined old Manhattan, many thousands of wooden wharves surrounding the shoreline where we lived.

"YoMike, you think this workin?" Carlos asked.

"*Circumambulate the city of a dreamy Sabbath afternoon. Go from Corlears Hook to Coenties Slip, and from thence, by Whitehall, northward.*"

I stopped Juan again. "Corlears, where you guys went to school. You know Coenties Slip?" It became a street near their old junior high school.

The boys were silent, then Juan said, "Corlears Slip was dug. Boats went in."

"Suckup!" Carlos teased.

"Where you learnt that?" Philippe asked.

"In history, you too."

"You never go ta no history."

"I pass, don't I?"

"Word-ta-the-nine!" Kindu said.

"What?"

"Word-to-the-nine, doggie-dog-dogs, what-ya-do, five?, smartest man in the world, Juan know New York, know history," Kindu rapped staccato and kept smiling.

"Yo, Kindu, you crazy," Carlos too smiled. So did the others.

"Juan-smartest-man-in-the-world," Kindu told us.

We'd gotten through one page in our half hour. There were 478 to go.

---

I moved home. Juan stopped coming when it was time to read *Moby Dick*. Phil started missing as often as he came. Kindu, Will, Carlos and I agreed to take our books to Casimir one Monday. Its wall of windows was peeled back in panels on account of good weather. We sat at the same table close to the sidewalk. The maître d' wasn't happy to see us in the front of his bistro. The boys wanted Cokes and Sprites. I heard skate wheels against concrete coming close. "Little Morgie," Will called in falsetto, sweetly torturing Morgan for his youth.

"Yo Morgan, Cam, what up?" Carlos leaned over the sidewalk, clasped hands and touched shoulders first with Morgan and then the other boy, tall and shaggy blond, as they skated up to our table. Cam was a year older than Ripton and a former classmate at the Earth School. He came to Tompkins sometimes and had played in Little League with Ripton. The bigger boys and Ripton didn't trust him, but he skated well. Morgan adored that, and they left to the park together. Ripton arrived and ordered a Coke.

"That nigga's a pothead, ya know that, rah? Ya want Morgie hangin out with him?" Will asked of the other boy. He didn't seem to be joking. The others were nodding.

"That boy doin crack-cocaine, buyin from my brothers," Kindu smiled.

"Cut it out, Kindu, if you don't know," I was stern.

He looked at his food.

Carlos didn't. "YoMike, you and Leslie blind? I don't understand you White peoples. That boy's messed up, you and Leslie lettin Morgan hang out wif him."

Leslie and I were concerned, more with Morgan being without an adult than that boy being a young stoner. We'd talked about drugs. It could happen.

"Let's start *Moby Dick*," I changed the subject.

We opened our books. Ishmael was contemplating a whiskey at the Spouter-Inn. Ripton wanted to read: "*Though true cylinders without-within, the villainous green goggling glasses deceitfully tapered downwards to a cheating bottom.*" He wasn't smooth, but he read better despite being four and five years younger than the bigger boys. They didn't seem to care but it made me suddenly sad at the failure of their educations, and with a fear for their futures. Kindu's and Carlos' attention drifted out the window to a man walking two Dalmatians. Will brought his head close to look at the menu on the table. The boys were gracious. But we were finished with *Moby Dick*.

---

Ripton and Morgan started sixth and fourth grades at the Earth School. I simply didn't know which grades the bigger boys started; where they were going was increasingly mixed up.

Ripton adjusted to the new school year by relentlessly talking about how wrong we were to forbid him from going to Baruch and making him leave Heschel though he, like Morgan, seemed basically happy. Morgan anyways almost always seemed happy. Leslie and I relaxed and let life pass. We walked with Ripton and Morgan and the dog to school in the morning. Leslie continued to work and I took Mr. Jenkins home. I'd spent the year since the Trade Towers fell shutting down the ruined public company, looking at new real estate projects and finally deciding to leave business. Leslie and I didn't know enough to pay attention to the ISEE, the Independent Schools Entrance Exam. Until she suddenly did and told me what should have been obvious; it was given in December and an industry of intensive study courses and highly paid tutors existed to coach children in preparation. We were late. Leslie learned which courses were available and they were full. The tutors she called were busy. The guilt of our failure set in. Ripton would be competing for admission against children in excellent private schools who were being tutored because they had good parents guiding them.

"Michael?" Leslie called. The rising she gave my name meant happiness. She had other sounds for anger, fear, disappointment, betrayal spread across the two syllables of my name as ants harvest aphids. I recognized the sound long before my name. "I spoke with a great tutor, Michael. He has great recommendations. He has time."

The young man charged a steep fee and taught Ripton twice a week. We decided to apply to six private schools: Fieldston, in the lower Bronx, where Leslie attended; Dalton, on the Upper East Side; the United Nations School and Friends Seminary, both close to home; Poly Prep, a sports-rich school far out in Brooklyn; and Brooklyn Friends, in downtown Brooklyn. We applied to ICE again, the Institute for Cooperative Education, where Ripton had interviewed the year before. He didn't push for Tompkins Square Middle School and didn't mention Baruch. He took the ISEE and did excellently. We started on tours and interviews. Our son was smitten with Fieldston and Poly Prep, both Country Day Schools teaching a century and a half of the city's children on gilded campuses; Ripton loved the playing fields. Leslie and I were impressed with the two Friends schools. Their student bodies, particularly at Brooklyn Friends, resembled the mix of our world.

# CHAPTER NINE

# Theft

*Early 2003*

Four letters to Ripton arrived on a Wednesday in mid-February. He was in the park playing and Leslie laid them on the butcher-block counter making a passageway of the kitchen. Private schools had mailed decisions on Monday.

I lifted the envelopes, reading where they'd come from. Each was regular-size, thin, not the bulk of optimism opening to a flat sheet on top, "*Congratulations, we're happy to welcome you to our community . . .*" and packets about the school, a contract where we'd promise to pay. These four would have a three-part folded sheet starting, "*Thank you for considering us. We received many qualified applications . . .*"

The phone rang while I was looking. Leslie answered and her voice climbed in a professional resonance. Then, "Oh," descending, "Okay . . . Thanks for calling," flat and she hung up. "The admissions director at Fieldston. Ripton's wait-listed, they've sent a letter." Where Leslie and her older sister had gone. They and their parents contributed to fund-raising drives, not enough to be benefactors but meaningfully. School gossip was a part of Rosh Hashanah and Passover dinners at Ria and Mike's. "Are they really wait-listing

187

him?" Leslie considered, because Ripton was our baby and we knew better. "*Maybe*," never "*no*," was a fund-raiser's way of maximizing money. "Bastards."

We'd applied to six schools and none of the letters on the counter were from Fieldston, which meant Ripton had one more chance at private school—the BFS letter would arrive the next day. ICE wouldn't make a decision till mid-August, which meant we'd apply to Tompkins Square as a fallback.

We were waiting for Ripton at the kitchen table, trying to seem as if we weren't when he walked in. He knew to look, dropped his backpack, picked up the United Nations School envelope, ripped it open, unfolded the one page with long fingers as if unfolding a brittle map, read and dropped it to the counter letting go of air, picked up the Friends Seminary envelope, ripped it open, unfolded the one page with attenuated fingers schooling as silver fish, read and dropped it to the counter. He didn't know about thin and thick envelopes, opened Dalton and then Poly Prep, his left hand Adam's reaching across the Sistine sky, long, drooping, not knowing. He said nothing, didn't look at us, picked up his backpack, walked to the TV room and started playing his video games.

Leslie showed me the Fieldston and BFS letters when she brought up our mail the next day. Fieldston was business size and thin, BFS nine by twelve and filled. She put Fieldston beneath BFS on top of the catalogues and bills.

Ripton saw the BFS envelope but didn't reach for it. "Did Fieldston come?"

"Underneath," Leslie answered, reading the *New York Times* she'd already read.

Ripton pulled it out, pried open the flap and started to read. "Fieldston accepted me to wait list," he smiled, handing the letter across the butcher block to Leslie, his hand risen to Michelangelo's God. "What's '*wait list*'?" but not listening, reaching for the larger envelope he'd pushed aside. "BFS accepted me, too. But I wanna go to Fieldston."

———————

"Shut up, Phil. You *deaded* me," Carlos told him as they came from the living room. He was missing something again. It always happened, to nearly each of us.

"Not me, nigga, probably Kindu," Phil protested.

Neither seemed bothered, Phil nearly clowning.

"They don't fit me," Kindu wasn't happy at the accusation as he sat at the table beneath the mezzanine.

Carlos looked at Phil. "It's you, nigga. You think I'm stuuupid? Give 'em back."

"I don't got 'em."

"What are you talking about?" But I knew they meant new sneakers.

"Phil deaded our Jordans," Carlos was matter-of-fact.

"*Our*" meant Air Jordan XVIIIs. The magical Michael Jordan had announced at the All-Star game that he was leaving basketball. He was immortal, but aged and worn enough for our boys to decide he was telling the truth. They believed he designed the sneakers, he wore them on court and the XVIII collection started showing up in our apartment. They arrived once a month in fancy boxes with slide-out drawers. Each came with a towel, brush and an Air Jordan "*Driver's Manual*" to care for the treasure inside. The first pair, Ripton's, was glistening white with navy blue piping and midsoles. The second, Carlos', was black with Egyptian blue. A third came white with Falu red. Then others. Carlos and Ripton made a line with their sneakers across the floor of the sports room and that's when I understood, momentarily the same size, that they were collecting and sharing them together.

"Them black and silver ones," Carlos insisted.

"See? They black," Phil shouted too loudly. "You know he be deadin everythin black."

Kindu had been borrowing black-colored clothes, including shirts and sweaters of mine. They turned out to be "*borrowed*" only after,

searching everywhere, I started asking the boys if they knew where
my clothes were.

"You a liar, Phil. Them don't fit Kindu. Ain't that right? Kindu?"

Deading wasn't only shoes. Once Ripton grew within their range,
his clothes became game. Even boxer shorts vanished. Ripton's first
iPod was an extravagance, beyond what the bigger boys would then
have. Days after Leslie gave it to him, Ripton was searching the TV
room, everywhere, till Kindu came home rapping to the new gizmo.

"Did you ask Ripton to borrow it?" Leslie was harsh because Ripton was clear no one had.

"Sure, Leslie. What you think?"

"Are you certain?"

"No."

Kindu had loaded his own songs onto it.

A short while later the iPod went missing forever.

So did sneakers and clothes.

---

Phil asked Leslie for a cell phone, insisting his mother couldn't get
him one. Carlos, Will and Juan soon wanted the same. Kindu had
one from his brothers, who ran their business that way. We'd given
Ripton and Morgan phones.

I didn't want to gift the bigger boys' phones and service. We
needed to teach them the responsibility of paying for things. Far
more than Leslie, I didn't want to be a free clubhouse.

We bought phones for those four boys, arranged basic service plans
and agreed to cover most of the cost for each month. They assured us
they'd pay a small amount. We asked, encouraged and they promised
to monitor their minutes. Each month they owed more. We lectured
and reprimanded. They denied fact and promised it wouldn't happen
again. It did. They paid us in weekly installments I tracked on sheets
of paper clipped again to the refrigerator door, but other and more
expensive needs mounted beyond extra minutes—clothes, sneakers,
movies, food, haircuts and shapeups, regular living money.

Getting paid back was good and awkward, taking money that they really didn't have. Not getting repaid carried failure, the torture of middle-class super-ego and sin.

Leslie and I eventually decided it was better to cancel their debts. I took the sheets of paper from the refrigerator door, ripped them up and threw the pieces in the recycling bin. We tried to be reasonable with how we spent money on the boys.

———

"Big Mike, what you doin?" Kindu called as I was on my hands and knees counting aloud, pointing to each ring with the tip of a sharp pencil—128 of an American elm the Parks Department had cut down near the Hare Krishna Tree. It had been planted at our nation's centennial, ten years after the Civil War and Lincoln's assassination. Tompkins Square had been a military parade ground through that conflict. I explained the years to him. "Slavery ended in the Civil War, nine years before this tree was planted. That's like from when you were nine till now—you remember when you were nine?"

"Damn. Big Mike gettin Aristotle, gettin Renaissance."

The trunk was nearly flush to the ground, root flange, damp sawdust and musk. "You want to count?"

"You crazy."

He helped me up and we started home past the holy tree.

"Remind you of your Vee-Tee days in the forest and pine?" Kindu asked. He meant my Vermont childhood.

"I guess. Hey Kindu, have you heard about your SAT's?" He'd taken them months before.

"Not yet."

"And colleges?" I'd heard from where I'd go by early spring thirty years earlier.

"I tolt you, the college advisor and me's pickin schools, she helpin fill applications."

"To where?" I asked as I had before. He never answered, not thoroughly, and whatever he said was lackadaisical.

"New York colleges."

"SUNY?"—the State University of New York educational system.

"Yeah." Apparently five schools.

Perhaps Kindu was telling the truth; he'd taken the SATs and hadn't heard the results. Time remained to apply to colleges and he was. Leslie and I didn't have the rights of parents to the bigger boys, but we'd grown to feel some, and often more than *some*, of the responsibilities. We'd often asked how school was. "*Ollrrot.*" About their grades. "*Good.*" When I pushed: "*What are you getting?*" The answers: *Cs, Bs.* We didn't ask to see report cards.

Who we are to each other might seem obvious, looking back, but clarity in transition from one way of caring and responsibility to another is mostly hindsight. Perhaps Ripton's school issues had focused us more on the bigger boys' educations. It came to us slowly that no adult was pushing Kindu towards college or that he knew how to push himself; he had no expectations for life after high school other than getting by.

"What do you think if I spend a day in school?"

"Wif me?" he slowed and turned.

If I saw Seward Park, sat in Kindu's classes, watched him in the hallways and at lunch in the cafeteria, I'd know about his education.

"Sure. Just me?" he asked.

I wanted to ask Carlos too but had trouble speaking with him. He was agitated that night, laughing in clips with the other boys and I caught only intermittent words, something about a girl, blood, the cafeteria. "What's goin on?" I finally asked.

"A fight, nothin. Don't worry."

"You said something about Jesus going to school?"

"Jesus? You gotta be kiddin? I protectin him. What you doin, listenin on us?"

"Do you need my help?"

"YoMike, I fine. Really." That was the end. Carlos agreed to let me visit his school too.

I wrote letters to Jayne Godlewski and Steven Satin, principals at Seward Park and Norman Thomas, as if from the boys' mothers.

They spelled their mothers' names. I was "*Dr. Rosen,*" a family friend wanting to spend a day in school.

Kindu brought a signed letter the next afternoon. Carlos promised to.

I called and Jayne Godlewski's assistant told me her boss was busy.

Carlos didn't bring his letter the next day and Jayne Godlewski didn't call. I left a message for Steven Satin.

Days went by and neither principal contacted me. I tried again and reached Jayne Godlewski. I explained my friendship with Kindu. "That's a great idea," but she needed permission from the superintendent's office and promised to call back the next day.

She didn't. Carlos lost the letter from his mother and I printed another. Steven Satin didn't call. Carlos said his mother signed but he forgot it. I called Jayne Godlewski, who asked for and I wrote an explanation. She emailed:

> Michael: Sorry we keep missing each other. I know
> Kindu and think this is a wonderful initiative. Will
> check with the Supt. office to let them know what you
> would like to do. Shouldn't be a problem. Will get
> back to you. Do you have any dates in mind? Please
> advise. Jayne Godlewski

I told her any day was good. She wrote again:

> Michael: One more question. I presume Kindu's
> parents have consented to you visiting our school and
> writing about him. please advise. P.s. We still have
> not heard from our district with regard to the
> approval. Jayne Godlewski

I reminded her that I had a letter from Kindu's mother.

Though I spoke with Jayne Godlewski's assistant several more times, and eventually with an assistant principal, I never heard from

Ms. Godlewski again. I made calls to the Department of Education, marshaled the contacts I had and couldn't find anyone to give me permission to spend a day with Kindu. Steven Satin didn't return my calls. Carlos didn't return the letter.

---

In all our family vacations, we'd never traveled back to Dallas with Morgan. Child-raising books about adoption recommended these trips. Morgan had hinted at visiting, but maybe we were avoiding some of the complexities. When he asked again about Jean and Dallas, we decided to go there in the spring of 2002.

Morgan started to join our family when his mother answered an advertisement in a small Texas newspaper; a good family looking for a second child to be brother to their son. Before contemporary communication technology, I installed a dedicated toll-free phone on my desk, didn't book meetings for the two weeks we ran ads, forwarded calls to home when I left work, stayed home at night and on weekends.

A woman from Grand Prairie called, she said next to Dallas, and gave me a number in case we got cut off. Adoption lawyers had told us to put in the toll-free number because a teenage girl, learning she was pregnant, sometimes called from a pay phone before telling her boyfriend or parents. This woman and her three children were living with her mother as she went through divorce. She was seven months pregnant, thought to keep the baby (fathered with a boyfriend) but decided it wasn't the right time. She wanted the adoptive parents in the hospital during the delivery, the first to hold him. She never wanted to. Most birth mothers asked for their medical bills to be covered, if not money for rent, food, clothes, travel back and forth from doctors and lost wages, whatever was legal and sometimes more. Morgan's mother wanted nothing other than a good family for the child she'd give birth to. She'd been the only woman so far not to end the conversation when she realized we were Jews. She liked that Leslie was a doctor. She liked that her baby would be someone's younger brother. She liked that we had an apartment with room for another child and a home on a pond in the country. "You sound like good parents. What's your son's name?"

I imagined her daydreaming, a boy with his older brother named what I'd say. Did she wonder at the color of the boy's hair, his eyes, clothes? "Ripton," I answered.

"*Ripken*. That's a good name, I like that man, with the Orioles, right?"

"That's Cal Ripken. Our son is Ripton, it's a town in Vermont near where I grew up."

"Vermont, that's beautiful."

She and I wanted things to be beautiful, this woman on the other end of a phone whose son might be our son.

"I like that," Jean said and asked to speak with Leslie that night. They did, when Jean suggested meeting, and for us to bring pictures of home and Ripton. We flew to Dallas the next week, rented a car and followed directions to her mother's, a shotgun house with a front porch in a neighborhood of shotgun houses with front porches. Her children were out, her mother poured sweet iced tea and the four of us spoke. She looked at our pictures. We walked no farther than the front room. She wanted to make sure, above everything, that we practiced driving to the Dallas/Fort Worth Medical Center. The four of us went to the airport and from there to the Grand Prairie hospital as Leslie and I were supposed to do when the baby was born.

Jean phoned with intermittent contractions the morning of Christmas Eve, hurrying to leave for the hospital. We were flying with Ripton that afternoon to visit my parents in Puerto Rico. "It's time," she said.

Leslie asked about the time between contractions.

"The doctor told me to come, he's gonna do a cesarean if the baby isn't coming."

"Don't, it's early," Leslie cautioned, knowing the weeks.

"The doctor said he should. You're coming?"

"Yes. Jean, listen to me. It's early for a C-section. Your checkups are fine, you've had three vaginal deliveries, don't let the doctor talk you into anything. No one likes to work on Christmas, so don't let your obstetrician hurry things up."

"I asked, if I don't go into labor. I don't want you to come up to Dallas and not have the baby."

"We're coming. Don't have a C-section unless the doctors say it's indicated, okay?" Leslie urged.

We cancelled the Puerto Rico flight, called my parents to let them know we were going to Dallas and bought two expensive tickets because they were the only ones available. We couldn't find Jean in the hospital. Her mother answered at home. Jean hadn't gone into labor and hadn't asked for the cesarean.

"I'm sorry. We were sure," Jean said when we got to her house.

Her mother brought cups of sweet instant coffee and sat beside Jean on the porch sofa.

"He needs to see you first. I don't want him to be alone in them bassinets."

"We'll be there," I assured her.

"I've been thinking, I hope it's okay with you, Justin Morgan was from Vermont, right?"

He made the Morgan horse famous. "Yup, he was."

"Do you like Justin Morgan Rosen? He should have a name on the birth certificate, I don't want him to be John Doe. If you think, I can say Justin Morgan when the nurse asks me."

We nodded, it was a nice name, that he shouldn't be John Doe. Her mother left to pick the kids up at an aunt's. They were four, three and one. I wondered if Jean explained where the baby inside her would go. "Oh," she dropped a hand to her belly, "he's been doing this." I looked closely, her alabaster skin, a raccoon band of light freckles from one hazel eye to the other across an aqueous nose; I'd come to know everything about this face, every move, rise and fall. "Long kicks, do'ya wanta feel?" her eyes generous.

I did, and not. "Sure," Leslie answered, her hand knowing.

"I'd keep the baby," she looked past the porch. "I tried but I can't work and we can't afford day care, anyway. My mother said it would be too hard." Her eyes stayed away until a tired Toyota pulled to the curb, her mother and children, light-skinned African Americans. "I know you'll be good parents," Jean came back. She didn't want my help standing, struggled up and hurried down the steps.

Leslie and I went to the airport and took the next flight home, re-booked our tickets and met my parents on Christmas Day. We called Jean the day after, Leslie and I both on the phone. "We want him to know you gave him his name," I told her. "Are you okay if we use '*Morgan*'?"

I heard her exhale, the phone against her face. "You don't like '*Justin*'?"

We didn't. "We do, but it's a Jewish tradition to name a child after a relative or close friend." We wanted to use another middle name for Morgan.

We called on New Year's Day to wish Jean, her children and mother well.

Her mother phoned from the hospital late morning, January 8, asking us to come. "They're inducing Jean," her mother said. It was a Friday.

"Let's go," I said to Leslie.

"Let's wait until she delivers," Leslie countered.

"We said we'd go." I wanted to be at a delivery of one of my children. I'd never had that chance.

"Let's wait until he's born this time. And healthy."

Jean's mother called again and we told her we couldn't get a babysitter. She suggested we take Ripton. We skirted issues. Morgan was born at 3:12 p.m. Leslie wanted to know his weight; eight pounds four ounces. She asked to speak with a nurse and learned his Apgar scores at one and five minutes; nine and nine of ten—a healthy boy. Then she said we could fly to Dallas. We drove the eight-lane commercial road framed by strip malls and gas stations to the brick plinth and stainless-steel letters announcing the medical center, through the berm and up the looping driveway of any proud corporate headquarters onto fresh blacktop with cars in sunlight. We stopped near the porte cochere and walked into an entrance of flow-ers, stuffed animals, balloons, magazines, get-well and newborn greeting cards guarded by youthful senior candy stripers smiling in pink and white searsucker volunteer shirts. Everyone was White. We found Jean through Information. "Have you seen him?" she asked, the exhausted optimism of birthing on her face, her mother beside the bed.

"We wanted to say hello," Leslie answered.

"Go to him," she smiled weakly.

"We wanted to thank you," I said.

She looked beyond the room, hazel eyes out the window. "I don't want him to be alone," and she didn't look back to us.

We saw Morgan in the line of bassinets, *"Baby Boy Brock"* swaddled in a white blanket and a light cyan cap. A nurse opened the door a little, "Can I help you?"

I pointed to Morgan. "That's our son."

Her eyes took in Leslie and me, neither postpartum. "Baby Boy Brock?" her voice kind, opened the door and took us to Morgan. "He's beautiful, isn't he? You can pick him up," and she walked away.

Leslie reached for Morgan, cradled a round-headed infant who couldn't open his eyes, held him to her cheek then handed him to me. Holding is my moment of becoming a parent. It was with Ripton. The nurse came back with a clipboard. "I need you to sign this," she said about a form. Leslie did, an acknowledgment we were taking Morgan. *"Justin Morgan Brock,"* it said.

We went to the elevator expecting . . . something, anything, stopped for our driver's licenses, proof we could parent? We passed the flowers and candy stripers to the parking lot away from Jean and her mother, as far as we knew away from the Dallas/Fort Worth Medical Center.

We drove to the suites hotel where we'd made reservations, bought tickets for Ripton and a babysitter and spent an uncomfortable night. It was illegal to take Morgan out of Texas, so Leslie called the local Four Seasons, part of the luxury chain, who had room for three nights and not after. She booked what she could. We met Ripton at the gate and found the new hotel. The Four Seasons allowed us to eat a late lunch. Leslie laid Morgan on a chair seat, two days old and too small to move. People stopped to watch. We used the hotel's luxuries. Morgan was on a seat top for breakfasts and dinners. Ripton slept in our bed and the babysitter with Morgan in the adjoining room. She took care of him. We asked the first morning and the next if we could stay but the hotel had no room. Leslie called her parents a couple hours before we were supposed to check out. Ria called a travel agent with an unlisted number, who arranged for us to keep our rooms for as long as we wanted to be in Dallas.

---

We reserved one room with two double beds in the Four Seasons for our trip back.

We planned to ask Kindu to stay in the apartment, but he'd been lonely. The bigger boys together would turn our home into a frat house. Anyone excluded would be hurt. We chose Kindu, Carlos and Will. They agreed to walk the dog four times a day, water the bonsais daily and the other plants when dry, feed the fish, feed the two turtles and two chinchillas. We asked Phil and Juan to leave by eleven. "Why can't we stay?" Juan was indeed hurt. We explained our decision had nothing to do with him and Phil, only that five boys was too much.

"It's not," he insisted.

"When my parents went away, I know what we did."

"We won't do anything," Juan promised.

"What you did?" Carlos asked.

We promised Phil and Juan that they could take care of our apartment the next time. We meant, but didn't say, with another of the bigger boys and even that wasn't comfortable.

"If we good enough for next time, what about now?" Juan asked.

Juan was smart; we'd not come to the same stage with each of the five bigger boys—not to the same trust, confidence, affection and expectations. Our differences wouldn't have much mattered if they'd stayed children, but the bigger boys were nearing the end of that.

Resentment and hurt would grow, at least for a time. Juan and Phil promised to leave by eleven o'clock. The five promised no one else would visit.

Leslie counted on them. I didn't see Kindu, Carlos or Will saying, *"It's time to leave."* They all spoke about girls we never met and Spanish parties in the Bronx. We wrote in the doorman's book that the five could be in the apartment and no others, but they were sharp enough to arrange what they wanted.

"YoMike, you know who the Yankees playin when you gone?" Carlos asked a few days before we left, looking at the Yankee calendar on our refrigerator.

I didn't.

"Four games, *IN* Texas?"

I shrugged.

"The YANKEES playin the Rangers, rah? That where you at?"

"We're going to Dallas, not the games."

"We should go," Leslie said.

"Hell-yeah!" Ripton shouted from his room. "I wanna see A-rod," the Ranger's shortstop, the highest-paid player in baseball.

"You takin me?" Carlos asked.

We should have been. We weren't.

"YoRipton, you goin wifout your sleepinbuddy?" he shouted to Ripton. They'd been sharing the TV room pullout sofa.

"Hell-yeah, if we can see A-rod."

———————

"This is where we saw you," Ripton announced when we walked off the plane. I looked at the waiting passengers, travelers hurrying by, airport concession stores and couldn't tell. Leslie couldn't. "Don't you remember that coffee place? You guys were there," Ripton pointed.

"Ripton's right, look Morgie," Leslie was proud. "This is where we were. Ripton ran off the plane to hold you."

"Mom let me hold you by myself."

"Great, you two were like? That's child abuse," Morgan was adorable.

"You were safe, Morgie, I kept a hand on you," Leslie said.

As the trip had come closer Morgan wanted us to try to contact Jean, then changed his mind. He did want to see the hospital where he was born but preferred spending a day there first to get used to Dallas. The concierge at the Four Seasons arranged tickets for the game and we sat along the third base line, able to watch expressions on the face of the highest-paid player in history. He was having a mediocre time and Ripton doubted A-rod was a god. My cell phone rang. It was a call from home, which I wanted to let go into voice mail but the game was only in the fourth inning, if something were wrong in New York. "YoMike," I heard Carlos. "Where you at?"

I tried to muffle the sound. "Okay," I answered, watching Derek Jeter at bat.

"Where you at?"

"Okay," I said again.

"Jeter gonna get a hit?"

"Who?"

"YoMike, I love you."

---

The concierge, a tall man of military bearing, a crisp uniform, blue eyes focused, looked down on us, opining that the hospital had closed a couple years earlier. "Is someone sick?" he asked.

We assured him we were fine.

"I wanna see it," Morgan said to make sure.

The concierge bent closer to Leslie and me, "It's not a good neighborhood."

We'd heard the same before Morgan was born. He gave us directions, Leslie drove and I navigated to Hospital Boulevard, where we couldn't find the hospital's driveway. I didn't see the plinth we remembered. "Why can't you find it?" Morgan asked on our third pass, rarely impatient. "You can ask there," he pointed to a gas station.

"Aw . . ." the man pumping gas shook his head to Leslie, searching through the windows to me, then Morgan and Ripton. "Aw . . ."

Everyone buying gas, the attendants, mechanics and the people inside the small store, everyone beside us was Black.

"That closed a long time. Ya'all need a hospital, ya got-ta go—"

"We want to see it, our son was born there," Leslie stopped him.

"Aw . . ." he paused again, then told us how to go. Although the plinth and pylon once announcing DALLAS/FORT WORTH MEDICAL CEN-TER were gone, "2709" in metal numerals had been pounded into the lawn by the driveway. It led us beyond the narrow manicured lawn and berm to a gray wasteland, what had been blacktop and fresh parking lines when Morgan was born, cracked with brown thistles, clusters of grass and deep potholes. FOR SALE—two signs larger than billboards, worn past abandonment were hammered high on the brick wall facing us. Tens of windows were shuttered in plywood. We stopped talking, riding in silence. Whatever we'd expected, this was worse. Leslie parked and Morgan got out, starting towards the abandoned building. "Morgan." He ignored us. "Morgan?" His shadow hugged steps, hands in his pockets, shoulders stiff. "Morgan!" I called a third time.

He stopped to look through an uncovered window beneath the porte cochere, raising a hand to the glare and looked into what had been candy stripers, patients, doctors, flowers, teddy bears, balloons and greeting cards. Leslie and I caught up but he hurried away. "Morgan," Leslie called. He kept walking and we looked inside— dust in a shaft of light, painted cinder block, a littered linoleum floor, piles of abandoned furniture.

We'd failed him. The hospital was unwanted. We hurried after Morgan and there was an "unwanted" in adoption. "It was beautiful, Morgy," Leslie said when he stopped. It wasn't except in the care people gave there, in the healing and birth. Morgan wouldn't let Leslie hug him and I didn't try.

Ripton was beside the car, impatient among the weeds. Morgan wouldn't talk for long after we were at the Four Seasons.

"*No*" finally came from Jayne Godlewski via an assistant principal, who told me she was head of the school's athletic program. So I asked to watch Kindu practice with his Seward Park baseball team. "You'll need to get permission from the Department of Education," she said, which I couldn't. When I called her back to say I was stymied, she told me Kindu had quit the team a few games before the end of the season, which was anyways over.

"Word? She tolt you that?" Kindu tried his million-dollar smile but couldn't bring it to success and shook his head. "We got two games left, I ain't dropped off nothin."

Carlos handed me the letter signed by his mother. "But . . . YoMike, I ain't goin to school. Since that fight," his voice soft.

I had to think—the cafeteria, but that was months ago. "*Good*," Carlos had kept answering over the weeks with the others when I asked about school. He'd been coming over well dressed at the end of each afternoon. "What do you mean?"

"I tolt you bout the fight."

"You didn't, really. You haven't gone in . . . months?"

"Somefin like that." He gave the story more shape, the bigger boys flirting with Dominican girls from the Heights, hanging with a group of Dominican guys. Carlos said "*Hey*" once too often to a particular girl.

"*Lookin tight, Fancy Boy, always pretty*," the biggest and loudest of the other boys said to his friends.

Carlos was supposed to hear. "*You wanna say somefin?*"

"*Lookin tight, what I say*," the boy jeered—he and his buddies were baggy.

Carlos set his tray on a table. "*You wanna say somefin now?*"

The boy got up, taller than Carlos, thinner, the same age, "*Lookin pretty, Fancy Boy.*"

Carlos stepped closer, senses quickening, smiles freezing around. They do in an instant.

The boy pushed Carlos, who rocked but kept his balance, pushed back and the boy fell into his friends, stood and threw a punch.

Carlos heard the kids. It could have been slow motion. He leaned away from the fist and flattened the boy's nose, felt it accordion and disappear, the crush of cartilage, and wondered at its ease. There was no nose and no blood. Then the emptiness burst. The boy's face, what it was, changed to confusion, a hand gone to what had been but was now only blood, pulling away, blood covering his sleeve, shirt, the floor. The police came. One tried to calm the boy and another hurried Carlos to the hallway, took his name and sent him home.

Phil recognized a girl from school through the window as their subway pulled into Union Square the next day. She looked into cars as they passed, pointed at Phil and called down the platform. He hurried with Will and Juan to the front, through the door and into the next car then to the front of that. They waited for the doors to start closing then rushed out, turned to watch as the train lurched forward, gained momentum and the car they'd been in rolled by with the boys from Washington Heights inside and older boys who'd graduated or quit.

Phil told Carlos about being chased. He decided to stay home the next day too—and the next till he stopped going to school, remaining at his mother's until three o'clock so the police wouldn't pick him up as truant, dressing to come to our apartment. He'd missed two months. He'd failed ninth grade once and was doing it again. He'd failed some other grade. I asked Leslie to talk in the TV room and shut the doors. "He's not gonna go back," I said, explaining what I'd learned. "He's dropped out of school—finished."

"He could go back." Leslie believed in the best things.

"He's not been there for two months. He's failed."

She made her dismissing face. "He should ask the school. Maybe they'll help."

"He's afraid for his life, Leslie." I thought about Carlos. He'd not been a student as long as we'd known him. His mother kept him home from the sixth-grade honors class. He wasn't attending three of five school days until we went clothes shopping the spring after we met. He failed some grade we hadn't known. He failed ninth grade and we hadn't known. He failed ninth grade again. How could we have been blind? We trusted the bigger boys' answers to our questions. "You know they're going to ring up one day, '*Is Ripton there? Can we come up?*' and we're going to have to say, '*No, not anymore.*'"

"You always think the worst."

"You think about it. Carlos is bright and he can barely read. God knows what the rest of them are doing—nobody tells the truth. Reading times, *Moby Dick*, the summer projects, everything, they're a mess. Kindu's brothers. That's what happens when they get older. I don't want to pass them on the street and look away."

We walked to the living room and told Carlos he had to earn a graduate equivalency degree, a GED. Leslie would bring home a preparation book. He'd come over each morning and study while I wrote.

He agreed, Leslie bought a book and we started.

---

"Big Mike, you gonna be happy," Kindu shimmered, holding out a sliver of plastic. He watched from a step away as I fingered the clear piece and it became a bronze medal on a ribbon sandwiched in display, a Ulysses Grant of a man, a broad face and beard, WINGATE MEMORIAL MEDAL across the top.

"Big Mike . . . Read the other side . . .

FOR THE BEST RECORD IN ATHLETIC IMPROVEMENT
SCHOLARSHIP AND CHARACTER

"That assistant principal gave it to me, the one tolt you I quit. It's to the best senior."

"I'm proud of you," handing the medal back, his fingers warm when we touched. A father, fatherly, a man should do more. I stood and hugged Kindu.

We held each other for a moment. "Keep it in the house," Kindu handed General George W. Wingate back to me.

"I'm sorry to ask, Kindu," I sat down again, "but have you heard from colleges?" It was early June. Leslie and I told ourselves that Kindu's colleges might be different. But we knew they weren't.

"Not yet, Mike."

---

I called on a whim, and Steven Satin answered his phone. I explained who I was, why I'd been calling before and about Carlos' fight. He didn't seem to know Carlos. I spoke about our family. I hoped he might welcome Carlos back, shepherd him through an education. He couldn't seem to place Carlos. He was in a hurry. "Sounds like the boy made a bad choice," Steven Satin said, and hung up.

---

Carlos' GED book was in our house but Carlos wasn't. He couldn't come the morning before because he visited his grandmother. The morning before that he left early to run errands—a shapeup with Phil in Washington Heights, new braids on Attorney Street. He slept late another morning. He visited his aunt. He took care of his brothers. He wasn't going to complete his GED. Leslie agreed I should take him to Ernesto Ferran, the counselor who'd helped us. I told Carlos we were going to someone who could help us understand what was best for his GED. We sat side by side on Ernesto's sofa facing Greenwich Village rooftops from a sixth-floor window, spoke for a bit and I left the two of them alone. Ernesto opened his office door a half hour later for the three of us to talk again. "Carlos can't go back to his school. If he passes every year, which he hasn't, he'll be twenty-one when he graduates. Kids will be calling him 'Mr. Suarez.'" Carlos couldn't study in his mother's apartment, a storm with three younger brothers who were already big, his mother and boyfriend, his older brother Jesus, Jesus' new girlfriend and her new-born twins fathered by a recent ex-boyfriend, and the girlfriend was newly pregnant with Jesus' child. On top of that, Carlos' mother and her boyfriend drank and argued.

Leslie suggested he study at the Door, a youth center for urban kids. She knew a woman there and called to see if they had room in their GED program and find out about SAT tutoring. Kindu also needed help, though we didn't know how to tell him. The woman said there were openings and she wanted the boys to come in for a tour and registration. "You have to give him credit," Leslie started about Kindu. "I know you're frustrated over the SATs and college—"

"You are, too."

"But he finished high school. Without our help."

She was right, and Kindu's mother was planning a celebration. She and his brothers gave him the money for a suit at Wallid's on Fourteenth Street, the narrow storefront between Second and Third avenues advertising DESIGNER MEN'S SUITS—$89.99, TWO FOR $139.99. Phil and Will helped Kindu pick out a tan polyester blend four-button jacket with pleated pants, a cotton and spandex white dress shirt with a deep pointed collar and internal stays, a tan belt and light beige suede Aldo loafers.

"Let's see," Leslie encouraged when they came home.

"I don't think so, Leslie," Kindu didn't want to put on his clothes.

"When Brenda and I went shopping, we'd always did a fashion show."

"That's so gay," Ripton shouted into the kitchen.

"Ripton!" I tried.

"It is," he walked in.

"They girls, dogs, wif a fashion show. Where you go shoppin?" Carlos asked Leslie.

"Bloomingdale's, Bergdorf," she blushed on her words.

"Word? Leslie? We goin shoppin to Armani Exchange, do some Pradas?" Phil asked.

"Zaras," Carlos said.

"Kindu, will you—" Leslie started.

"KinDUUU—" Will mimicked her.

Ripton, snorting, loved when Will played with our voices.

"I wanna save it for graduation," Kindu said, and left to hang his new clothes on the rack in the small room behind the living room.

"Looks splivy, for sure," Phil assured us, combing through the refrigerator unsatisfied. "Can we order Chinese? Any niggas hungry?" He always was.

Elaine called Kindu at our apartment the next afternoon—a letter had arrived from school. He borrowed my bike, came back a few hours later and said nothing. I asked. He walked away. I followed. He kept his back to me. I pushed. "I failed English," he said to the air. But he'd spoken with a guidance counselor, who said he could walk across the stage for a rolled piece of blank paper. A diploma would wait until after summer school.

"What about colleges?"

"She say it's okay, long as I pass the class."

"Did she say when you'd hear?"

"No."

"Fuuujuu'an," the doorman said when I answered the house phone midmorning one day the next week.

"Who?"

"Fuuujuu'an," I couldn't understand what he repeated. "Kindu's brother."

"Mr. Rosen. Say, hey, what up? It Fuquan, Kindu there? We waitin on him for graduation."

He'd gone out with Carlos. I had no idea where. I ran to the small room—the suit and shirt were hanging there, his dress shoes laid out below.

Kindu and Carlos didn't come back till late. Kindu wanted to be left alone.

---

We hadn't figured how to get Kindu to agree to the Door, and though he said he'd go, Carlos never managed. We should have understood sooner, he was afraid to go alone. The two agreed when Leslie suggested Kindu keep Carlos company. When Kindu arrived, however, we hadn't solved how he'd miraculously decide to sign up for SAT tutoring. But it didn't matter, they never went. After a week I asked them to meet me at noon on a street corner nearby.

Sixth Avenue towards Canal is Holland Tunnel trafficked. Exhaust, horns and inch bursts of speed. I hurried my bike through the angled intersection between buses, long- and short-haul trucks, angry taxis and cars and two policewomen in diesel exhaust midlane conducting traffic. The shape of my boys emerged. One moment they were silhouettes, Spanish and Black teenagers, then they were mine; Carlos' shoulders and chest, his braids, Kindu's height, his round head and close hair.

We crossed Sixth Avenue to the Door and the group standing outside was from any urban high school; loud, Tompkins Square Middle School at dismissal grown a few years older. Carlos and Kindu took seats inside the front door and I went to the woman perched behind the counter. I explained our appointment for GED and SAT tutoring. She handed me clipboards with forms to complete.

"What you do'in, Mike?" Kindu's face showed a dawning realization.

"Mike gotya, son," Carlos was a puppy-wagging his tail, slapping his clipboard to Kindu's shoulder, slapping his thigh.

Kindu glared ahead.

"It's the right thing," I said.

He watched the wall in front of us, watched it more then slowly started writing. The woman we had an appointment with came. She was White, dressed in a tie-dye skirt and peasant blouse. She let us into the main space behind the turnstiles, described the Door and went to show the place to the boys.

She came back twenty minutes later without Carlos and Kindu, who were getting free physicals, a requirement for participating in programs. "The boy with the braids, he'll be fine. But the short-haired one, he won't keep coming. I'm sorry, but I'm not wrong about these things. He's angry."

"That's Kindu. He says he applied to SUNY colleges but hasn't heard back. Is that possible?"

"Decisions go out in May. Kids have known since then." She seemed to understand.

The two boys and I walked home through Soho. We were an odd troupe in a rich person's shopping playground strangely mixed with a few hip-hop homeboy boutiques they knew. I felt comfortable when we hit the old Italian streets and then the Bowery. I asked Kindu to stay with me. We left Carlos at the Christodora and went around the corner to a small Cuban place with café con leche. Kindu ordered a Coke and said he hadn't taken the SATs or applied to colleges. "I plannin on it. I ain't gonna sit around wif my life. There nothin to worry about cause I know you and Leslie worry."

"When?—are you planning on college?"

"Sometime. Later."

"What were you waiting for?"

He couldn't explain.

"We expect you to go to college, there's nothing to wait for. Unless you want to get a job?"

"Big Mike . . ." and he tried different stories. He didn't want to work, and agreed to go to the Door each afternoon for the SATs and take the English summer school class he needed.

---

Carlos' GED classes started at nine each morning. He'd have to wake up, attend school, study and get to bed for an honest sleep. On his own at his mother's. He wouldn't. "You have to move in," I told him and Leslie agreed.

*What did his parents say?* Parents? We never asked his mother.

Years later, I asked Carlos what he had said to his mother. "I tolt her, '*If I stay, I'm gonna end up a bum. Look at Jesus—he's a bum.*' She got upset, she said, '*You can motivate yourself and work hard here.*' I tolt her I'm too lazy. She understood."

Though he'd spent years coming to our apartment, sleeping over nearly each weekend and months of summers, some things we long knew about Carlos' habits gnawed freshly at us when he became a constant part of our home, and without logic, surprised us. He refused to clean dishes other than those he'd eaten from. He refused to unload the dishwasher. Clothes piled for weeks on the floor around the bed he slept on and he rarely did laundry. And more than any other habit, confronted with his daily effects, Leslie and I were shocked at the ritual, expense, labor and acute discomfort that came with Carlos' braids. For a long evening once a week he sat on the living room sofa undoing tens and more of thin tight braids while each slowly freed strand frizzed and joined in an explosion of hair. He scratched relentlessly, then shampooed, stuffed on a winter hat or Yankees cap the next morning and went to the same woman religiously for thirty-five dollars of fresh braids in tight new zigzag traverses of fashion on his scalp. Carlos said tears ran as the woman pulled. The pain passed, but as the days went by, as he played, exercised and sweated, particularly in the worst heat and humidity of summer, Carlos' scalp itched fiercely and he couldn't scratch or wash for fear of loosening the woman's work, pulling out strands and being denigrated as styleless. He slapped his head instead, as if killing an army of gnats, fast snaps and no rubbing to avoid freeing ends. We'd seen him at it, but hadn't realized the constancy. Carlos tied a tight du-rag six of the seven nights to keep the braids from rubbing the pillow as he slept. Watching him from the time he fastened it till he went to sleep, eating a goodnight bowl of cereal, making a ham and cheese sandwich from the cold cuts Leslie ordered so he'd phone for less Chinese delivery, was like watching a deeply disturbed young man twitching both eyes together every half minute or less, a grand tick to the fabric pulling into his forehead. He didn't have thirty-five dollars every week, but he got it.

"It's silly, you know, this pain and effort with your braids. And the money," I said as we sat at the kitchen table together one night, each of us eating bowls of cereal.

Carlos twitched and slapped at his hair safe beneath the du-rag. He spooned another mouthful, smiled and didn't answer. I'd said the same thing to him for weeks on end. He knew I was silly. "Girls loves it," he finally humored me again.

----

Their ways were uncertain, more than they could know in that confidence and ignorance of childhood, but Kindu and Carlos did understand dangers in the life they had the chance to cross from, Will, Juan and Phil the same. The five, young boys among the others we'd met, kept coming to our home, put up with reading time and more of our creeping educational intent. They had placed their hopes, we understood, on routes to their futures we'd help lay. Carlos and Kindu dreamed of college baseball while the others didn't, but they came to this thought differently. Kindu would take the SAT, apply to colleges and try out for the team wherever he was accepted. Carlos counted on being recruited, baseball his North Star. We approved both routes, both equally uncertain. And we found we were proud parents as each of the five boys took steps forward.

I was certain that the baseball leagues along the East River were precious, the local men running them heroes because baseball after high school meant college and any way of getting poor kids there helped break poverty's cycle.

We'd picked a different league for Ripton then Morgan, the Stuyvesant League for boys for Stuyvesant Town and Peter Cooper Village stretching north from the other side of Fourteenth Street, a White bastion of middle-class housing built for World War II veterans in 110 redbrick high-rises. Their children's children played on the greenest grass fields I'd seen anywhere in Manhattan. Kids south of Fourteenth Street weren't ostensibly allowed into that league, but Ripton, Ricky and three other boys we knew from our side of the street played on the A's with a coach who lived around the block on Avenue C. Jeff's team had been going through the season undefeated and as victories mounted Carlos, Kindu and Will started coming to watch games with us.

"Oh shit!" Carlos burst the first time he walked onto the Con Ed fields, meticulously maintained in the shadow of the electric power plant, visiting and home teams on scoreboard lights in deep center field. "YoMike, why they got grass?" he smiled lovingly.

Ricky was the league's dominating pitcher. Ripton was powerful at the plate, hitting for average and the only over-the-fence home run we'd seen in our two years sitting in the aluminum bleachers. Jeff made him the team's MVP, reminding us that boys south of Fourteenth Street, no matter how good, weren't allowed on the autumn traveling team.

I knew, watching Ripton, that he'd gotten strong competing with the bigger boys. He and Ricky played fiercely.

Jeff lived in his mother's apartment, a round and oddly dandy man in his midthirties, round face, round glasses, dark brown skin and a sharp goatee. We'd met him that week walking his toy Doberman pinscher in Tompkins Square. He reminded Leslie and me that his A's had twice beaten the opponent they were facing that weekend. His dog lunged at Mr. Jenkins.

An inning in and a run down, the A's started chanting,

> *Hubba hubba ring dong ding*
> *pitcher's got an arm like a washing machine.*

the line of our boys pressing against the dugout chain link,

> *Boy's in a hole ten feet wide*
> *can't climb out cause he's got fat thighs.*

Stuyvesant League parents had complained about our children's poor manners all summer long. We hadn't, the victors, particularly cared. But that day Ricky didn't pitch, Ripton didn't hit and the A's didn't win. The sides lined up, shook hands then sat on the good grass as the commissioner made a speech and handed out first- and second-place trophies. He was the winning team's coach and ran the hotdog and candy concession when his kids weren't playing.

Every boy was honored. Ricky was awarded the league's best pitcher. Ripton clapped and slapped his friend on the back, high-fived when Ricky returned with his trophy. The commissioner started speaking about the MVP and Ripton sat straighter, nearly on his feet. The commissioner spoke about the MVP's great year at the plate, his power, average and play at first base. Leslie gnawed at the inside of her lip. ". . . and for his play today . . ." and Ripton's shoulders drooped. The commissioner called his own son. We clapped. Ripton hung his head. Teammates came to him, slapping hands, saying he'd deserved to win. Ripton hurried ahead when we left, his mitt in swoops to his steps and slaps against his thigh, gripping the aluminum TPX at the joining of tape to barrel. He and Carlos had spent hours together mimicking Paul O'Neill's diamond tape swirl. "You had an amazing season," I caught up. He wouldn't pay attention. "You know you were great. No matter what happens, you have that forever."

"Leave me alone."

I slowed a few yards behind. At Avenue C most everyone kept across to Stuyvesant Town and we turned south towards the Lower East Side. Ripton stopped hurrying when the victors were gone. "I had a better season. Everyone knows."

He and I were first into the pizza shop in Haven Plaza on Avenue C. Pitchers of Coke and Sprite were on the tables in back. Other A's, Jeff and a few parents came, Leslie, Morgan, Carlos, Kindu and Will. The boys were loud and crass and no one shushed them.

———————

Leslie was in her bath when the boys came from the living room and surrounded me at the kitchen table on a Sunday night. "What we doin this week, Mike?" Kindu smiled his smile and shimmied his shoulders.

"Yeah, Mike, what we doin?" Carlos enjoyed Kindu's silliness.

"What we doin, Mike?" Kindu asked again, stepped down to the passageway of the kitchen and fast-marched to the living room in the way he'd been perfecting—round shoulders, stiff torso, straight arms, a new shuffle.

"Kindu crazy," Carlos said.

"Dad?" Ripton drew out the word.

"What do you guys have in mind?"

"Six Flags, I mean—" Kindu shouted from out of sight.

"Six Flags is a whole lotta fun, don't you think?" Carlos asked, adding his vote for the amusement park in New Jersey.

"All of us?" I knew that answer. "How much is it?"

"Fifty dollas, but we have these Coke discounts, see?" Phil said, holding out a Coca-Cola can with a *BUY 1 GET 1 FREE* coupon on the side. The boys had four cans. They needed me for transportation, food and ancillary expenses. I knew it would be fun, but the Puritan in me saw nothing transcendent in the adventure. I prepared to bargain. "Sure, let's go." The boys were happy. "But we have to go to DIA: Beacon first."

"What that?" Phil sensed danger.

"A museum north of here, along the Hudson." A turn-of-the-century Nabisco factory converted into a permanent home for much of the DIA Art Foundation's collection of Andy Warhol, Donald Judd, Dan Flavin, Richard Serra and others. I imagined the bigger boys would look at that art and, wildly inspired, write in the notebooks we'd started back with *"pick a topic."*

"That's not fair," Will complained. The others grumbled.

The Door was closed for a staff meeting on Tuesday and Kindu didn't have to be in English class till the evening. So we had a window for a DIA trip and the same the following Thursday for Six Flags. Our car was being repaired and Martin Motors assured me we could pick it up Tuesday morning. We had all the bigger boys stay over Monday night. I put their notebooks on the dining room table, turned the lights off hoping they'd get to bed and woke them Tuesday morning for breakfast. I went to DIA's website for directions. It was closed on Tuesdays.

"Six Flags, dogs, meant to be," Phil gloated.

We took two cabs to Martin Motors, filled the elevator to the second floor and I wrote my name on the list at the counter. Employees and customers stared at the eight of us. The staff, save for the middle-aged White cashier, were Black. The man who called "*Rosen*" and I recognized each other. Mr. Clarke apologized for our car not being ready. I explained that I was taking the boys on an adventure, describing Six Flags and DIA. He was sorry that he couldn't help, Martin Motors didn't rent vehicles. I pointed to the boys, listening from across the room. "A church group, Mr. Rosen?"

"We're family."

Mr. Clarke called someone who had to call someone and we waited. "We have a van for you," Mr. Clarke said at the end.

The boys enjoyed Six Flags. We delivered Kindu to class.

Everyone stayed the following Wednesday night and boys were spread across the ground floor the next morning—on the sofas, oversized chair and ottoman, on the carpet beneath the stuffed dogs. They wouldn't wake up. They wouldn't get dressed. Ripton wouldn't decide what to eat and the others ate slowly. I pressured them to hurry; no one did. Eventually everyone except Ripton was ready, who still hadn't decided what to eat. He'd stayed as selective as ever. "Come on, Ripton," Will said. I reminded the bigger boys to take their notebooks, Ripton opened a small, candy flavored yogurt with rainbow sprinkles in hues unknown to nature and we took two cabs to Mr. Clarke. "Culture's good, you guys pay attention," he told the boys.

The older ones nodded. Along the West Side Highway, beside the Hudson River near the George Washington Bridge, I reminded them, "You guys have your notebooks, right?"

"Damn," Kindu said from the back.

"You didn't take yours?"

"Sorry, Mike."

I pulled off to a feeder road then back to the highway home. I didn't say anything and turned off the motor when we came to the Christodora.

A cigarette in his hand, his wife pregnant, Dennis waved from the stoop. That's when the boys noticed. "Why we here?" Phil was confused.

"For Kindu."

"I was jokin. I gots it," Kindu said.

"Joking?" The kids were giggling. "It's no joke. I drove here."

"Oh, shit," Carlos was gleeful back beside Kindu. "You fucked up, Kindu," loudly.

"Mike, I love you. Who am I?" Kindu started.

"Didn't you see me turn around? Didn't you notice I drove all the way back?" My streetwise boys had maneuvered me around **the** block. It was driving me crazy driving them nowhere.

"I'm the Wolverine, Mike. I don't forget nothin."

"You stuuupid!" Carlos shouted.

"We wasn't lookin, Mike," Will said.

Juan and Ripton needed to use the bathroom. "Remember to eat something, if you're hungry," I meant to remind Ripton. He wouldn't know his hunger till it was beyond his control. Morgan, Phil and Will decided they needed to use the bathroom.

"Mike, who am I?" Kindu asked again when we were with Carlos.

"I'm not in the mood."

"The Wolverine."

I started driving again nearly an hour and a half after we'd first left home. "Why we do'in this?" someone grumbled an hour of urban highways later.

The frustration escaped. "You want to be idiots running around amusement parks? Is that what you want? Flipping burgers at McDonald's, that's what you're gonna do."

"YoMike, calm down, you Oh-Dee'in," Carlos tried to help me.

"Dad had to kill it," Ripton complained, his tone when Leslie or I embarrassed him.

I grew angrier. "Yeah? You think I'm Oh-Dee'ing? If you don't read, you don't have any curiosity, you don't care about the world beyond fuck-ass public housing and the Yankees, you don't care about art or painting or politics, your life, if you don't care about anything more than fucking video games, WWF and getting laid, what are you qualified to do when you grow up, when you have to take care of children? What are you gonna be able to do beside flip burgers?"

"Gonna call my moms, tell Elaine," Kindu teased me. "I ain't gonna work in no McDonald's. We gonna play baseball, Mike, you know that. For what we gonna get from a museum?" Kindu was rarely less than honest.

"Major Leagues," Carlos boasted. "Major-Leagues-dogs-Yankees don'tneednomuseum."

"Yan-Kees, Yan-Kees," Kindu started chanting, Carlos joined and the others. I glanced behind. Only Phil was quiet, our Red Sox fan.

Finally, we started into Beacon, a factory town like others forgotten along the Hudson, given a small rebirth by antique collectors, weekenders and DIA opening, one of the country's largest contemporary art collections. Black teenagers and languid elders we passed on the streets spoke of the Great Migration north for jobs that would never return. "Is anyone hungry?" I asked. No one answered and I followed directions to the museum.

"I'm hungry," Ripton said as we started into the parking lot.

The reception building sold tickets, cappuccinos, dainty sandwiches, salads with locally grown vegetables and pastries. But after the travails of the trip I didn't want to stop again for anything. I didn't want to feed Ripton and not ask the others if they were hungry. I didn't want to offer delicate food. I marched the boys into the museum, evangelized about the Walter De Maria squares and circles flat on the center concourse floor and insisted we go to the Warhol room, where 102 canvases were hung side by side along the walls. "What this?" Phil asked and I saw the others wondering. "This art? I can do this."

"Shadows."

"I don't see shadows," Will watched the paintings, a long series of rectangles and zigzags in changing colors.

Juan walked away along the paintings.

"They blurry, like, out of focus," Kindu said.

"This is bullshit, bee," Carlos said, somewhere between playing and complaining, watching me.

"What do the colors mean?" Will asked.

I saw a tenement roofline and chimney. That's what I'd seen the last time I'd come. "Hell if I know. It's famous, he's famous, Andy Warhol. He lived Downtown."

"Nigga is whack," Carlos teased me.

"Was whack. He's dead."

"Same thing. White people like this stuff?"

"It's priceless."

"This is crazy. You know that, rah, crazy shit," Phil was loud and the guard watched us. He looked like one of the old men we'd passed on the street. I think he smiled.

"Shhhhhh," I ran a finger to my lips.

"Crazy shit!" Phil was louder. But the guard didn't care. We were alone in the room.

"Look at the paintings, and write what you think." I meant the bigger boys. I saw Juan along the opposite wall, sitting and writing.

The boys liked Dan Flavin's lights and were wondrously in awe walking the Richard Serras. "How nigga do that?" Phil asked about the steel standing where it shouldn't.

"I'm hungry," Ripton reminded me inside one.

I snuck him away for a snack. He didn't go for locally grown vegetables. He didn't eat pastries, fruit or sandwiches but agreed to throw out the bread and eat the cheese inside one. I wanted him to finish before we went to the other boys.

We met them walking back in the front door near the De Marias. "Where you at?" Kindu asked.

"What do you think?" I waved around the museum. They understood I'd been feeding Ripton.

"NiggaMike," Phil teased.

"Those round steel things," Juan answered. The other boys agreed on Serra. "And the crazy car strips." John Chamberlain's *Privet*.

We drove to a deco diner downtown, DINER flashing in big red neon. The host sat us at a large table beside the old-fashioned counter and spin-around seats. The terrazzo floor, chrome clamshell wall panels, tabletops, banquettes, everything glistened.

———————

Leslie and I called the boys to a family meeting in the living room: Kindu had refused to return the Chiefs jersey he hadn't paid for. We gave Morgan a dispensation on account of young age and Juan hadn't showed up for a few days.

Late that summer Carlos had pushed Kindu and Phil to join a baseball team with him that was short on players. The league, in Central Park, was filled with Latino and Black kids down from Harlem and Washington Heights. Our boys apparently convinced the coach that they couldn't afford the two-hundred-dollar team fee and, without talking with us, agreed to pay in installments. The coach gave them jerseys and pants and they started playing.

I picked up the phone one evening to a man asking for Kindu. Who wasn't home. "I need my uniform," the caller said, explained that he was the Chief's coach and said he'd asked Kindu many times to get back what was his. Kindu wouldn't talk with me. Carlos told me what he knew, I told Leslie and she suggested the meeting. We sat in a circle on dining room chairs, stuffed dogs, the sofa, blue chair and ottoman. Ripton wouldn't turn off his portable CD player or take out his earphones, insisting he could hear past the music. Phil kept dozing. I took notes.

Carlos: Phil! Yo, look at Phil go to sleep.
Leslie: Phil, don't go to sleep, it's not sleeping time.
Kindu: Mike, Mike, why you writin topics, Mike? Why you writin topics for?
Will: [To Ripton, about listening to the CD] Can I hear it? I want to hear it. [To us] What this is all this about?
Carlos: Frank's jersey, Phil paid seventy dolla. Phil didn't get to play much and Frank cut him so Phil is goin to keep the jer-

sey. That I understand. This guy [Kindu] paid ten dollas. He played a lot then.

Will: He got his money's worth?

Carlos: He played a lot. He got benched like one game. Now Frank wants his jersey back and he don't wanna return it. What good does the jersey do him, dogs, when in fact every time you see Frank for—

Kindu: Carlos was knocked sense into by Mike. That's the reason Carlos is sayin—

Carlos: It is, I just said that . . . I was gonna keep the jersey last mumf, when Frank cut me. Mike said 'it's not yours, it's stealing, take it back.' I tookt it back.

Kindu: Dogs, dogs, this is what I said.

Will: Carlos, you pay that moncy?

Carlos: No I didn't pay nothin.

Will: Oh, oh ollrrot, cause if you paid that money, then you deserve the jersey, I mean if you quit but you only paid ten dollas.

Will: So Phil, why Phil pay seventy?

Carlos: Cause Phil pay seventy, you was suppose to pay two hundred. Kindu, give him your point of view.

Kindu: My point is, if I didn't know Mike, I would still kept the jersey—rah?

Will: That's true.

Kindu: Now, cause I know Mike, that means I wouldn't kept the jersey.

Carlos: Dogs, you know what, I don't get that right there?

Kindu: Carlos, if you didn't know Mike, you would have kept the jersey.

Carlos: If I didn't know Mike—

Kindu: If I didn't know Mike, I woulda kept the jersey.

Michael: The point is, inherently you're not a thief, but you're acting like one. I don't want you to be that way.

Phil: He inherited a thief?

Michael: Inherently a thief, meaning not—

Kindu: All I say—

Phil: Because he's Black?

Michael: No! I don't give a shit if purple—

Ripton: Nobody gives a shit if he's blue—

Michael: I'm talking about a kid who's saying *"I'm keeping something that's not mine. Somebody's pointing out to me that it's not mine, but I'm not going to listen, cause I know that guy."*

Phil: Kindu doesn't get that, cause the reason Carlos try'in to say—

Kindu: I know what Carlos tryin to say—

Phil: If I did not know Mike, I would not have knowledge like that I have now—

Carlos: But that's the whole point. Kindu be'in stupid—

Kindu: All I'm try'in to say—

Carlos: But we do know Mike—

Phil: We do know Mike, and he put knowledge into our heads.

Carlos: —and no knowledge is go'in into your head!

Phil: —and you're doing things for no reason.

Kindu: Will, Will, you get what I'm tryin to say?—

Will: I get it but you're not make'in sense.

Phil: Niggas on that team play'in white tees, ain't got no jerseys. Cause you got the jersey.

Carlos: Just give 'im back the jersey!

Phil: Give 'im the jersey.

Carlos: What the hell does it do you? You gonna go practice with a Chief uniform? *"I used to play for the Chiefs—"*

Kindu: Mike, Mike, what you writin notes for?

Will: What you gonna do if you see Frank? Are you gonna—

Carlos: You know what you do? You give him a jersey, that's how easy that guy's left your life, just cause of a jersey. That's it.

Kindu: I don't care, dogs.

Phil: It's Frank's jersey.

Carlos: You know why them kids don't have jerseys? Cause
    people like you didn't want to bring them back to the team.
Kindu: No, cause Frank, he operate wrong, dogs. Cause I made
    one error?
Carlos: Bein a good coach and givin back what's his is different.
Kindu: Look, dog, you're talkin bout one bad play.
Carlos: He done one bad thing to Kindu. Other than that,
    Kindu played somethin like thirty games—
Kindu: What you have done?
Carlos: I would have been mad, but I would have give him
    back his jersey, I don't care about it, the jersey's not all that
    cute—
Kindu: Jersey don't mean nothin to me—
Carlos: It mean a lot to you cause—
Kindu: What matters is he took the jersey off me and put it on
    a kid that no one knew. A kid he never saw practice until
    the day that he came to play.
Carlos: What that's got to do wif it?
Kindu: That got to do with me havin to take my jersey off and
    give it to that kid. Now he got to feel that shit. If we didn't
    know Mike, we still do the same things we do, dogs, rah?
    Come on, Will.
Will: But you know them, son.
Carlos: That's the whole point, and we know right—
Kindu: But we know them and that mean we change?
Will: And you can't say "if you didn't know them." You know
    them, that's it—
Kindu: We know them, that means change, rah?
Will: [To Kindu] You goin to the Door now, rah?
Kindu: [Nods his head]
Will: So if you didn't know them, you wouldn't be there now,
    rah?
Kindu: That costs nothin to me.
Carlos: That change your life? Change your bad ways—
Kindu: I know what's right and what's wrong—

Carlos: Are you doin what's right?

Will: He knows it's wrong.

Kindu: He took the jersey off my back—

Carlos: So what?

Will: You know how I woulda do it? [Morgan runs into the room] Oh, Morgan, come over here, yo, oh I missed you, son, come over here! Look at this nigga, son. How you been, son? [Hugging Morgan]

Michael: I'll sit here all day, Kindu, but I'm not going to drop it. I'll sit here all night, but we're not leaving until I get a legitimate reason why that jersey's yours.

Kindu: Because I want to pay back, Mike. Want to pay him disrespect—

Carlos: You gettin 'em back by not playin for him. Do you know how much Frank is shitting on himself right now? I bet you, you go bring him his jersey he tells you "Forget it, I want you to play for me."

Kindu: Will?—

Carlos: And we, we all hit bombs yesterday. Kindu hit a home run, Robinson hit two home runs, I hit a bomb—

Ripton: Robinson hit two?

Carlos: Yeah, hit it out of Central Park—

Will: Frank asked Kindu for the jersey, right?

Kindu: First he goes, first he goes, "Kindu, I got to speak to you." I said, "Frank, I got a game, dogs. See ya later."

Carlos: One of the main reasons why Kindu wants to keep it is cause of what it looks like. If it would of been a Tides jersey he would of gave it back.

Ripton: That Chiefs jersey is nice.

Will: I thought it was payback. I didn't know it was—

Carlos: He said it was payback, but if it was ugly. I can't care cause that jersey ain't takin me nowhere in life. I give that whack-ass shit back.

Leslie: Can I, can I, um, say something for one second? Will, do you have all day or do you have any plans that you can't change to go shopping, cause I don't want to lose you. [Leslie and Ripton wanted Will to go shopping with them to outfit Ripton for his upcoming bar mitzvah.]

Will: Nah, I got all day.

Leslie: Do you have any recommendations about where we're going?

Phil: Prada.

Ripton: Will, Will, I'll go to Prada.

Leslie: We can visit the store. We've never been there.

Will: I'm gonna go over there with basketball shorts and Jordans. Where's it at?

Kindu: Let's go to Prada.

Carlos: We're go'in to Prada. We're go'in to Prada, we're go'in, we're go'in to Prada. But, back to the, back to the task at hand—

Ripton: Alright, people, be quiet, we're finishing the conversation at hand.

Phil: I understand Kindu, dogs, bein disrespected. But Kindu, you didn't pay the league fee that you was supposed to pay to actually have ownership over the jersey. You's just play with it. You playin wif his shirt. And he had to pay for all the empire, he had to pay for everythin, all our competitions.

Carlos: That's what I say, if you would'a gave some money—

Phil: I gave seventy dollas—

Will: You supposed to pay for transportation and umpire. You didn't pay.

Kindu: Carlos, Will, come on son, would you, how would you have felt, dogs, if he tell you to take your jersey off and give it to some whack-ass nigga, son.

Carlos: I would have said "Keep your fuck'in jersey." I wouldn't'a tookt it back.

Will: But do you think you deserve it, Kindu? You didn't answer my question. Do you think you deserve it?

Carlos: The point is, yo son, you know the bad people start stealin? That's what my mom told me. When I was a kid I brought home a eraser, my mom said that's how you start stealin, dogs. Made me bring that shit back. First it's a eraser, then it's a uniform, then it's bats—

Will: It's right, dogs, you start little first, then if you don't get caught you go on to bigger things.

Carlos: That's true—

Kindu: Like I'm, like, I'm gonna rob a bank—

Will: Do you really think you deserve it?

Carlos: This isn't a game. He could call the cops.

Kindu: No he can't.

Carlos: Yeah he could.

Kindu: I signed a contract with this nigga.

Carlos: He could actually call the cops on Kindu Jones.

Kindu: That's what it's gonna be.

Carlos: Alright, Mike, what you got'a say?

Michael: To me, there's no question. It's clear you have a right to be angry at that coach. He has the right to do as he wants. It doesn't mean that he should. Your right is to decide not to play for him. You also have the right to tell him that what he's doing is wrong, and why. You don't have the right to steal. Your right is to take off your jersey, and walk off the team.

Will: When you think about it, you are better than the people that are playin now. They the one losin. He's the one losing out.

Kindu: Will, you're right, Will, you're right—

Will: But I'm sayin—

Kindu: —you're all right, you're all right—

Carlos: So do the right thing—

Kindu did call Frank, and gave back the Chiefs jersey.

———————

"Did you take money?" Leslie meant from her wallet. We were sitting at breakfast.

She'd been leaving her wallet inside her purse on the foyer floor next to our unlocked apartment door for years. She took money from it almost nightly to pay deliverymen for food. Everyone knew.

I hadn't taken anything.

"Two hundred dollars are gone. I went to the bank yesterday. I counted, twice."

We didn't want to think any of the bigger boys would steal. Each had been home the night before. Missing clothes, sneakers, even an iPod wasn't raw like money. The missing dollars were large for Ripton or Morgan. Anyways, they'd ask.

"What do you think happened?" Leslie lowered her voice.

We didn't want to answer that, but had to. Only the bigger boys had been over. We danced around whom we thought might steal; even suspecting any one of them felt like a violation of their trust in us.

She asked again a few weeks later. "Did you take money?" her face already forlorn.

I hadn't. "How much?"

We'd both forgotten her purse downstairs.

"Three hundred."

I spoke with Carlos. Not all the bigger boys had been over.

"Not me," he said. "I don't steal."

"That's why I'm asking you."

"Don't ask me."

"It's the second time in a month."

"How much?"

"Three hundred. Two hundred the last time."

"Jesus. I don't know. You gotsta put her wallet somewhere."

I told him we'd forgotten.

"Why didn't you say somethin?"

"We wanted to make sure it didn't happen again."

"You know who came last night?" He meant one of the boys.

I didn't.

Those who hadn't been came over for Chinese once Leslie and I had gone to bed. Carlos was certain who'd done it. He spoke with two others, who thought the same.

Leslie took her purse upstairs each night. We never confronted that boy. We hoped the years would change him.

---

Carlos didn't have the opportunity to spend high school in a rarified baseball academy in a warm part of the country under coaches honing his skills for a chance at college play and after that a minor league career and the slimmest shot at the major leagues. Norman Thomas didn't offer baseball. The Door didn't have sports. He came home beaming from the East River Tides' summer award dinner with the news that he'd earned the Félix Millán Little League's Triple Crown award for the most home runs, highest batting average and most runs batted in, as well as a Gold Glove for outstanding defensive play. He'd get the trophies in a few months. But the Tides weren't competitive; scouts didn't watch their games. Carlos' coach, supportive, knew little about colleges because few kids went. Carlos wasn't on a route from being a star along the East River to his dream. "Is there a more competitive league?" I asked him.

"Robinson been talkin wif some guy bout Bonnies. And there Youth Service."

I'd never heard of these teams. He told me they were in Brooklyn and I found them on the Internet, storied members of the Parade Ground League for a century on fields in Prospect Park: Sandy Koufax, Manny Ramirez, Joe and Frank Torre, Joe Pepitone, Willie Randolph started there. Carlos liked Youth Service League more than the Bonnies so I called Mel Zitter, the man in charge. I didn't hear back so emailed and didn't hear back. Carlos was too shy to contact Mr. Zitter and I decided to wait before pushing.

I had been thinking for two summers of sending Carlos to baseball camp, and finally pushed myself to stop wasting his opportunity.

He would practice, meet coaches, a step might lead to a step and I found a camp in Cooperstown near the Baseball Hall of Fame. Leslie agreed we could send him and I asked Pastor Phil (for whom I still cut onions across the street) if the Lutherans would be our front. We didn't want Carlos to know we were paying for him. Pastor Phil agreed. I reserved a spot online, filled out the form, we made a donation to Pastor Phil and he forwarded that to the camp.

"You remember Pastor Phil?" I asked Carlos.

"Yeah?" as if I were asking him to go to Sunday service or cut onions.

"They want to send you to baseball camp."

"Word? Like, Chelsea Piers?"—the sports complex on the Hudson River.

"In Cooperstown, Upstate."

"Where that at? Wait, the Hall of Fame? How they know me?"

"Near there. I think they saw you in the park."

That satisfied him, but he refused to go alone and worked on convincing Ripton. Then I was left with the fact I'd arranged a gift for Carlos and not the other boys. I told myself it was okay. Beside Félix Millán and playing occasionally in Tompkins Square, Juan and Will were drifting away from baseball. Phil said he cared but had things to do whenever Carlos, Kindu and Ripton went to practice. But Kindu—sweet, responsible, easy to take for granted—also wanted to play in the majors and I hadn't tried to send him to camp. It wasn't just that I was stingy; Kindu didn't have the same hunger or talent as Carlos. He was also one year too old for Cooperstown, but I hadn't tried to find alternatives. Kindu understood why he couldn't go—he always understood.

We loaded the campers' suitcases, bags, loose sheets, blankets and pillows, baseball gloves, bats, batting gloves and cleats into the back of the car and started north, switching to blue highways past the Tappan Zee. New York becomes rural and Main Street towns not far northwest of the city. Family farms struggle to survive. "Cows!" Carlos screamed. I jumped. He was pointing at fifteen or twenty heifers in a field.

"They're cows," Ripton dismissed the apparent as extraordinary.

"I nevva seen cows," Carlos was jumping. "Lookit them niggas!"

"Never?"

"Nevva been outta New York. The LES, the Bronx, baby."

We'd traveled with Ripton and Morgan. Never out of New York? "What about horses?" I asked.

"I seen cops on horses." The Holsteins were fading.

We found the camp at the end of a dirt road up the rise from two beaver ponds. Carlos wanted the top and Ripton accepted the bottom of a bunk in a room they'd share with a dozen others behind the dining hall. They put their gear and clothes away while I made their beds, fluffed their pillows, spread their blankets and turned down the top sheets. We went to the dining room and they started through the tees, caps, hoodies, nylon pullovers and jackets logoed with COOPERS-TOWN BASEBALL CAMP AT BEAVER VALLEY. "Are you coming on Thursday?" the director asked me. She'd helped with the church arrangement and suggested donating enough for Carlos to buy clothes, sodas and candies through the week. I didn't know anything about Thursday and had planned to pick up the boys on Friday. She said parents could stay in the bunks the night before, have breakfast with the campers and watch the grand finale game before dismissal.

I asked if Kindu could play. She said *yes* and he wanted to. I wanted a note from his English teacher allowing him to miss two nights of class, which he brought. I asked to see his syllabus and realized he wasn't keeping up. "I'm not taking you unless you've finished the reading."

"I know, I know. Don't worry. Hey, Mike, who am I?"

I didn't answer.

"The Wolverine!"

"Great. Do your reading." He assured, I harped, we packed and he hadn't finished by Thursday evening when it was time to leave. I'd watched him fold his East River Tides fire-engine red jersey, place it in the suitcase beside his cap, glove, batting gloves and cleats. He wrapped his toothbrush, shampoo, hairbrush and Vaseline in a plastic bag—Kindu rubbed Vaseline into his skin each night. "I'm not taking you," I said.

"Don't, please, dogs—"

"A deal's a deal. You're playing me. Your reading's not done."

He stood taller than me, silent. "Please."

I needed to teach responsibility. I wanted to figure a compromise. I wanted Kindu to be happy. I wanted Carlos and Ripton to be with him. I wanted his company. "You can come, but you have to read in the car. No talking, nothing."

We started driving, he asked questions and I didn't answer. "Who am I?" The sun set and I turned on his reading light. I stopped at a diner Upstate, but it was closed and I drove to a McDonald's, the only thing open. Kindu finished reading a little before Beaver Valley. The camp director gave us our own bunk room for the night.

We met Ripton and Carlos at breakfast, tanner than a week before, relaxed and happy. Carlos took me to meet the head coach. "YoMike, Coach O'Keefe, all them want me in St. Louis. But," he dropped his voice, insecure, "I tolt them yesterday I was doin a GED." Coach O'Keefe was in his twenties, a large man, affable, blond curled and red from summer. The best of this country. Both my hands would have fit into one of his, blue eyes looked down on me. Anything was possible. He and his friends coached community college teams and American Legion summer ball around St. Louis. They wanted Carlos to play Legion with them next summer and stay for college. He was better than good enough for a scholarship. But because he'd dropped out of high school no coach could yet risk a slot on him. Carlos first needed to complete a community college semester with good grades at home and Coach O'Keefe would find the best place for him in St. Louis.

Carlos was disappointed.

I was elated—we had a plan.

Coach O'Keefe gave me his phone numbers and email. "I've told Carlos, he's too old for camp next summer, but we want him back as a counselor. He's great with the kids."

Carlos and Ripton dressed in their Beaver Valley royal blue shirts and caps. Kindu wore his fire-engine red shirt and cap. My guys were on the same team. They won.

We spoke about St. Louis on the way back home. I didn't know the place—somewhere along the Mississippi, Mark Twain's America, Louis and Clark, past New Jersey. I didn't think there would be many Latino students. Carlos knew less and didn't care. The coaches stroked his ego and that mattered. He planned to finish the GED in the fall, enroll at Borough of Manhattan Community College and complete the one semester by summer. It was a plan. Cocky, naïve or both for someone who didn't complete grades, but a good plan.

Kindu moved in when we got home that night. We thought he had to. Much later, I asked if he spoke with his mother.

"Yeah, I did. She saw me movin my stuff out and askted me what I was doin. *'Ma, you know the neighborhood is bad around here, drug dealers everywhere. I don't like that and you don't want me to be around that. Leslie and Mike, they're makin me go study the SATs and do summer school. I know I won't do that here.'* She said, *'I understand that's what you want to do.'* She knows I don't want to be around what my brothers are up to. Just as long as I come over every day, she's okay."

"But, did you say that part about *'drug dealers everywhere'*?"

"Yeah, I did."

"Your mother knows your brothers deal, right?"

"Yeah, course. But she can't switch their minds up. They're grown. Even Fuquan tolt me I should move in wif you. He said, *'There's nothin over here for you.'*"

---

Carlos said his teachers were impressed with his progress. They planned to give him the Predictor test earlier than the other students, because they thought he was ready for the actual exam. I assumed the exam came at the end of the courses but it wasn't that way. A student began anywhere appropriate to his or her knowledge and remained in a course loop after loop until the teacher felt the material was learned. His teachers—math and science from one, English and social studies from the other—said he could probably take the GED exam in a couple of months and start at BMCC in January, on Carlos' schedule for St. Louis in September.

"We gots a parent-teacher conference next week," Carlos flapped a paper while Leslie and I ate a Sunday supper omelette. The boys, as usual, had refused my cooking and were waiting for the Chinese they'd ordered. Leslie and I knew we had responsibility. We made sure there was milk in the refrigerator and cereal on the shelves, bananas, frozen food, I offered and was rarely taken up on cooking. We provided beds, paid for takeout, but I'd not thought we'd be *"parents"* to the bigger boys at school conferences. Carlos had never had one before. Of course we'd go.

Carlos borrowed from Phil to dress tight for the Door, Zara jeans and a baby blue Armani Exchange polo. He smelled of the Axis Homme deodorant the bigger boys fumigated themselves with. It seemed we were supporting that company; when its scent carried through downstairs to the second floor and up to our bedroom, we knew a bigger boy was readying himself for something special. Carlos went to a Lower East Side woman for fresh braids at thirty-five dollars and to Washington Heights for a fifteen-dollar shapeup. His mother gave him money once in a while, we did and he played pretty boy to girls for jeans, sneakers, sweaters. It worked for him. "This is my mom, Leslie Gruss, and my dad, Michael Rosen," he introduced us to his teachers. They were late middle aged with the aura of second or third careers about them, I thought public school refugees now in a more peaceful place. The math and science teacher stooped the way tall and thin men can look older, his chest disappearing into years, his narrow face framed by salt-and-pepper Einstein hair. The years had worked to fill Carlos' English and social studies teacher's lilac print summer dress, tight across her waist seam. She smiled down on Leslie and me, black and gray curls to midback. I couldn't place her accent. She said Brazilian. She loved Carlos, both of them did. "He's very bright," the math and science teacher said and I was suddenly sure he'd grown up watching Carl Furillo play the dead spots and angles of Brooklyn's right-field wall.

"He's our class leader," the English and social studies teacher bragged.

"But he's too impatient," the Ebbets Field man told us.

We all agreed Carlos needed to be patient. But it wouldn't happen, not yet, "*I always swing at the first pitch,*" Carlos argued with me time after time.

"*That's ridiculous. They're gonna throw you crap.*"

He didn't care. Carl Erskine said Furillo always swung at that first pitch, but Carlos had never heard of either man.

"It's a little early, but Carlos wants to take the Predictor," the math teacher told us.

"It's early," the Brazilian woman agreed, "but Carlos' attitude is great. He told us about St. Louis. You must be proud," looking to make sure we were.

"We are," Leslie offered tentatively.

We were.

"It was nice to meet you," the Brazilian teacher said. "We had no idea . . ." and catching herself, "I mean, your family."

The math teacher was nodding along. "Carlos'll do great."

———————

Dennis was on the stoop when our cab stopped.

"It's so bad for you," Leslie's contempt had grown more vocal because Dennis was soon to be a father.

"Iknowleslie," sliding the cigarette behind his back.

"How's Olivia?" I asked.

Dennis took a half puff, crushed the half-smoked cigarette on the gray granite baluster and threw it to the street. "Good, shesgotmorningsickness," to a trail of smoke, "allthetime, thedoctorsays itsnormal," embarrassed by what his lungs were disclosing.

"What week is she?" Leslie asked, watching the disgorgement.

"Eight."

"In three or four weeks she'll be better."

Dennis reached towards his back pocket, his eyes away on the thought of his pregnant wife, pulled out his pack and jostled a cigarette before reconsidering, pushed it down and the pack away. "Igottastop, withthebaby."

---

"You goin to the cafés in the mornin?" Kindu asked a few nights after summer school ended. In the afternoons he went to the Door, working with a guidance counselor to complete the omnibus application to SUNY's community colleges. I was going to the café on Ninth Street where I'd asked the owner to hire any of the bigger boys. "How bout I go wif you?"

Kindu pulled the foil top of a cream cheese single-serving size to a "U," sliced the dollop and lifted to a bagel half he held with fingertips, spreading hydrogenated white across the toasted top, plastic serrations corning to rows and crosshatchings. White played on the maroon of Kindu's lips as he chewed. "Thanks for the food," writing on the top sheet of a small stack of lined pages with a blue ballpoint pen.

"What are you working on?"

"About me and my family, *Part of the Struggle*. All we gone through. I been thinkin—I wanna go ta college outside'a the city. If I stay around Will and them, I'm not gonna work hard enough. And seein my brothers, seein my moms, it's too hard."

"What's going on at home?" It seemed time to ask, though I feared the answer.

"Jamar got picked up, for we workin on that." He meant getting his brother out of jail.

"The first time?"

"Nah," shaking his head. Kindu never elaborated; he offered blurred, quarter pictures about his family. "Now that I bein here, it harder bein there. Peoples ain't goin nowhere," there was emptiness in his eyes. "My brothers was in a fight. A guy cut up Fuquan pretty bad, his face," brushing the fingertips about the edge of his mouth. "But we got dat guy."

"You, too?"

Kindu started a smile and went back to his paper. "I tolt you, I wanna go away."

---

Morgan began fifth grade at the Earth School and Ripton started seventh at BFS. Getting to Brooklyn wasn't walking down the street. Leslie printed the Avenue B bus schedule. She kept watch to see it turn the corner at Fourteenth Street. One or the other of us would be ready to take Ripton and "*Bus!*" became an alarm. We'd been waking him earlier than Morgan, breakfast was Rice Krispie treats or chocolate chip cookies in front of ESPN on the sofa in the TV room. Like the bigger boys, he'd begun showering the night before and sleeping in boxers. I went back upstairs to wake Morgan while Leslie kept an eye on the clock. "Five minutes till it's time to get dressed." Then five minutes later, "Ripton, time to get dressed." We fed Morgan. Then a reminder to Ripton and more till he was ready. "Five minutes to bus time," Leslie shouted but they came earlier and later and Leslie stayed vigilant. A white truck or yellow school bus poking into the intersection could first seem a blue and white MTA bus. "BUS!" Leslie yelled. She and I alternated taking and picking him up from school. "Are your teeth brushed?" Leslie asked because they normally weren't. The parent staying for Morgan made sure Ripton and his backpack got to the elevator, the parent taking him was waiting in the hall holding the door, both of us hoping the red lights and passengers kept the bus enough for us to catch it across the street and ride to Delancey. Or we'd walk to Avenue A, where buses ran more often.

The Delancey subway station was a labyrinth of turns, stairwells, passageways and switchbacks. Three stops later, Jay Street was the hourglass neck of trains into and out of Brooklyn, enormous but straightforward.

We started letting Morgan walk home alone after school, old enough for the 433 steps from the Earth School to the Christodora, sufficiently safe and most days he went to the gated playground inside the park along Avenue B with DJ, Miles, other friends and parents. Leslie met him there on days she took Ripton to Brooklyn, and looked for him later on days I'd done the morning bus and subway trips.

Two weeks into the new year Ripton said he didn't want our help going to school. I rode with him the next morning, checklisting through steps and turns he needed to make. I reminded him to be careful on his way home. Is "*remind*" strong enough for what a parent does turning a twelve-year-old loose in New York? He promised. That afternoon Leslie tucked behind a corner at school and trailed our son through his first trip alone.

Ripton did fine.

————————

Jeff called wanting Ripton and Ricky on the Stuyvesant autumn all-star team, competing across the city.

"I thought our kids couldn't play?"

"It's okay, Mr. Rosen. Ripton and Ricky are the only ones." He explained that there were almost no practices, the games were on weekends and began right away. Leslie and I drove Ripton and Ricky to Upper Manhattan for the first one, searching for a baseball field through an enormous park we'd never heard of, passing baby strollers, hotdog stands and ice cream carts till we happened upon our Stuyvesant team. Jeff slapped Ripton and Ricky on their backs as heroes and introduced us to Paul, whom I realized was the Jack Russell–sized man I'd watched bark and scurry the baselines and dugout losing to the A's. He hadn't liked our team's ways. Leslie and I sat on the concrete bleachers, dirty and disintegrating. The game wasn't special, except Ripton hit the go-ahead run-batted-in with a line drive to right field.

The next weekend I drove Ripton and Ricky to somewhere we'd never been in Queens. I sat in serried bleachers pressed against the visitors' dugout, the bench at field level behind a chain-link fence the same as Tompkins Square and the East River fields. Ripton and Ricky began their A's chanting two or three innings in with a teammate on base:

> *Hubba hubba ring dong ding*
> *pitcher's got an arm like a washing machine . . .*

Jeff, coaching third base, was smiling. The same as I. The summer had been fun, sunshine on grass. Paul, coaching first, began to snarl. The boys kept chanting. They probably didn't realize, and wouldn't have cared. "Stop it," Paul screamed, kicking at the first base bag.

> *Hubba hubba ring dong ding . . .*

"YOU'RE BENCHED!" Paul charged the first base line yelling at the two. "Go to the end!" pointing to where he wanted them.

Ripton and Ricky looked to Jeff. I looked to him. He looked at the ground.

"Go!" Paul stomped and when the boys didn't he started towards them again.

Ripton and Ricky went to the end of the bench, close to me. "It's BULL-shit," Ripton turned and tried to explain. "We did it all summer, BULL-shit."

Paul heard. He came the rest of the way, banged on the other side of the chain link from the boys, a snarling show. "One more word and you're outta Stuyvesant. You understand?"

"It's BULL-shit," Ripton complained during our ride home.

"Jeff don't do nothin, rah?" Ricky said.

"Jeff's whack."

"He pussy."

Jeff was. The sentiment.

Neither Leslie nor I could go the double-header the next Sunday. Jeff called to tell us that Paul wasn't terribly angry, and he wanted to make sure Ripton was playing. I asked if he could take the boys. He said there was room in a van Paul drove.

"It's BULL-shit," Ripton came home that evening. Paul had pulled off the FDR somewhere north in Manhattan and kicked Ricky out.

"For what?"

"I don't know. *Bad language.*"

"What happened?"

Ripton didn't know or wouldn't say.

"Did he swear at Paul? Or Jeff?"

"HELL no."

"Did Paul call his mother?"

"HELL no. He kicked him out."

"Did he make sure Ricky had money?"

"No. Jeff sat there. We told you he was pussy."

The FDR is the major expressway along the eastern length of Manhattan. I phoned Jeff and Paul and neither would tell me what happened. They didn't have to; I was certain Paul would never kick a White twelve-year-old with English-speaking middle-class parents (including a father at home) out of his van by the side of a busy highway. Racism didn't have to come sounding like Bull Connor or Edgar Ray Killen.

Ricky was a Dominican kid with messy braids from public housing. His single mother spoke broken English. His father came to one game a year, if that. I'd met him once in all the years.

Ricky could be as loud as Ripton. He was crass as a typical twelve-year-old Lower East Side boy with no malice. He could have been hit by a car, mugged, kidnapped, molested and should have been terrified by the side of the highway. I should have reported Paul to the league. I should have reported him to the city's Administration for Children's Services. I wrote an email to the list of players' parents and read it to Leslie.

"You sure you want to send that?"

I pressed *Send.*

Another father wrote back minutes later—traveling team players, besides Ricky, seemed to have fathers at games:

> I'm extremely grateful my son gets to play for guys like Paul and Jeff . . . Respecting the coaches is a part of being on a team. If that respect is not there, then there is no team . . . If a child has a difficult time treating coaches with respect, then being on a team may not be for him or her and perhaps they should look to individual sports like golf or tennis.

*Golf or tennis?* I wanted to ask that father if he'd seen the Jacob Riis golf and tennis teams recently. An email flurry started. Most all parents said that Leslie and I were misguided, Ripton and Ricky poorly raised and ill behaved. Our boys were dropped from the team and we were dropped from the e-mail list.

---

Ripton's first BFS parent-teacher conference came in early November. My stomach fell as the date approached. His advisor was BFS's French teacher, Madame *pe-REE*, a round-faced and solid woman with curled and dark hair. She looked up and smiled when we knocked, invited us to sit around her table. "Our *rip-TONE* is a good young man," she started happy. "*Rip-TONE* and another boy were in a fistfight the first week of school." I glanced at Leslie; reddish blond hair about her face, blue eyes shifting deeper when fierce or terrified. Her smile was frozen. It wasn't a smile at all but a place saver, a segue to fear or concern until she judged the other person right or wrong, generally the latter. "I took him aside, hugged and told him, *"You belong here, rip-TONE. We love you. You don't have to prove anything."* Leslie's smile unfroze. Her eyes emerged. She came closer inside her face. Madame Perry grew up in Paris, moved to San Francisco to teach in a private school and sought a job at BFS to be in New York. She was a Buddhist and lesbian. She had good things to say. Ripton was in a good place.

―――――――――

Daniel Bell was my favorite Baloo of a man; a belly arriving before the rest of him, black hair full like it was the late 1950s, the smile and kindness from Disney. But when he spoke it was Kipling; poetry, pragmatism, biblical exegesis and history tumbled from his thoughts. He'd left high school at sixteen for a community college, dropped out, drifted to New York and taught himself the guts and nuances of computers. He'd been hired to run the hardware side of our IT department, making sure traders' and bankers' machines operated fast between markets and time zones. Ours was his second job in the financial industry. He built a computer for Ripton when I moved into Red Square. He built another for all the boys when I moved back home. He had to constantly clean it from file sharing clutter, viruses, worms and porn-site infections, knew where the boys went, judged us all human, liked us and forgave people their ways.

When Daniel started a computer consulting business, Leslie's practice became his largest client. We met every few weeks in various cafés to talk about poems, religion, business strategy and raising the boys. He knew about Jayne Godlewski and Steven Satin, Jamar in jail, *Part of the Struggle*, Carlos' GED and hoped-for escape to St. Louis. "It's hard," I finished my coffee.

Daniel nodded behind his coffee mug, put it down and swallowed. "Of course it is. If it weren't, the people downstairs would have their own Carlos." He liked the Beaver Valley story. "Is Carlos good with people?"

He was, to the point of suave, regardless that he thought himself shy. The girls did chase him.

"Does he know computers?"

He didn't, more than messaging girls and friends, looking at ESPN and porn. Daniel asked and I told him that Carlos could certainly learn. He offered Carlos a part-time job and spent a midafternoon to evening teaching him to build and get a computer online, then sent him home with components to do it again. "This is the case," Carlos told me when he walked into the apartment, and it was, metal sprayed beige with a built-in power supply, a medusa of black, yellow and red wires challenging with black and white plugs. "This is the processor and this is the motherboard. We got screwdrivers?" and set up in the living room. Leslie had gone to bathe, Ripton and Morgan were watching TV and Carlos wanted me to watch him clamp the processor, metal heat sink and fan to the frame. "You gotta put in this memory chip," showing me a thin slice and prying it into the motherboard, "FUCK," in the staccato when a Yankee pitcher threw ball four, a batter struck out, an umpire missed a call. His rage frightened me, not cute from when he'd been small. He was waving a finger, pinching flesh to blood, sucking a cut. "FUCK." He pushed the chip to where he wanted and twisted small gold screws into an arrangement in the case. I started reading a T. C. Boyle story about Catholic miracles and realized I'd let the time slip to get Ripton and Morgan to bed. When I came back down Carlos was lowering the motherboard into the case. He secured it, told me what he was going to do with cards and peripherals, added colored cables, snapped the black and white plugs where they belonged, announced he was finished, plugged the computer in, turned it on and nothing happened. "FUCK."

I winced at his voice. "We should both go to bed. You have to get up for class."

"I want it to work."

"Tomorrow."

"But it worked at Daniel's."

I came home the next night to the computer running and Carlos facing an information stream. "Wow," I heard myself. I'd never taught Carlos to build anything.

"I'm loadin software," he pushed a button to slide out a drawer, replaced one disc with another and typed. "Yo Mike . . ."

I was proud of the breadth of his back.

"Daniel payin me ten dollars an hour, that good, rah?"

It was. Daniel struggled to find clients and pay his bills. He had no other employees, couldn't afford ten dollars an hour to train a kid and wouldn't consider doing otherwise.

"I love Daniel," Carlos said to the screen and his elbows moved as he typed.

Daniel started sending him to clients' offices, first to deliver then to also set up machines. He came home pleased a few weeks later from a small hedge fund's office. He and Daniel had worked by cell phone to integrate a new workstation into the network. "He give me this," Carlos held out one of the phones. "Sometime peoples stuu-upid. Don't plug in they computers and they callin Daniel. They gots'ta pay him ta go plug in a computer?"

Daniel sent Carlos the next week to reinstall software in a work-station in Leslie's practice. She'd come home for the day by then and the office manager called to say how courteous and good he'd been. Daniel called to say the same, wanting to help make a better world. He didn't care about braids and swagger, vocabulary or ca-dence. "But does he have any other clothes?" Daniel asked during our next coffee. I explained "*baggy*" and "*tight*" and spoke with Car-los, who borrowed Zara, Armani Express and Diesel from Phil.

---

We noticed after a while that Carlos didn't have a bank account. "What do you do with your checks?" Leslie asked.

"The check cashing in Red Square."

"You have to open a bank account," she told him.

"It two dollas?" seeing no reason.

"Who do you see in line there?" I asked.

"What you mean? You making no sense," he passed into impatience.

"Dominicans, Puerto Ricans, Blacks, Mexicans?"

"What you botherin me for? You makin no sense, it two dollas?"

"You see any White people?" I didn't back off.

"Yeah. Sometimes."

"Really? In suits?"

He laughed "YoMike, you too much," pulling me to him and no one that large had hugged me in longer than I could remember. My father lifting me into the air.

Leslie explained savings and checking accounts—depositing his paychecks without being charged and earning interest. The rates she and Carlos found online were so low he'd earn essentially nothing and he wasn't moved by pennies—the boys left coins scattered around the apartment. He lost interest altogether when Leslie explained that he couldn't deposit a check and withdraw the money immediately.

"That what check cashing do."

"But you have to start saving. For your future," I said.

"YoMike, most peoples ain't rich. I needs my money."

"For what?"

"Stuff. Helpin my brothers, clothes, Jasmine, you know."

"*You know*" meant other girls. He knew I knew and Leslie didn't, at least on the surface. A guy conspiracy.

Leslie explained the fees if his savings or checking accounts were too low.

"That like two dollas, rah? What the difference?"

"The point is to save enough not to live paycheck to paycheck," I said.

"Easy for you," Carlos made eyes around our apartment.

"I worked, nobody handed me anything." I was sanctimonious.

He and I knew it was more complex. "But you neva been in the projects. Leslie grown up rich, don't you, Leslie?"

"I was very lucky. But that's why we want to teach you to save," she answered.

Leslie and he opened a bank account with his next paycheck. He promised to save. Then a credit card tied to the account arrived a few days later. Leslie wanted to take it away. Carlos loved his name printed in plastic, put it in his wallet and promised to keep it there.

---

"*The task at hand*," Kindu crafted his new phrase into answers, questions and statements, elongating consonants and one-vowel "*hand*," an officer to his troops, a coach at halftime. "I don't know, Mike, the task at hand . . ." because I'd asked what was on Carlos' mind.

Carlos wasn't focusing on the task at hand. He'd passed the Predictor and grown more distant. We'd asked him and Kindu to come home by eight-thirty on school nights for Ripton and Morgan's quiet at bedtime. Carlos regularly came home later. We'd asked him and Kindu to call by eight o'clock on nights they wouldn't be home. Kindu always came home. Carlos disappeared some weekend nights and wouldn't call. He'd stay at Jasmine's or another girl's. He'd stay with Phil, one of Phil's cousins in Washington Heights, at Will's, at any of too many places. He wouldn't say. "You're worse than my moms," he answered when I reminded him what we'd asked.

"Those are our house rules."

"Maybe I shouldn't be here."

"You're not studying the way you used to. You can't take the GED for granted."

"You beastin. I passed the Predictor, I'm goin to class. You actin like a girl."

His English and social studies teacher called because he'd missed a school day. She figured he was sick and wanted him to have the assignments. But he'd left at the usual time and came back when class ended. "Where did you go this morning?" I asked when he came back.

"Why you askin?"

"The lady teacher called. You promised you'd never skip school."

"She calt?"

"She thought you were sick."

"I passed the Predictor. It don't matter."

"You promised."

"You actin like a girl. I'm telling ya, you a clown."

I wanted to kick him out. I didn't want to. His baseball season was ending. The GED exam was coming. He was volatile, which we feared for ourselves and him.

"Nigga can't throw fastball to Carlo? Stuuupid. Challenge me? I rock that nigga. Spanish pitchers stuuupid." He was bragging because his A's had won another playoff game and he'd come home with a home run, double and single. He was planning his heroism for the next afternoon's game following the morning GED exam. Timing hadn't been auspicious.

"You don't see Jeter bragging." I was superstitious about hubris.

"Fuck Jeter. This the LES." He didn't tell me about his plan to meet Phil and Kindu outside the Door two and a half hours after the three-hour test began, leaving time to get to the game.

I discovered that situation in the morning as he rushed to pack his baseball uniform and equipment, unable to find his lucky batting gloves, edging close to late for the most important test of his life. "You're sure that's a good idea?" We were in better moods.

"I'll do fine. I'll rock that sucker." He meant the exam.

Kindu and Carlos walked in together after the game. "Kindu was a star, make Bernie a girl," said about his friend and the Yankees' center fielder. "You shoulda seen one dive," he bragged. The boys were proud, mud flaking from their sneakers and uniforms, falling in a shadow around the bags they dropped to the floor.

"How was the test?"

Leslie came down in her nightgown and sat on the steps.

"It were simple," Carlos started unpacking his baseball bag.

"Leaving early?"

"I rocked that sucker, I tolt you, fo'show'er." His cell phone rang and he answered. "Don't be stuuupid. Put Baby on . . . Hello? Listen, you niggas ain't doin nothin till I gets there, you understand?"

"What's going on?" I asked when he hung up.

"Fuckin Jesus. Stupid. He the oldest, rah? Niggas pickin on my little brothers, jumped 'em on they way to school, all Jesus had ta do is fuck 'em up but he pussy, keep callin me the whole fuckin test—"

"You answered your phone?" Leslie asked.

"In breaks, Leslie. Jesus calls and I calls back in breaks. I haf to—my little brothers? I gotta go wif them to school tomorrow."

"To beat up kids?" I asked.

"What you think?"

*"Take care of your brothers,"* his father told Carlos before the murder. Carmello, Pedro and Baby could play him to run home.

"I don't want to hear this," Leslie said and walked upstairs.

"Don't forget school," I said.

"I tolt you, that stuuupid." The test results wouldn't come for almost a month and we wanted him to continue class. He said kids never did.

"I know you're gonna pass, but to be safe—"

"You don't listen."

Carlos left early the next morning and I reached the teacher from Brazil before class began. She was surprised Carlos wasn't coming. She'd told him he should attend for himself because it helped the GED program. The curriculum was funded by the Department of Education, and while free to students, the Door was paid its expenses only for students completing a course.

I was cleaning the mezzanine and heard wood scrape across tile midmorning, someone in a dining room chair below me. "Back from the ghetto," Carlos said softly.

"Who are you talking to?" I asked.

"Shit Mike, you scart me. I didn't think nobody here."

I came down. His eyes were wide. I explained what the Brazilian teacher had said. "Not for a momf. I gotta work wif Daniel."

CHAPTER TEN

# KINDU | *Early Spring 2004*

Kindu loaded the stacks of dirty dishes filling the sink into the dishwasher, ran it, scrubbed the kitchen counters and sink to shining once Leslie and I went up to sleep. We asked the boys, pretended to tell them, to do their own dishes, but only Kindu listened. He vacuumed downstairs when he thought the rooms needed cleaning.

I'd never known anyone as sanguine, sweet as his mother had said.

He'd lived with us for months, the pressure of our expectations, the everyday frustrations of family, and he never showed anger. We were reminded, as playful as any of the boys, that he never seemed unkind, curt or crass. If we pushed about something that probably upset him—SATs, the Door—he became silent and walked away.

As well as we knew him, as open, loving and talkative as he was, the ends of stories Kindu told about his family didn't weave together. I could have left him to his privacy—if he were an adult I should have. But he was still growing up, a boy in our home and, beyond curiosity, Leslie and I had a responsibility to know about him. It was late autumn and I asked Kindu's help moving boxes from an

249

accountant's office in New Jersey to storage on Avenue B—relics of my real estate. I couldn't do it alone, but also wanted to sit with him. We loaded the Volvo and were driving a local road wrapped by strip malls when Kindu asked me to buy him a set for a going-away party his family was throwing him.

"If you tell me the truth about your family."

"You jokin?"

"If you tell me the truth. Elaine called you an '*adopted son.*' And your sister said '*my cousin.*' Your father lives Upstate? It doesn't make sense."

"You bribin me?"

"What do you want to buy?"

"I seen this Drifter set at Michael K, button down and pants."

"Explain your family."

"That's . . . ahh . . . I ain't never wanted the other guys to know. We raggin on our moms and I ain't want no one feelin sorry for me."

"Okay. But it's important to understand inside families. You know Ripton and Morgan were adopted."

"Okay. I'll tell you. Elaine ain't my moms. She is like Leslie is Ripton and Morgan's moms, she raisin us. Thank God for Elaine, I tell you that. Except my real moms is Roberta Jones and John Collier is my real dad. They were together, but they never got married. That's why me, Jamar and Fuquan, we Jones. The other guys gots they fathers' names and they parents weren't married. But that's how we done it.

"Elaine raised us since I was nine momfs. Our moms couldn't take care of us and our dad was in jail most of the time. Fuquan was three and Jamar was five."

"Who are the other kids—the girls answering the phone?"

"They my sisters, but they cousins. See, Elaine raised three of her own kids, two girls and a boy, they you and Leslie's age now. My moms had a sister, she had, like, nine kids. Elaine tooked in seven plus me, Fuquan and Jamar, and Elaine's youngest daughter tooked in the two. My moms tried to raise us but it was too hard. She weren't healthy and with my father, it was constant, constant in and out for drug possession, drug dealing, gun possession, things like that. I never hated him, Fuquan hated him because for him, he felt, he were just not there. To him, he weren't bein what his name is. He weren't a *father*. But me, me, I was young. If he comes I'm happy and if he doesn't come I'm not sad because I still have my moms, my mom's still around, Elaine's still around, her husband's still around. He was basically the father figure. That was Alonzo, that's Jimmy, the man Upstate I tolt you about. I went to visit my father once. I remember that, I really remember that. I remember it because I can remember the alarms and you haf to take your belt off and all that, I saw him in the booth where people come to see their wives, somethin like that. That's the only time I went. He'd come visit when he got out of jail, take us to see our grandma and take us back to Elaine on a Sunday. But he couldn't come often, I'd say the most, six times, maybe, over the years.

"My moms would visit when she could. She wanted to take care of us but she couldn't get on her feet, and wif my father in and out. She would leave us wif our grandma, then my grandma got very sick, very ill. Elaine and my grandma were sisters-in-law but they looked at it beyond that, they were like sisters. My grandma askted Elaine to take care of us. Elaine and Alonzo were on Euclid Avenue in the Bronx, but it was terrible, drug dealers, drug infested. We stayed there till I was three, then we moved down here to Seward Park Extension. That when Elaine took in the first four of my mom's sister's kids, my aunt weren't able to take care of herself. Elaine had a job in New Jersey but she had to quit that and we started public assistance.

"When my moms could visit, she took us on the subway to Coney Island for weekends. She lived with a friend in the same building with my father's mother, for whenever she pick us up, it weren't only to see her but to see our grandma too.

"She died in January, 1996, two and a half, almost three years before I met you, of AIDS. That's one thing I regret, I weren't goin to the hospital. The hospital calt, my aunts and uncles calt and tolt us she was in the hospital. I was ten and I was nervous, I was scared, and I didn't want to go. Bofe my brothers went and my aunt and my uncle, Elaine's daughter and her husband. They went and came back that night and they tolt me she was like, she didn't know anyone, so I askted my brother, '*Should I have gone?*' He said, '*You wouldn't have wanted to go, it was like she didn't know us.*' The only thing that keeps me regrettin is that I didn't get to see her when she was alive, even though she wouldn't known who I was. And my father was in jail when my mother died, he couldn't see her at the end, like, and they loved each other. That gotta be hard.

"My father calt from time to time and tell us he loved us. Some days he come around he could look good, then suddenly we get a call he were in the hospital not doin so well. He was very frail. The downhill was not this summer, it was last summer, we had a barbeque and he was, like, the surprise to come around. Everybody knew he was goin to come around but me and my brothers. He come around and he was very frail, you could see it in his face and in his hair. Not that he was goin bald, but he was frail. He was on a dialysis machine, three days a week, and he calt, days before he died, and he sounded good and everybody said he was alright. A couple of days after, I get a call from school, Elaine calt the school, my counselor calt me down and tolt me to go home. It's not like we think he was goin to pull through this because we knew he weren't. We knew it was goin to come, so it was like, *Just take it easy. Just calm down.* As soon as I got the call you know what it is, you know what the call is. *Just take it like a man, try to stay focused like you can.* The day I found out was the day of the prom. I would'of gone, but I just changed my mind. That was the beginning of last summer. When I said my uncle died last June, I meant my father, he was forty-four or forty-five. I just didn't want to tell you guys, I didn't want anyone to feel sorry for me. Then last November, Johnny died, Elaine's second husband. He was a great man, he made sure he was another father figure to all of us, especially all of us boys.

"My father was basically livin in, like, a home for like, elderly people. He had his own room and stuff like that, room service and stuff like that, a home for people that really can't take care theirselves. His kidneys were terrible.

"Thank God for Elaine, I tell you that. She kept us all together, or else we'd be all split up by now. That's number one. So that's somethin she tried not doin, separatin us.

"The dealin, that starts because we part of the struggle. My aunt who's a Transit worker, her son Damian started, Jamar and Fuquan start workin wif him. Tyquan, he the oldest of us ten, he and Jamar are one year apart, he got his diploma at Murray Bergstrom where I started. He went to college, everythin was smooth, they seen how good he was playin basketball so they tookted him. But then, it were the love of hustling. Cause Upstate, he was gettin like a hundred dollas from the school a week. You can make more than that in a day. Elaine was very happy, his mom, his real mom was very happy, *'He's in college he's in college he's in college.'* The summer he came back, when he seen how everybody was livin, the way they were dressin, the clothes, shoes, chains, rings, bracelets, that made him say, *'Fuck that up there that's only payin a hundred somefin a week, fuck that.'*

"Jamar stopped dealin in 2000 cause he went to jail, and if he would have done it again he would have gone for years, five years or somefin, not months, so he stopped. But he started again.

"Even Fuquan, he get caught, he'll get years. He tries his best to outsmart the cops. So he doesn't stay outside. He got a phone, so he give the drug addicts the phone number and they call and say they want a ten or a twenty.

"That's why I chose to go Upstate, I didn't want to be around drugs. If I pick a city college I'll still be comin home every day, livin wif you but I be comin home to visit, to the same things I'd been comin home to since high school. Then I'd have Will and them guys. But if I go upstate I get focused, I get the job done, I don't blame no one.

"Me and the other guys, you know we don't smoke or nothin. But they ask, *'Yo, Kindu, son, would you ever smoke, would you ever smoke weed?'* My brothers all tolt me, *'Don't ever do this.'* I've always stood by that answer. In the summertime, doin what they do, you can make so much money, but when it come to a time like this, gettin cold and very cold, it comes very lonely, you really depend on a drug addict comin. That sad. The first of the momf, you can bet there's a lot of people comin, they just got their social security or their checks, they not just comin for one, they comin for four or five. I ain't gonna do that.

"Elaine's proud I've got the opportunity to meet people like you, to move into your home, if I say '*Mom, I'm goin home,*' it sounds good, but it makes me feel . . . It's an odd thing, somefin I never thought I'd be in.

"I tell you enough?"

I wrote out what he'd said when we got home, printed the pages and left them with others beside my computer when I went to bed. Will read my notes that night, showed the other boys and they went to Kindu. "Nigga, why you never tolt us?" Will asked.

CHAPTER ELEVEN

# ROSEGARDENS | *Early Spring 2004*

A large envelope from Morrisville State College came addressed to Kindu Dupree Jones. He was at the Door. Leslie and I searched for Morrisville on the Internet because the school didn't send an envelope that size to wish him a good life. It was 250 miles upstate, dipping as a light weight on a string 30 miles between Syracuse and Utica. The college offered baccalaureate and associate degrees and had a baseball team. The pictures on the website showed happy students of multiple colors on a green, almost colonial campus. The animal barns spoke of an agricultural past. The directions said it would take us four and a half hours to drive, which meant more.

"There's a letter for you," Leslie said when Kindu walked in.

He dropped his backpack and hurried for the envelope on the butcher-block divider, opening it and his face calmed to happiness. "*We are pleased to accept you,*" he read aloud, took a breath and asked, "Where's Morrisville?"

We explained.

"That mad *brick*, ain't it?" He meant the winter cold. "I'm goin ta college."

We hugged him. He borrowed my bike to tell his mother and brothers.

Morrisville was his one acceptance. We asked him to call the number on the acceptance letter to arrange a tour. He couldn't enroll at a college none of us had seen. I wanted to make a college adventure of the trip. Kindu, Will, Phil, Juan and I took a day and drove to Morrisville.

I was excited that Juan asked to come. He didn't want to go to college, didn't want our lectures and started stocking shelves at Toys "R" Us after graduating high school at the same time Kindu hadn't. He'd stopped spending much time in our home. I hoped coming with us meant a change.

Snow started fifty miles out of Morrisville, deceptively gentle flakes while we drove into a blizzard. I couldn't see the road and what should have been an hour more than doubled. When we found the main parking lot we stepped into winter, snow above the boys' high-tops, a cold wet in my sneakers. They wore hoodies and I had a light autumn jacket. "Mad brick," Kindu slid his hands up opposite sleeves.

"Nigga crazy ta go here," Juan stated what seemed momentarily obvious.

"This isn't a place for a Black man," Phil shared his thoughts. "Ya see any Black peoples here?"

We could hardly see anyone. The admissions office assigned a blond sophomore to give us a tour deeper into campus, through three- and four-story redbrick buildings with small windows and adjacent parking. We did pass African American students. "See?" I said for Kindu, White, Black and Asian students dressed for winter and we weren't. Perhaps Latino students, we couldn't tell.

The guide left us in a second-floor office overlooking the storm for Kindu to fill out registration forms and pick spring courses. He and I walked up to the third floor to meet Thomas David from Financial Aid. His office was caring, Rotary Club and chamber of commerce awards beside pictures of his wife and children, him and his friends duck and deer hunting. Thomas David was the department head, born and raised in Morrisville. He started through the details of forms and calculations. "And because you're an orphan, you're entitled . . ." —*"orphan"* seemed wrong for Kindu, who nodded that he would get several more thousand dollars a semester from a state grant because his mother and father were dead though Elaine raised him, Jamar, Fuquan and his cousins were family and he was part of our home. Kindu was an orphan. "I want you to make me a promise," Mr. David laid his pencil down on his calculations, looking up earnestly, black hair Brylcreemed, beginning to close the deal, "I want you to sit in the front row in class. Will you do that?"

Kindu was silent. He'd probably never sat in the front row.

"You see this?" Mr. David reached for a ream-thick printout in oversized computer paper, turned it for Kindu to see the names and numbers, pointing with his pencil to a column of grade point averages, circling those he meant, a salesman's skill reading upside down. "You know what these are?" everything below a 2, Slinkying through a few pages. Kindu didn't. "Kids who took financial aid, signed their names to loans, thought Morrisville was a party and failed their courses. You can't come back, you don't have an education and you have to pay back the government starting now. The government, mind you, you understand? This morning, where you're sitting, I had a young man with a 1.99 average. His mom sat where you are, Mr. Rosen. And a 1.99 isn't a 2 or above, is it, Kindu? You know what you're qualified to do after failing here? Making burgers at McDonald's, that's what you're qualified for."

Kindu hurried a glance at me, his smile. "That what my dad says, he talks about McDonald's."

"Your dad's right. That's why I want you to sit in the front row. Nobody in the front row fails out of here. You promise?"

"Yes, Sir. I do," Kindu said.

———————————

Will and Phil wanted me to meet with their guidance counselors. They explained details I couldn't follow and the morning after returning from Morrisville we took a cab to Norman Thomas High School. Steven Satin's school was one of the largest and most crowded in the city, hidden inside a luxury office tower at the crest of a hill on the southeast corner of Park and Thirty-fourth Street, at 556 feet the tallest building around beside the Empire State Building several avenues over and designed in the international style by the same architects. The Emporis Building cried power at a diagonal to the wide intersection and rose from a pedestal plaza in light orange brick and glass. I'd known Norman Thomas was inside but not where until Will and Phil walked me to Thirty-third Street, down the hill and in back to *NORMAN THOMAS HIGH SCHOOL* in block letters not obvious beneath an overhang and above a one-story wall continuing the plane of the plaza. I saw an entrance to the underground passageway for 3,003 students, a contemporary hypogeum, the rectum of a luxury building. If entering the back end didn't impress these students that they weren't quite the same as the shoppers and corporate folk working, sculpting themselves and drinking lattes above, the phalanx of uniformed school guards and New York City policemen, computer banks, turnstiles, X-ray scanning machines and metal detectors hinted that something was afoot beside education. Will and Phil funneled single file into a feeder line and I stepped in behind. Hundreds of teenagers were wearing black North Face parkas. Those in front of us swiped ID cards through a reader and photographs emerged onto a large screen for a policeman behind a tall desk matching face to child, pushing a key to let the boy or girl through the turnstile. "My dad," Phil told the policeman when it came his turn to swipe.

"Doesn't look like your dad," the officer looked down on a middle-aged, short, thin, balding White man, and didn't smile.

"I'm raising these guys," I indicated Phil and Will.

"We meetin guidance counselors," Will said from in front of the man's desk.

"Do you have an appointment?" he asked. I felt impatience at my back, a din in front.

"Yes, Sir," Will answered.

"Sign in over there," the man ordered me, pointing past kids in other lines waiting to put belongings through X-ray scanning machines. He released the turnstile and we went to one of those lines, waited for our turn and put our coats, hats, gloves, shoes, backpacks, wallets, cell phones, change and whatever else potentially concealing threat in trays and pushed them into the machines then waited to be called by another policeman to pass through the metal detector. Phil and Will each set it off, were ordered to collect their things and walked in stockinged feet across the wet terrazzo floor to join the longest line yet. "Take off your belts," an elephantine policeman commanded there. Boys held their falling pants in one hand and grasped their gear in the other. "Get in line, be quiet, take off your belts," the big man caterwauled, his voice hovering above the whir of people and machines. Girls passed through another line and released students stood alone and in groups pulling on sneakers and boots, lacing them up, hiking up pants and threading in their belts, putting on coats, putting themselves together. I took a photograph of the mayhem, and quickly another. Policemen surrounded me. "Give the camera," the elephantine one demanded.

"No."

"Give it. Pictures is illegal."

Phil pried his way to me, put his hand to my camera and I let him have it. "My dad don't know," he told the policemen and to me, "Let them have it till you leave, Mike, it'll be good."

"I'll get a receipt?" I asked the elephantine one, thinking he'd never chase a mugger, thinking I wanted Phil's help.

"Yes, Sir. You sign there, get an ID card and they gives it back for you," he pointed to a table by the exit.

Phil and Will went with me to the visitors' desk. I completed a form explaining why I was trying to get inside Norman Thomas. The woman there photocopied my driver's license and called the guidance counselors' office to make sure someone was in, wrote my name on a pass and watched to make sure I posted it to my chest, told me to fill out a receipt for the camera and handed me a copy.

The boys and I followed the line of kids through the *up* side of the escalators. I was contained in shrieks and shouts and black North Face. Some few students were flowing *down*. Beyond the whir of stairs and rails we were sliding towards an odd rattling I couldn't figure till the first landing where glass and plastic bottles rolled endlessly into a thick bullnose of chewing gum. We stepped across, up another level and on the same past bottles, chewing gum, and other debris till the sixth floor and exited into a hallway. "That's the cafeteria," Phil pointed and I saw a room filled with North Faces sitting on benches and tables, standing and talking. I wondered where Steven Satin might be.

"You might want this," Phil handed me the memory chip to my camera.

The guidance department was a rectangular holding pen with a few chairs and rubber-bumpered steel tables, walls covered in smiling students on verdurous campuses. Three steel and glass partitioned offices opened into it, one counselor for every 1,001 students. It had the architecture of a police precinct. The tables and chairs were olive green.

Will's counselor answered his knock. She tried but didn't know him, asked his name twice and pulled up his transcript. She was in her late twenties, distracted, a hint of lavender to the room, her shelves filled with snapshots in pastel frames of a smiling toddler and police-uniformed husband, large as she. I explained that Will was a friend, nearly one of our sons and we were trying to help. "You're not doing well this semester, are you, Will?" she looked and he hung his head. "Or other semesters."

It was hard to keep Will's school story straight. He was in his fifth year, but he'd never say which grade he'd failed. A semester earlier he told me he needed one course to finish. Which we assumed he was taking until he and Phil asked me to Norman Thomas, when Will explained he was taking seven courses and getting As and Bs. "No, Miss," Will kept his head low.

"Can he finish school this semester?" I asked.

"Impossible. He hasn't taken required courses that need to be se-quenced. You're at least a year from graduating, Will. Aren't you?"

"But, Miss—"

"Geometry then algebra, American then world history—"

"Miss—"

Will must have been at fault, a failed student fodder for rebuke, but I'd seen the entrance, escalator and cafeteria and years of glimpses into the bigger boys' lives. It's simple blaming children as failures in a system that never worked.

He'd shown me an essay for an English course he was taking and occasionally participating in.

> I want to go to college because I want to challenge myself with something meaningful in life. So far no one from my family has graduated from college I want to be the first, to set the example for my little sisters. So they too can go on to achieve their dreams in life.
>
> One day I want to be able to have a family, to support and give them anything they need.
>
> I was born on July 12, 1985 in the Dominican Republic. I was raised there until I was 6 or 7 years old. At which time my grandmother, who was raising me, sent me to New York to rejoin my parents.
>
> My mother and father divorced when I was 12 or 13. I was shocked because until then I would have never thought that could happen with my family. My parent's divorce gave me a whole different look at life. It forced me to grow up, because I was the oldest child, and my father leaving forced me to take a lot of responsibility.
>
> During that time I loved playing baseball in a local park called Tompkins Square Park. I met one of my best friends there, a young boy named Ripton. I don't remember how it happened, but Ripton invited me to come to his house. At that time I think he was about 8 or 9 years old. I remember

seeing his mother Leslie Gruss, sitting in the park but never being introduced to her. Ripton introduced me to her and she said "hi" and the first thing she asked me was "Will would you like some homemade cookies." Of course I said "sure." That was the first time I ever went to a pent house apartment, so I was amazed at the life that Ripton was living. I never saw his father, Michael Rosen, around, but I met him later on because I made a habit of going to Ripton's house. At that time I was also confounded with everything that was going around me, so I got attached to how perfect Ripton was living life. And I wanted to be part of it. Soon enough I did become part of his and his family's life and they became part of mine. His parents in my eyes are my second parents. Leslie always wants you to learn and do more and Mike always wants you to know that life isn't all about one thing. You have to expand your horizons and see what is out there. They have us read books and help us out with our school work if we need any. If there was ever any problem I had I believe they would help me. To be honest, if it wasn't for them I don't think I would even have wanted to go to college. I have considered college but it wasn't my first choice after high school. I had thought to join the marines. As my older brother joined the army. But his military service has been traumatic, and my mother very strongly encouraged me to continue with my education. To best achieve my dreams. As have Leslie and Michael, Leslie is an Obstetrician gynecologist, and Michael used to be a university professor, then a business man, and now a writer.

I want to be successful not only for myself but also for my mother, Brijida Torres. I want to repay her for all the hard work she puts into me and to let her know she hasn't done all that for nothing. I want to give her everything she wants in life so she doesn't have to work anymore.

I don't know exactly what I want to study, but I'm leaning towards sports marketing or perhaps other aspects of marketing. I love sports. I like baseball love basketball and football I'm also pretty good at playing each of these sports.

I know that I would exceed at sports marketing, because I understand the beauty and business of sports in America. A college education is a critical step in entering this field. To expand my understanding of not only marketing, but also of a broad range of areas a student learns.

Will's guidance counselor starting fidgeting about her computer, the floral of potpourri tipping beyond tolerable, lavender candles aflame and said, "Come back the day after tomorrow. We'll try to figure something out."

"Thank you, Miss," he said in the whisper of "*Ollrrot*." Will didn't look up but stood and walked out slumped shouldered. I shook the woman's hand.

Phil was at a rectangular table reading nothing. "She there," he whispered, rising to knock on his counselor's door. "Miss Kaplan, hi, this is my dad, Michael Rosen." They knew each other.

A BA from the University at Albany hung on her wall. She bookended a handful of counseling and psychology titles on a shelf. Miss Kaplan was the same age as William's counselor and gregarious, black haired, brown eyed, nothing pastel or floral but lavender followed us. "Phil has at least two years left," she answered my question. "I've explained this to you," she said to Phil. "You've failed too many courses. Phil's bright"—she looked to me with affection then back to him—"Too bright for your own good." Phil was holding a wide smile trying not to. "Because you don't try."

Phil nodded. "I'm serious now, Miss Kaplan. I'm growin up. My dad and my moms, Dr. Gruss, helpin me focus on college."

It was a display from *Cool Hand Luke*. The three of us in her room knew better, unless Phil told stories so often he believed himself. He'd told us he had a semester left. "If you take that co-op program, and work, you could graduate this semester. But not like you've been doing, Phil." His name was a fine word. The counselor explained the co-op program to me, offered at city social service providers. High school kids took morning classes and did afternoon office work for accelerated credit. Courses relied on home study packets and assignments. "Let's see about Bellevue," and Miss Kaplan started on her computer to see if the large city hospital near us, known for its psychiatric ward, had room and offered what Phil needed. It did, except for a science lab—I thought odd for a major medical facility. "You'll have to take that in night school," and she called trying to reach Bellevue, listened and hung up, dialed again, hung up. "Busy." Miss Kaplan wanted us to stay until she reached a Miss Parker. She told us the only place offering the science lab was at the eastern edge of Queens, more than an hour by subway each way. She tried Miss Parker several more times.

"Maybe we should go there?" I suggested.

Miss Kaplan told us where to find Miss Parker, wrote a note and said she'd keep calling. I handed in my ID and picked up the camera. We easily found Miss Parker, who asked Phil curriculum questions he couldn't answer and told us about her grandchildren. She hadn't heard from Miss Kaplan, called and couldn't reach her. I wrote down her questions and we hurried back to Miss Kaplan. Three students were waiting before us at the rubber-bumpered tables. A half hour later Miss Kaplan reached Miss Parker. Phil and I transported bits of information between Norman Thomas and Bellevue for five days until he was accepted there.

Will and I were back in his guidance counselor's office as directed. He would be granted a diploma if he passed the seven courses he was taking. She didn't explain how that could be. We didn't ask. The lavender was welcoming.

Phil's mother took a morning from work and went with him to Queens because an adult was required to register. The lab, it turned out, wasn't being offered, but was at a school on the Upper West Side. Phil was given a dispensation for needing an adult, went to that school the next morning and was told the course was full. He called to tell me from a pay phone.

I found the number for the Upper West Side school and called the administrator who'd told Phil there wasn't room. When that went nowhere I called the principal. "This is Dr. Michael Rosen. My son Phil . . ." and I explained our situation. He made room in the class.

Phil wasn't going to wake up for school unless he moved in, so we asked him to. Leslie started working with him for hours each night at the dining room table, completing his study packets and assignments.

---

Carlos' GED scores arrived. He'd succeeded in some parts but failed the exam. He went back to class.

---

Autumn passed into New Year's a few days before Kindu left to college. The boys wanted a goodbye dinner with chocolate cake and candles, which we decorated to say *Congratulations Kindu!* His favorite was shrimp grilled in a peanut butter and hoisin mixture. I made them with hamburgers, hotdogs and salmon. "Kindu, you sit here," Phil pulled back the armed chair at the head of the dining room table, where Ripton normally sat with his long legs draped over the upholstery. We passed the food—hotdogs for Ripton because he ate nothing else, fed ourselves till Phil stood and went to Kindu. "We known Kindu for a long time, dogs," he smiled.

"That's rah, that's rah," the others agreed.

"Juan, Will and Kindu was in class, I was in the other eighth grade. We was in the cafeteria doin The Rock and this Black kid come over and start do'in The Rock, '*Do you smell what The Rock is cookin?*' givin the eye, nigga, the big eye," mimicking the people's eyebrow.

"That rah—"

". . . and we start becomin cool. I love Kindu, rah? We proud of you, dogs, the first go'in ta college, who woulda thought? Rah?"

Tears started in my eyes. Who would have thought.

Carlos walked to Kindu, bent and hugged him. "Remember, Kindu, back when I was fourteen and you sixteen, before we lived in the Rosegardens, like, before we moved in. We was hungry one day,

Leslie and Mike was away. We counted our money and had us one dolla. We went into the Koreans and found them oatmeal cakes wif cream in the middle. They was one dolla but it was nine cents for the tax, peoples wouldn't sell it to us."

"I do," Kindu said, nodding. I was wiping tears. We were smiling. *"Rosegardens"* was Kindu's invention, from the beginning of basketball season two months earlier, watching TV highlights of the Portland Trailblazers in their Rose Garden stadium.

"We looked over the floor and found us a dime. We bought them cakes and went to my apartment. We had bread and you had tuna at your house, for you went home, all the way to Broome Street, nigga, got tuna and come back. We made us sandwiches and ate them cakes. *Part of the Struggle*, and here we are, livin in the Rosegardens and you go'in off to college. It just amazin."

The Rosegardens.

---

We gave Morgan a BMX bike for his eleventh birthday, a beauty with shining chrome rear wheel pegs, a frame in bright blues, yellow and white. We went to Tompkins Square so he could ride, then he pedaled away to try tricks in a quieter playground on Third Street. One of the older boys he'd learned to skate with was there hanging with some others. I'd been running into him on the streets with older kids far from school while class was on, a goth- and punk-leaning group. I called his mom the first time because I'd want someone to do the same if they saw Ripton or Morgan. She thanked me, knew, and I didn't call the other times.

"Let me ride it," the boy held the handlebars, took the bike and Morgan eventually walked home.

"Why aren't you riding your bike?" I asked the next morning.

He explained that the boy had it. Leslie called his mother. She knew that Morgan had lent his brand new birthday bike to her son, who'd left it unlocked in the hallway overnight. Someone had stolen it from there.

"He took it," Morgan insisted. "I didn't want him to."

Leslie called the mother again, who searched the stairwell; the bike wasn't there. Leslie told her that her son had taken it. She seemed unconcerned.

---

Ripton bought tickets online with Leslie's credit card and took Will, Phil and Ricky on a Saturday night to see *The Passion of the Christ*, the controversial film in Aramaic, Latin and Hebrew coproduced, directed and cowritten by Mel Gibson about the crucifixion of Jesus. The media had been filled for months with accusations and disavowals of the movie's anti-Semitism. Leslie and I would have been happier if the boys hadn't wanted to see it.

"It was nasty," Phil said when they came home.

I was at the kitchen table and Leslie had gone upstairs.

"Will says *we* killed Jesus, like the movie. We're going to Hell." Ripton was bothered.

"Unless you believe in Jesus," Will said.

"It's a story. The Romans crucified thousands of people, sometimes in a day. We don't know a lot about Jesus. People debated whether he was part of God, or an inspired man. But religion shouldn't breed hate."

"It ain't hate, Mike. It the truf. It's the *Bible*."

"You think if Ripton and Morgan are good people, if Leslie and I are good, we'll burn in Hell because we're Jews?" We'd had the same conversation years earlier, with different names and sins, about Jonny McGovern.

"I love you, you know that. Your peoples kilt Jesus and you don't accept him, so you have to go to Hell." Will, to his credit, wasn't happy about it.

---

Carlos took the GED exam, attended class for the month and failed. He took it again, attended class and failed. He'd stopped studying hard, said he wanted to pass but wouldn't do more. He hadn't accomplished the steps to St. Louis. A new girlfriend from class kept failing by larger margins than he.

"He'll be fine," Leslie said.

I saw the slumped shoulders, an edginess more given to anger infecting the house. "*Simple*" hadn't been and he wouldn't admit but certainly knew didn't make reality. He must have been disappointed, frustrated and afraid. "I don't like it. His attitude sucks. It's our house, and Ripton and Morgan see."

"We'll make more rules. Don't worry, he's smart and he'll motivate himself. It's good for Ripton and Morgan to see the studying."

"He's not studying."

"He's doing well. You believe in baseball but that's not realistic. You don't want to hear it, but nobody makes it, you know the chances? We need to teach him to study."

I did know the chances. There are 16 National League, 14 American League and 246 minor league teams. I believed in Carlos. I was pushing baseball because I'd push nearly any dream. Carlos told me baseball was his way out.

# CHAPTER TWELVE

# GETTING OUT

*Late Spring 2004*

Kindu came home from Morrisville on the occasional long weekend. His college chartered a bus and though I knew, the elevator bell ringing, the drop of his bag on the hallway floor to Kindu's "the Rosegardens" moments before he turned the doorknob astonished me each time he returned. Leslie and I folded into him, he'd grown that big and walked through the apartment hugging everyone. "You hungry, Mike?" which meant he wanted steak sandwiches from Avenue D. "It's good to be home," he said, or some variation. We had become his home.

After he settled in, no matter how late, Kindu went down to Broome Street to visit his family. Then came back to sleep. "It's a little odd," I'd whispered to Leslie one morning watching Kindu, wrapped in his comforter asleep on the living room sofa.

"We're a little odd," she smiled.

Kindu told us he was coming home for spring break. With Phil and Carlos in the house, it didn't feel right to leave them for our vacation. Leslie and I spoke about driving near New York, to Boston or Philadelphia, the Catskills, but friends invited us to their suburban tract mansion outside Chicago and we bought plane tickets for everyone except Juan, who couldn't leave his Toys "R" Us job.

Kindu and Carlos had never been in a plane. "Is the sun real big when you get up there?" Carlos asked as we were packing the night before we left.

"It's the same," I explained.

"But we're way up."

"It's like, a hundred million miles away. We're about a mile up. The sun's still nine—"

"I got the idea."

"Hold it," Ripton called from the TV room. "Did Carlos ask if we're close to the sun?"

"Dogs, I don't know."

---

Leslie hurried us downstairs when the van arrived the next morning.

Will had been in an airplane when he was six or seven, coming to the United States. Phil flew back to the DR every few summers with his mom and sister. Ripton and Morgan were only taking another in a line of flights. Kindu was silent and observant. Carlos was wide eyed as we rose into a threatening cumulus sky, lifted towards its ceiling into gray and cut into sunshine on a cotton-ball cloud. He squinted, turned from the window and leaned to me. "YoMike," Carlos leaned across the aisle, "does it rain above the clouds?"

---

"Oh shit," Phil blurted when we drove through the gates into the subdivision then the driveway of our friends. "Shit," the other boys save Kindu and Morgan mimicked in a mantra. Baby maples were planted in thin lines between awkwardly large houses in what would have been a farmer's field. The bigger boys had never made a pilgrimage to the American suburbs. Our friends were doctors, the house owners around also all White.

We forced the boys to the Field Museum and once we got there the dinosaurs suited them. At lunchtime they hurried to the cafeteria and filled their plates. I slid mine after Kindu's at the cash register and the others lined up behind. I asked the woman there to put us on one bill. She smiled, a large woman wearing large Tuareg silver earrings and inches of lacquered horn, elephant hair, bone, Tuareg silver and beaded bracelets jumbling. "Are you with a church?"

"They're my sons."

"All them?"

"Yes, Ma'am."

"God bless you."

"Can we see a Cubs game, if the tickets aren't too expensive?" Will asked when I sat down. Sammy Sosa was the home run hitter in Wrigley Field then.

"You a Cubby fan, Will?" our friend Erik asked.

"Dominicans," Carlos explained of Phil and Will.

Erik explained that the Cubs were out of town. But we drove to the stadium anyways, parking on the street parallel to the third base line. The boys walked the circumference of the exterior to stand outside Sosa's right field.

We followed Erik through Highland Park past other subdivisions along Half Day Road till he stopped before 23 Point Lane. We parked and the boys rushed to an unscalable steel gate showing a few hundred feet of curving driveway evaporating into evergreens, a brushed steel "23" was bolted to it as tall as Ripton, looking like basketball jersey numbers. "Damn," Carlos caressed the shining metal. "Damn," Phil said. "Michael," Kindu mumbled. "Ollrrot," Will whispered. They posed for pictures. "This is big cold cash money. You know that, rah?" Carlos declared at Leslie and me, as if somehow we didn't respect Michael Jordan. I thought of all the sneakers they'd bought.

———————

We'd waited to buy Morgan a new bike, which looked like his old bike, and on a cloudless Saturday in spring he took it to Tompkins Square. Its chrome pegs flashed as he tilted and turned, blues, yellows and white glistened.

Baseball was still new, Mariano Rivera was two outs into the tenth inning of a tied home game against the Red Sox that day. "I don't feel good about this," Carlos shouted from the TV room for me on the bike.

"I don't either," I shouted back, expecting a broken bat bloop to a Red Sox win when Morgan slammed the front door hard.

"My bike's gone." He'd rested it against the iron fence inside the playground next to other kids' bikes.

"You're sure?" He was and we walked back to the guys.

"Morgan was in the playground—"

"Your bike?" Carlos jumped.

"Where you at?" Kindu asked.

"Playground, stupid," Carlos shut him up.

The boys rushed to the door, the elevator came and they jump-jangled in, half on and lacing untied sneakers as the doors closed.

I saw Carlos, Kindu, Phil, Will and Ripton jog into the park. Mariano was walking back to the mound for the eleventh inning when I went out. I pedaled through the park and came across Carlos, Will and Ripton in the large oval beneath the baby leaf canopy of the Hare Krishna Tree. "Junito got it, but he ain't in the park no more," Carlos told me; one of the boys Ripton's age we'd met the first day, who'd come with us to the Chinatown restaurant then drifted away. "We lookin for Phil."

Whom we found beside the Temperance Fountain looking at girls sitting on a bench. Ripton insisted on going when the boys decided to walk to Junito's.

"When you bigger, dogs," Will told him.

"I'm as tall as you."

"When you get bigger," Carlos said. "That buildin dangerous."

Ripton and I went back to our stoop, the granite warm from where the sun had been.

"Whaddayawaitinfor?" Dennis started a cigarette to his lips, thought better, darted his head like a turkey for Leslie, saw she wasn't there and gifted the cigarette and lighter in smooth arcs.

We explained Morgan's second stolen bike.

"Thesekids . . ." Dennis shook his head exhaling, meaning the dozen to fifteen he'd been watching inside the handball and basketball courts along Avenue B. "Theybeatthecrap outtaaskateboarder," smoke flowing from his nose, "Yaseethat?" he inhaled. We hadn't. "Beattheshitouttahim. Withhisskateboard. Icalledthecops, fuckthecops. Kidsgonnakillsomeone," Dennis ground the cigarette on the baluster and flicked it to the street. His cell phone rang. "Olivia," he said to us, "gottago."

Ripton and I stayed. Carlos and Will came jogging back a few minutes later beside Phil bouncing on Morgan's bike, pirouetting as best he could. "Junito had it in his apartment," Will said.

"Nigga *borrowin* it," Carlos said.

"What you think? Was inside the little dude's 'partment?" Phil circled us on the sidewalk.

"The El-Ee-Es," Carlos said.

The Yankees had lost by the time we got back upstairs.

---

"What we doin for summer?" Carlos asked as we sat for dinner that night. "We goin to Puerto Rico, rah?"

"We goin to DR, dogs," Phil was too quick.

I had dreamed about the Silk Road, or Ankor Watt, and described them to the boys.

"No way," Ripton said.

"Where that?" Carlos asked.

"I wanna go to Italy," Ripton continued. When we were separated, Leslie had taken our sons to a Club Med south of Rome. Ripton's biological father was Italian American, though he professed not to care.

"All us, rah?" Will said.

"Is Italy in Rome?" Carlos asked.

Ripton laughed.

I didn't want to go to Europe.

"I'll go anywhere that makes everyone happy," Leslie said.

"You stuuupid nigga," Phil said. "Rome peoples from Rome, it's a city, nothin to do wif Italy."

"Let's drive to California in one of those RVs," Ripton suggested.

"Dogs. Cali. Like rock stars. Let's get a big-ass RV, go Lux-U-Rie," Phil encouraged us.

"Like sports stars," Ripton said.

I started googling RVs, figuring for nine of us and the dog. Thirty-two-foot ones seemed to work. The guys wanted to see pictures. The Internet said we were joining a new world by renting an *"estate on wheels. A tribute to your success."* We saw buses. I thought of disaster, driving a thirty-two-foot vehicle from a rental office in New Jersey back through the Holland Tunnel hitting cars across Canal Street, terrorizing people, spinning the ship-size steering wheel and reversing the trip into America. *"No special license requirements,"* the websites assured us, a disaster and testament to industry lobbying. "I can't drive that," Leslie was adamant.

"You can, Dad," Ripton encouraged.

I thought about the maps the bigger boys carried, their cartography of the Lower East Side, Washington Heights and the Bronx, small parts of the DR for Will and Phil, the world largely uncharted. If we lived in a RV and drove across America, stopped in cities, visited museums and ballparks, toured historic places and ate differing foods, we'd expand the bigger boys' horizons. They might not yearn to read Melville and Dostoevsky from one trip, but it was a step on the road to encourage inquisitive minds. We decided to travel for three weeks and that Miami was more practical than California. Carlos called Kindu on the cell phone Morrisville provided him. "YoKindu, we goin on a trip. Three weeks, drivin a Es-Yu-Vee to Miami," he started.

"We can go to Gettysburg, my parents took us there," I said when Carlos hung up.

"What that?" Will was wary.

"From the Civil War," Ripton answered.

"That fought here?" Will asked.

"Nothin educational. Just Miami," Phil looked for agreement.

"Yeah, Dad. We're not stopping anywhere, just Miami."

"Miami is awesome. Girls," Phil offered.

"You've been?" Leslie asked.

"My cousin there."

The RVs slept only six, even the forty-foot one. We were nine. I figured we'd take sleeping bags, boys could share beds and push into corners. We started reading about RV travel, getting into the cities we wanted everyone to see, the realities for campgrounds.

The boys checked with Juan. He couldn't take three weeks off. Carlos, after our first excitement, had to pass his GED before coming.

Leslie and I decided to try to get as far as Key West.

———————————

When I asked, Carlos still wanted to try out for Youth Service League, the oddly named team in the Brooklyn Parade Ground league I'd tried to contact before taking him, thus also Ripton, to baseball camp in Cooperstown. Plenty of YSL players had graduated from there to the major leagues, and many more to minor league careers. I wrote, called and Mel Zitter answered one of my emails; Carlos could come to a high school off Prospect Expressway in Brooklyn on a Saturday morning to try out.

A few mornings later I found myself sitting beside Spanish-speaking mothers and fathers along the basketball court sideline with Carlos filling out forms. A coach threw him some ground balls and Wiffle ball pitches. A short man and I were the only ones without darker skin. We had the same build. Mel Zitter wore a navy blue YSL tee shirt and baseball cap, blew a whistle and commanded his players to hurry to the hallway. He ran them for forty-five minutes. Carlos crept back wet, hardly able to stand and said he was allowed back the next day. We came and it went the same. He was invited back the next day and the next and that's how the week went, morning class and afternoon tryouts, Carlos hardly able to stand when he came home, eating, doing a little homework with Leslie, going to bed and the final cut was coming on Friday.

The elevator rang when it was already dark outside that evening, Mr. Jenkins barked and our apartment door didn't open nor did our neighbor's. Then the door handle slowly turned. Carlos leaned into the foyer, his feet in the hallway, his face and uniform dirt and sweat stained. "I made it," he said with a peaceful voice, crumpled to the floor curling into a fetal position and he wouldn't move.

I sat on the step beside him. "Do you want some Gatorade or milk?" He hated water. I was dreaming of Manny Ramirez and Julio Lugo, who'd made it from Carlos' new team to the major leagues. I was dreaming about Carlos' possibilities.

"You believe that? Youth Service."

"Do you want to go to the living room?"

"I can't. YoMike, I gotta cut my hair. Youth Service Rules. Girls loves it. I gotta cut my hair," he mumbled to the floor.

He sat in the living room for hours that night, angrily undoing the braids he'd worked years to grow. He seemed not to remember the pain, the itching, the distraction in the quest for his wonderful hair, that the girls loved, that he'd put more money into than any aspect of his life, including sneakers and jeans.

"How you doing?" I asked sometime when half his hair stood on end.

"I don't wanna talk about it," he mumbled, surrounded by the other boys, who'd heard about Youth Service and had come to keep him company. But Carlos started singing somewhere into his shower. The boys took pictures while he shampooed.

"Let me drive the Volvos," Phil said when we walked to the garage the next morning, planning to drive to Washington Heights.

"You gotta be kidding?" He was still too young for a license and didn't have a permit.

"You know I drives my moms car."

He took it without her knowing. "You're an idiot."

"YoMike, Phil's a great driver," Carlos was trying to be a cheerful version of himself.

"Give me them keys, Mike, I got ya covered."

I didn't know, except Kindu, that the boys made a pilgrimage to that barbershop weekly. Phil said it took them an hour by subway. "More," Carlos corrected.

"What are you going for?" I ignorantly asked Carlos. I only knew of his weekly braids. He explained shapeups each week, yet more money. "Why not Kindu?" I asked.

"Black peoples hair," he answered.

Their hair was the same, kinky and wavy, to me. "What's the difference?"

"You stupid? We can't go to no Black barber place, that's whack," Phil answered.

They'd never driven so weren't sure which streets I was supposed to take. The signs and billboards along Amsterdam Avenue were in Spanish, the buildings low, many in disrepair. "That's it," Phil pointed to a shop in a row of one-story shops across from a block-long construction site. The plywood safety fence around was red and blue the length of Amsterdam and free of graffiti, MANNY RAMIREZ and BOSTON RED SOX painted in Red Sox font beside a pair of dangling red socks. Two empty barber chairs faced a mirrored wall taped in Valentine's Day cards, red and white balloons, paper lace and streamers. A dozen or more men sat on folding chairs and benches drinking cafe con leches and bottles of beer in brown paper bags. Carlos said something I couldn't understand to one of the men, except *Youth Service League,*" the room approved and the man who would be the barber motioned to the chair nearest the window. He put his bag and beer on a shelf, looked at me but spoke to Phil. "*El es mi padre,*" Phil answered. The barber said something else. One of the men stood and the group insisted I take his chair.

The barber wrapped Carlos in a baby blue plastic smock matching the Valentine's décor, reached underneath to pull out handfuls of hair, wrapped its collar in a folded paper towel and buttoned the front. Carlos was the focus of the room. The barber took his clippers from a hook and asked something. "Third base," Carlos answered and the man patted him on the shoulder. He almost smiled and the moment evaporated when the barber turned on the clippers. Carlos' face lost itself. Hair fell in strands and piled in a circle. Gradually, he was cut to scalp. "*Cerveza?*" a man asked, holding out a paper bag, pulling up the green bottle and candy cane label of a Presidente beer. "*Nieto?*" he asked, his eyes bloodshot, his face red. "*Padre*," Phil corrected him, and looked to me smiling. "Are you our grandfather?"

The barber brushed Carlos' neck and head with talcum, tidied his cutting, put away the clippers, reached into a tall jar of blue liquid for a straight-edge razor, dried it on a hanging towel, snapped the strop and stoked the razor a few times, spread the edges of Carlos' haircut with shaving cream foaming from the bottom of a dispenser I knew was warm against skin and shaped up the cut. The man said something and Carlos finally looked up into an open space in the mirror. He pursed his lips, frowned the way he did for anger but the barber patted his shoulder again, rubbed Carlos' head and drank his beer. "Youth Service," he said to the room and Carlos smiled. I paid the man twenty dollars and a tip for a new cut, sharp lines and Carlos' baseball dreams.

"I can't go on the trip, yaknow that, rah? I can't miss games," Carlos said as we were walking to the car.

I knew that, but hoped he could be in various places at once. He also had to juggle the GED. I didn't want to admit he couldn't come with us.

"Let me drive," Phil held out his hand for the key again. "Lease expirin, what you care?"

The lease was almost over. Only near its end did I learn that our oldest son would be selecting our next family vehicle. "Mom promised," Ripton insisted.

"I never thought he'd remember," Leslie explained why she had given a child control over a major family outlay.

Naturally, Ripton insisted on a Hummer. Or a black Escalade, Cadillac's mammoth SUV. I rode my bike everywhere. I still hung wet clothes on railings and banisters and tried to forbid anyone from using our dryer, though the boys did when I wasn't around. I washed our dishes, pots and pans and let then dry by the sink rather than run the dishwasher. I printed on the reverse of paper. I wasn't going to pull up in front of our apartment building in a SUV. "I'm not riding in it," I said.

"A promise is a promise," Ripton reminded me.

Leslie reiterated to me that a promise was indeed a promise. She and Ripton visited Manhattan's Hummer dealer, then the Cadillac and other dealers of SUVs. They went on test drives, learned about lease options and came home with brochures and souvenirs, primarily from Hummer—Hummer miniatures, Hummer key chains, Hummer cologne, Hummer body wash.

"I'm not riding in it," I whined to Leslie.

"I never thought he'd remember," she explained again.

We needed a larger car. Boys sandwiched themselves on the floor to fit in the one we had. So I tried to reason with Ripton for a gas-efficient alternative. I showed him photographs of vans, which consumer reports said were also safer. He wasn't swayed. "Nobody can hurt us in a Hummer." I showed him a *New Yorker* article demonstrating the opposite. "We'll crush anyone," he disagreed.

Mr. Clarke left a message for Leslie suggesting she test drive Volvo's SUV. "I think you'll like it," she called from his desk. "It's smaller than SUVs and it gets mileage like a car. If we trade, we'll get a good lease. And it seats seven."

"*Seven*" clinched it. Everyone I'd spoken with about driving an RV the length of the country questioned our sanity; other than the boys, who thought the idea marvelous.

"You're crazy," my father said.

I agreed with him. I couldn't get beyond the fear of driving a bus into cities, parking at restaurants and finding campgrounds. Leslie bought a guidebook to dog-friendly hotels. She bought a seatbelt for Mr. Jenkins. The new Volvo would work for America if we were seven plus the dog.

---

It was my job and one I wanted—to pick Kindu up when summer started. Leslie and I kept in touch with him through the semester, making sure he got to classes, studied for quizzes and tests and turned in his papers. He said he was keeping his promise to Mr. David. Morrisville gave each student a laptop, as well as the cell phone. We took advantage of the technology, calling, emailing and IM'ing. Kindu sent his papers for us to review. The boys IM'ed among themselves.

He met me outside his dorm then introduced me to his roommate and friends, all Black. I hadn't thought what to expect. I'd passed White students hanging out among themselves. "This is my dad," Kindu said. He had more belongings than he'd brought, including a small TV from his roommate, who was graduating. Kindu had been Morrisville's center fielder, and promised us he was at the gym and library. "For Yankee games," he rose to my skepticism.

I hadn't had a TV through college and grad school. "You shouldn't have time to watch the Yankees. They'll win and lose without you."

Kindu tried not to show how ridiculous I was.

We carried his things down to the car, including nearly a dozen boxes of sneakers he said were cheap in Syracuse. His older brothers wanted and were paying for them.

"Who's that?" he asked about a CD I kept playing as we drove.

"Savage Garden," pop we enjoyed till New York and I gave him a copy when we got there.

---

Making Youth Service bettered Carlos' mood. He stopped grumbling, except for bad days at practice. He unloaded the dishwasher once in a while, slept home some weekend nights and focused again on studying at the Door, sharing space with Phil and Leslie at the dining room table. He failed the Predictor but by a slim margin. The Brazilian teacher called and explained that his courses were ending. He'd have to repeat what he'd already sat through if he were to stay at the Door and they didn't think he would. "He should have passed by now. I want to sign him up for the exam," she told Leslie. It was in a week.

Leslie told Carlos. He understood, or said he did. "You know what *'cram'* means?" He didn't. "If you have a lot of studying left, all the time till you can be ready, that's *'cramming.'*"

Leslie and Carlos started cramming.

"YoMike," I came home to them at the table, "you ever cram?"

"Yup," I nodded, days and nights in the library.

"So you wasn't ready!"

"You heard Leslie. If the test's really important, you keep studying."

"She didn't say that. I bet you wasn't ready."

They crammed for the week, Carlos promised to turn off his phone, not to leave early and we gave him money for a cab to get to the test on time. He came home mimicking Kindu's shuffle through the kitchen. "I rocked that nigga. What you think?" he looked back and forth between us.

"I don't want to jinx it," I said.

"What you think? Say what you think."

I wanted him to pass. I thought he wouldn't. I'd bet he would. I was afraid of jinxing. I didn't want to know what I thought. Leslie was certain he passed. "You passed," I said, knowing I'd taken on my father's face, pursed lips and tight jaw. I was convinced he'd passed. Leslie hugged him, then I did and he lifted me into the air.

"I'm not goin to class," he said.

---

Phil explained, when we started going to Norman Thomas, that he knew when the school sent report cards and warning letters home. He made sure to take them out of the mail. His mother must have wanted to be tricked. Leslie and I made sure to keep in touch with Miss Parker.

Leslie and Phil were at the dining room table each night, completing the independent study packets and studying for tests. Leslie had been at the table since Carlos moved in.

We had planned our summer adventure to start when Phil's co-op program ended, until Miss Kaplan asked him about his progress in a second science lab. I told her I'd never heard that. She disagreed. She'd explained that he needed two labs when we first met and was surprised he was taking one. I reminded her about the adventure with Phil's mother in Queens and the Upper West Side school. She told me to look at the "*FS*" on the transcript she'd given us to take to Miss Parker. "That's the other science lab."

I found the transcript and wasn't at all clear what "*FS*" meant because the other science lab was "*Sci Lab*."

When I called back, Miss Kaplan explained that despite how proud she was of what Phil was accomplishing he couldn't graduate until after the second science lab. Meaning he couldn't go to college in the fall. I asked for an appointment and told Phil I was going alone. "How ya doin, Sir? No photographs, right?" the elephantine policeman welcomed me when I passed beneath him. I told Miss Kaplan about Phil and Leslie sitting for hours each day at the dining room table. I told her about the other bigger boys. I explained driving across a swath of the country. Miss Kaplan phoned Miss Parker. She called a counselor she knew at BMCC. They agreed that Phil could enroll in the fall if he took the missing science lab at night. She wanted Phil to be prepared for the extra load so found the title of the lab textbook that would be required and asked me to make sure he studied during our trip. Leslie and I spoke with Phil, who promised. Leslie ordered the book and packed it.

---

Will finished the semester and graduated from Norman Thomas. He'd followed Carlos and Kindu to the Door, worked with a college counselor and was accepted to the two-year program at John Jay College of Criminal Justice in New York for the fall.

---

Our new Volvo had little space in the back when the last row of seats was in use. We'd need to leave people behind or purchase a roof-rack storage container. We reminded the kids to pack the minimum. Mr. Clarke had explained to Ripton that his Sony PlayStation 2 plugged into the SUV's DVD and stereo system, so the boys were accumulating movies and games for the excursion. Leslie bought wireless headphones for each of them. She ordered books on tape, including *Cold Sassy Tree*, Ripton's assigned summer reading. She bought a portable cassette player and plenty of batteries. She practiced strapping Mr. Jenkins into his seatbelt, which was more a harness. The dog would have to rest on someone's lap attached by a buckle to the same seatbelt as the person he was sitting on. The very rear of the SUV sat two uncomfortably. The middle seat fit three tightly with the sandwiched passenger elevated and missing legroom, fine for a trip to the mall but probably painful for a cross-country outing.

Leslie and I planned to stop every couple of hours and have the boys rotate seats.

Will decided he couldn't go because he needed to find a job. Ripton said Will didn't want to leave his girlfriend. Phil and Kindu said she was pressuring him. I told Will it was important to see the country. Leslie told him we wanted his company. "I gotta find a job. You say that's important, now I ain't gotta?" he responded.

"Angie doesn't want you to leave?" I asked.

"That not what it is. You say we gotta work."

"Everyone wants you to come. Ripton would be really disappointed."

He did. We left Tuesday morning, June 29. Leslie strapped Mr. Jenkins into his seatbelt, clipped him to the leash and he waddled beneath the weight. Carlos, who would not miss a single practice session, and Juan, immured at Toys "R" Us, helped carry our bags to the sidewalk. The boys filled the roof container and rear of the SUV till it was clear we had too much. We made a pile on the sidewalk of what had to be left behind. The bigger boys and Ripton had more than Morgan, Leslie and me. We asked them to cull again.

We said goodbye, hugged Carlos and Juan and crowded ourselves into the car, Morgan unhappy in the middle shotgun seat. We explained again that everyone would rotate. Leslie drove and I turned to see Carlos and Juan carrying bags up the steps. Dennis sat on a baluster smoking. We left by the Holland Tunnel into New Jersey and it was time for lunch. Leslie pulled into a diner off the highway past Jersey City. We took turns walking Mr. Jenkins in the parking lot while the boys ordered and ate. I called home. "It's mad lonely," Carlos said, watching TV. Juan had left for work.

Passing exits, remembering back to our trips as college students, Leslie and I felt our way to the Benjamin Franklin Bridge into Philadelphia. We parked along the Christ Church burial ground at Fifth and Arch beside an iron fence cut into the brick wall so people could see Benjamin Franklin's grave inside. "Why we here?" Phil asked.

Leslie mentioned Independence Hall and the Liberty Bell. I pointed out Benjamin Franklin's grave.

"We don't care bout no grave," Phil said.

"Do you know who Ben Franklin was?" I asked.

The car was silent, then, "Some dude wif Lincoln," Will said.

"Phil?"

"Yeah, like that," he answered.

"The Revolutionary War!" Ripton shouted.

"Yeah, like that, wif Lincoln and them dudes."

"Let's look at some things," I said.

"We wanna go to Miami," Ripton reminded Leslie and me. He, Phil and Will had been pushing. Kindu was noncommittal in his normal way, but probably agreed with them. Morgan was young. Leslie and I insisted on keeping the trip as we'd planned, seeing what we thought they should. That meant Independence Hall and the Liberty Bell.

"We don't want anything educational," Ripton tried to convince us.

We started to Independence Hall, where the Declaration of Independence and then the Constitution were formulated, debated and signed. The sun was obnoxious. Mr. Jenkins walked a few blocks but pugs weren't bred for heat and humidity. He panted loudly, found a few feet of shade beneath a ginkgo tree canopy and dropped splay legged, rubbing his belly into the concrete. I carried him to Independence Hall, which was closed for the day. I went to a man in gray and green, shaded and sweating beneath a four-dimpled campaign hat, who could have been waiting for Old Faithful. "Cutbacks," he explained at 2:45 in the afternoon, the federal government reducing staff. I called the boys close, held the dog and talked about the Continental Congress, representatives risking their lives to treason, self-evident truths and the Constitutional Convention delegates negotiating a country wearing coarse clothing in summer heat before air conditioning—

"Like now?" Phil said.

"Can we go?" Ripton asked.

"Are you a school group?" the park ranger asked.

I wanted the boys to understand the bravery involved in risking execution by hanging, that Jefferson read Rousseau, Locke and Montesquieu, that Franklin was in tears at the 1787 Constitutional Convention when it was his turn to sign, "*I have often and often in the course of the Session . . . looked at that sun behind the President without being able to tell whether it was rising or setting. But now at great length I have the happiness to know that it is a rising and not a setting sun,*" I did my best to paraphrase for them. They didn't care. I'd hoped they'd see the smallness of the room inside. "We're family," I told the ranger.

"Can we see the Liberty Bell?" Kindu asked. It had been moved since Leslie and I were in college, enthroned inside a building probably designed by shopping mall experts. I hurried through to take Mr. Jenkins so Leslie also could go in. The bell was behind shelves and displays jammed with miniature bells and more bells on wooden bases, framed photographs of the bell, calendars, brass key chains, pewter plates, ceramic plates, ice buckets, golf putters, thimbles, ceramic tiles, trivets, tin pennywhistles, patriotic posters of the bell, posters on the history of the American soldier, six-inch busts of Abraham Lincoln and Benjamin Franklin, recipe books, bell wind chimes, bell pencil sharpeners, bell disposable pens, bell goblets, bell necklaces, bell bracelets with little bells hanging as charms, Liberty Bell souvenir spoons, tee shirts, caps, tote bags, plates and bowls, place mats, refrigerator magnets, coffee mugs, silk and rayon scarves, neckties, bowties and more things I didn't remember.

We left Philadelphia for Washington, D.C., two and a half hours, 150 miles. I drove and Leslie read through the dog-friendly guidebook and made our first reservation for three rooms in a hotel on the border of Chinatown. The boys laughed at a comedy. "That's Baltimore," I said, hoping for attention past their headphones. "That's Baltimore," I waved out the window. We'd emerged from the tunnel passing downtown. No one noticed so Leslie turned down their volume.

"The fuck?" Phil yelled.

"That's Baltimore. You should see it," I said as we were driving by old warehouses.

"Beautiful," Phil said.

"We're not stopping?" Ripton made certain.

"Is anyone hungry?" Leslie asked.

They were and we pulled into a Ruby Tuesday beside the highway. I gave water to the dog and walked him. Leslie ordered dinner for herself and me, ate quickly and came out to take her turn with Mr. Jenkins. "What we gonna do in Washington?" Phil asked when I sat down in front of my Jumbo Lump Crab Cake and cooling Chicken Bello sautéed with baby portabella mushrooms and artichokes. His tone was *why* rather than *what*.

"Congress. The Lincoln Monument. The Vietnam War Memorial."

"Why we doin them things?"

I looked at him and the others, tight faces, eating burgers and fries, Ripton his hotdogs. "We don't want to," he said. "Mom says she doesn't care." That couldn't be true, quite.

"It's the capital of our country."

"So what? Why we gotta?" Phil said.

"Can we go to Miami after?" Ripton pressed.

It was Phil's turn to rotate through the dog seat after dinner, the last row on the driver's side where Mr. Jenkins had been sitting on laps, but he insisted it was Kindu's.

"You know it, Phil, you know it," Will grew obviously frustrated as we stood waiting beside the Volvo.

Morgan, quickly uninterested, climbed into the rear row on the passenger's side and started playing with his Game Boy.

"I'm not, it's Kindu," Phil said earnestly but inaccurately.

"I'm after you," Kindu corrected him.

"You can't skip—" Will grew angry.

Leslie and I got into the car with the dog between us and waited. Then waited more. The boys argued more. Ripton, frustrated, came to the front passenger window. "Tell Phil to get in," he said to us.

I went to the boys. "You know whose turn it is."

"What you mean?" Phil was shocked.

"You guys'll work it out," Leslie said through her window.

The boys argued. Phil grew more shrill. "Get out," he finally barked to Morgan. Kindu helped strap Phil in with the dog.

"Everyone needs to help," Leslie reminded the boys as we came close to the hotel, struggling with them to turn off their electronics. The hotel was on a busy street. Phil was impatient with the dog seat-belt, murmuring. The others started taking suitcases from the back and top. I waited on the sidewalk to change Mr. Jenkins into his regular harness and leash. The straps fell away, Phil grabbed the dog and threw him across the seat and out the door. I froze, imagined missing, Mr. Jenkins running into Chinatown traffic. "What the fuck are you doing?" I caught the dog to my chest.

"I'm not sittin wif it," Phil blurted, pushed out of the car brushing furiously at Mr. Jenkins' fur on his clothes. "Not no more."

"You don't throw the dog."

The others stopped. Kindu and Will came near.

"I'm not sittin wif it."

"Yo, dogs, we all haf to," Will insisted.

"I don't see Ripton."

He hadn't rotated through the dog seat.

"You threw the dog?" Leslie faced Phil.

"You could'uv hurt him. He could'uv run into the street."

"It's a dog," Phil dismissed me.

"He must'uv been scared."

"I'm gonna, tomorrow," Ripton said.

"Everyone has to sit with him," Leslie said.

"I don't like 'im."

"I don't either," Ripton said.

"I'll send you home," I told Phil.

"I don't care."

"You don't care?"

Leslie placed a hand on my shoulder. "Take the luggage inside."

"I'm gonna send him home," I said loudly enough for the boys, but went into the hotel. I don't know what Leslie said to Phil, and we were civil afterwards through the little there was left to the evening. We started the next day with the Lincoln, Vietnam War, Korean Conflict and World War II monuments the next morning and then the Holocaust Museum. We looked at Congress from outside. Ripton sat in the dog seat as we passed by the Washington Memorial and the White House on our way to Colonial Williamsburg, the Rockefeller-financed restoration of a village that was once the capital of Virginia. We spent the next morning walking through that re-creation, watching dozens of people leading their seventeenth-century lives: bakers, blacksmiths, dairymaids, planters and passing ladies in silk taffeta anglaise gowns with bodices and ruffled sleeves. I'd been enthralled with the blacksmith when I was a boy, sparks flying as the strong man pounded red iron into horseshoes I'd insisted my parents buy in the gift shop. We'd gotten a baker's dozen of gingerbread cookies in the bakeshop. "This is mad borin," Phil announced.

"What do you notice?" I dropped my voice to my chest.

"It's boring," Ripton answered.

"What's missing?"

"Cars," Will said.

"Electricity," Kindu answered.

"You see any Black people?"

"So?" Phil asked.

"Slaves. Who do you think did the work here?" because I'd done my homework. Over 50 percent of the people in the Chesapeake area then were slaves. They kept Colonial Williamsburg running but were absent from the white-painted colonial houses and tree-lined streets we walked. "Slaves," I repeated loudly as a group of bodiced ladies walked slowly by watching us.

"Dad!" Ripton hissed.

"It's disgusting," I was insistent. I'd loved this place as a kid, but hadn't understood whitewashing and tourist dollars then.

MORE THAN 200 years ago, the
pursuit of equality, freedom, &
independence began a
movement that continues
to shape the world . . .
Welcome to the
REVOLUTIONARY
City

. . . I read to the boys from a brochure.

"That sounds good," Kindu said.

"This mad borin, Mike, can't we go?" Phil asked.

We drove to friends in North Carolina. We floated on inner tubes the next morning in a very cold river through the Great Smokey Mountains. We headed towards Charleston afterwards, hoping to spend the night in the Gullah country of the South Carolina Sea Islands.

"My mom's from Charleston," Kindu said as we neared.

"Do you want to call anyone?" I turned back to him.

"No."

"Should we call your mom?"

Kindu had no interest.

The thermometer said 102 degrees in sunshine as we followed directions into the parking lot beside an old church. Our tour book said we were centrally located for the walking tour we insisted the boys would enjoy.

> The Historic Downtown District has stood throughout Charleston's history as the cultural capital of the South and is considered by many to be a living museum, with a wonderful variety of things to do and see . . .

. . . I read loudly.

The boys insisted on seeing nothing. They complained about the heat before we left the car. I carried the dog to a strip of grass by the side of the church. He tried and refused the sidewalk. The boys grumbled, Leslie and I explained what the guidebook said was interesting; antebellum mansions, narrow houses turned away from the street with porches along their sides, climbing wisteria, azalea and shade trees. The plants were in purplish bloom.

"It's too hot," Ripton complained.

The dog panted, suggesting he'd heave apart as I carried him. We hurried into a convenience store for the air conditioning. Mr. Jenkins pushed his belly and nose to the tile floor and squirmed, leaving a wet trail. He was swimming. "Warm day, in't it?" the saleslady asked behind her counter.

"Sorry," I apologized for the dog.

We piled sodas, juices, teas and waters next to her register. "Visitin?" she asked.

"Goin to Miami," Phil said.

"We're from New York," I said.

"A church trip?" she asked.

"Family," Kindu answered.

"Brothas from the same motha," Phil lifted a palm towards Leslie and spread his arms to the others. Leslie turned crimson. I followed the woman's gaze to Ripton's blue eyes, Morgan's alabaster skin and blond hair, Kindu's darkness, one boy to the other.

"Brothas from the same motha," Ripton repeated, all gums. The young woman laughed. We walked back into the heat. North Atlantic Wharf and Mid Atlantic Wharf streets caught my imagination. I pointed to the street signs. "Remember '*Circumambulate the city of a dreamy Sabbath afternoon*'? I asked the bigger boys.

They didn't.

"*Go from Corlears Hook to Coenties Slip?*" I was too loud.

"I'm not feelin ya, Mike," Phil shook his head.

"Dad's crazy," Ripton made eyes.

"I'm feelin the heat," Kindu said, sweating. We all were, the dog breathing hard.

"I thought you were the Wolverine?"

"That's the *Moby Dick* guy?" Will asked.

"Do Black people get hot the same way? Because of Africa?" Morgan asked without a measure of malice.

"Melville."

"We're all the same, Morgy," Leslie answered him.

"Wolverines from the cold. The North Pole, like that."

We turned to the cobblestones of Chalmers Street and the old slave market, "*temporarily*" *closed for many years*, the guide book said. We noticed its haint blue doors, as instructed, a magical color also called Gullah blue, warding off the evil spirits. "*Approximately 75% of the African Slaves brought to America entered through the port of Charleston*," Leslie read. Charleston was afterwards a gateway from the upper to the lower South while more than two million slaves were traded after importing was outlawed. Morgan, Ripton and Kindu, Leslie and I were rapt. Will seemed that he could be but Phil was leaning towards him and whispering as Leslie read. They laughed. "What are you guys talking about?" I asked.

"Nothin," they tried to calm themselves but kept laughing.

"You aren't listening."

"We ain't Black," Phil said. "I don't care bout slaves."

We'd had this conversation often; *"Look at yourself. Millions of slaves were sold in the Caribbean, raped on ships, plantations, had babies with Tainos and Caribs, Europeans. You think your skin and kinky hair just happened?"*

*"We whatever they got in Dominican,"* Phil said of himself and Will. *"Africa got nothin to do wif it."*

"Lots of your ancestors were slaves," I preached to disinterest.

A Black man across the street waited to sell *NIGGA* tees and hoodies from the back of his car.

We started to the coast with Leslie's daily half hour of *Cold Sassy Tree*, set in a rural Georgia town in the early 1900s. The boys wouldn't turn off their entertainment, questioned why they had to do Ripton's homework, made fun of the actor's Southern voices and Will Tweedy's narrative.

"It's half an hour," Leslie insisted. "Have you read your science book?" she asked Phil, the other six of us knowing he hadn't and wouldn't.

"I will," he said.

I think he believed himself. *"Phil's a scammer,"* the bigger boys had said to me.

We ate on the veranda of a Beaufort restaurant a few feet from tall grasses and birds fluttering along the waterline. Leslie and I were captivated by the life before us. The boys were bored. We drove to St. Helena's Island the next morning. Kindu and I bought beads and I picked out a book of Gullah poetry, we ate Gullah food in a Gullah restaurant and heard no Gullah. I don't know what we should have expected. The boys were unimpressed with the concept of descendants of slaves speaking an African Creole and we started towards Savannah.

"What we gonna do there?" Phil asked.

"It's beautiful," I answered.

"That's what you said bout that other place," Ripton said.

"Charleston."

"Whatever."

Leslie decreed a new rule to turn off the DVDs, music and Game Boys ten minutes before a next destination. So we could talk, but each day remained a struggle. She read about the twenty-four squares historic Savannah was built around. We found a bookstore recommended to us, *Midnight in the Garden of Good and Evil* spread through its window display and surrounded by postcards, posters, photographs, walking-tour maps and guides to the esoterica of the city. Customers waited at the register. "Mike, what that? *Midnight Good and Evil?*" Will asked.

"It's a book, stuuupid," Phil said.

"I know that, dumbass."

"It's about a murder," I said.

"And a movie," Leslie answered.

"It takes place here," I waved my hand in the short and long distance. "The guy murdered and the guy who killed him, maybe they were lovers. There's a drag queen who's transsexual. It's written like Truman Capote."

Phil started, hesitated, started again, "He was president, rah?"

"That's another one. This guy wrote *In Cold Blood*. They're like novels."

"That mean they ain't true?" Will said.

"What's *truth?*"

"What happens."

"The characters were real, but they're characters. The murders happened."

"It's true or it ain't," Will said.

Leslie and I bought books. We walked around the neighborhood and the boys were happy to leave. The dog squirmed into a strip of grass between the sidewalk and street underneath a tree and wouldn't move. Leslie, equally tired, volunteered to sit in the shade and wait for us. The boys thought it was safer to stay with her. I gave Leslie the books and went for the car.

We were miles out of town when she mentioned the shade tree, which reminded us of the bag of books beneath it. I turned and hurried back to Savannah. I hoped the police car coming near was speeding for someone else. "Oh shit," Phil and Ripton echoed each other. "Dad?" Ripton accused.

"Vermont?" the officer looked at my license, which seemed a long way from Georgia. I explained our trip and the books. He looked through the car as the boys watched. "You're crowded in, aren't you?" he said to them. "That's a cute dog," on Phil's lap.

"We okay," Will answered.

"You're enjoying the trip?" the officer asked.

"Yes, Sir," Kindu answered.

He was a big man, his skin the color of Kindu's. "Hope your books are there. Drive safe," he let us go.

The books were.

We drove the coast to Jekyll Island, once America's wealthiest summer resort and now largely a nature preserve. We rented bikes, raced each other and Ripton disappeared. We searched for an hour then went to the hotel desk. The lady explained that all paths looped back to where we were. I feared those photographs on the sides of milk cartons. We started talking about calling the police when Ripton rode back thirsty. He'd followed a path into the preserve and out.

We left by Captain Wylly Road across the water and onto I-95 South for 410 miles to Miami Beach. Leslie insisted on *Cold Sassy Tree*. I tried a *"Later"* between us and she volleyed her *Don't undermine me* look. Leslie wanted to stop for the night along the way and the boys insisted on the seven or eight hours to get there. She negotiated a second half hour of Rucker Blakeslee, his progeny and romance in return for sitting in the car all day.

"Nigga's voice," Phil mocked as Richard Thomas read out Blakeslee's elderly twang, slid to his Southern softness in the old man's replacement bride, Miss Love, and shifted to an adolescent clip for Rucker's fourteen-year-old protagonist grandson, Will Tweedy.

"That's one guy. He's famous," I said.

*"Rucker!"* Phil imitated Thomas, "can't stand that."

*"Rucker!—"* the back of the van started chanting. *"Miss Love—"* the way we'd traveled down the coast of America. *"Will Tweedy, you get back here!"*

"How do Chinese people name their kids?" Phil asked at Leslie's click of the Off/Eject button of the cassette player.

Boys giggled. My vision flared and my neck stiffened at the nape. Nothing Phil answered would be good.

He waited the cadence of comedy. "They throw pots and pans down the stairs and listen, *Ching Ching Chong*," his voice tangoed.

Boys laughed, Leslie laughed and I could have. Phil was funny. His joke was funny. But we'd not raised the boys to be racists. I pulled from the left lane across traffic. "It's not funny," our right tires hit the rumble strip, shaking the Volvo.

"Holy shit!" Phil screamed, the others shocked.

I pushed the brake—

"Dad's Oh-Deeing," Ripton shouted—

"It's a joke," Will pleaded.

Our left-side tires hammered the cuts and I pressed till we jolted to stop. I spun around. "I've had it," I pointed at Phil.

"It's funny, it's not racist. You think it's racist?" he brought his argument to the others.

We'd been speaking earlier that day about Shaquille O'Neal, still a basketball star with Los Angeles, who'd displayed ethnic sensitivity and a captivating mélange of lovely Chinese and Japanese sounds when he'd commented to journalists about Yao Ming, the touted Houston Rockets center recently come from China, "*Tell Yao Ming, 'ching-chong-yang-wah-ah-soh.'*"

The boys found Shaq hilarious. So I went back to the conversation. "No? What happens if a White player said, '*Tell Shaquille O'Neal, Ooh ooh ooh ooh,*' and jumped around like a chimpanzee, would that be funny? I give up. I don't know what to say to you."

"We Spanish," Phil said. "I don't care about Shaq."

"And Kindu? He's Black."

"Kindu, you care, dogs?"

"Phil's jokin, you know that," Kindu said. I realized he was brokering a peace.

The joke seemed harmless. Everyone else was laughing. It was stupid and funny. They were boys. A lecture seemed way too teacherly.

"Kindu dates Spanish girls. You don't like Black girls, rah?" Phil asked.

"Black girls are nasty," Ripton said.

"I'm not listening to this," I got out of the car. I was certain Ripton wouldn't grow up talking the way he just had—but Phil's joke wasn't a help. Leslie came out and I asked her to drive. The boys were wearing their headphones by the time I got in again, drowning me out, watching another comedy. Phil and Ripton laughed loud in synchronicity as we neared Miami. I hoped for the best.

We checked into one of the hotels on Collins Avenue where tourists dressed in crisp-pressed distressed jeans, navy blue or bright white blazers and wraparound sunglasses finished business and lazed for meals, lazed through the night on linen-draped mattresses and chaise lounges around an Olympic pool mellowed with kerosene lanterns hanging from poster beds and arched poles. The bigger boys and Ripton emancipated the casual clothes they'd brought across America—the reason their bags were heavy—called housekeeping for an iron and board, pressed their pants and shirts, shaved, showered, cologned themselves and walked out to Miami for the trip they wanted. I was proud of how they looked, handsome. Ripton and Will were back near 2:00 a.m., Phil and Kindu invited to a club with girls they'd met. Will had forgotten his ID, Ripton was too young.

We let the boys sleep the next morning. We didn't go to museums. Leslie gave them a break from *Cold Sassy Tree* and Phil from the untouched promise of his science book. We reminded them about sunscreen when they woke at lunchtime, gave them pocket money, reminded the bigger ones about condoms, made sure they ate. Thereafter, we spent the day and evening with Morgan and the dog.

We woke the boys midmorning the third day, packed them in a car, started to Key West as they slept. Leslie read about a public beach with snorkeling near shore and rented equipment for herself and the boys. Kindu and Will had never touched the ocean. Ripton loved catching fish, but none of the boys had watched colorful ones in their reefs. I wrote in a café across from Hemingway's house. A salesperson told Leslie about a music festival on the Mallory Square public wharf. We'd been to the waterfront by then, lacquered in a seaside kitsch reduced from the same vernacular as the Liberty Bell, a promenade of cobblestones and faux wharf piles luring pedestrians to sidewalk stalls and trinket shops, talking parrots, jugglers, bars, acrobats and painters colored in a pallet of Caribbean green, flamingo pink, Mediterranean turquoise and Caribbean copper.

We ate dinner early in an open-air restaurant beside our inn. The bar and a few of the tables were sheltered beneath a thatched roof. Tequilas and rums filled the backsplash. During the 160 miles, crisp jeans and blazers had given way to Hawaiian shirts, flip-flops and pastel shorts. "The book says we should watch the sun set from Mallory Square," Leslie told us. Save Morgan, the boys refused because the Home Run Derby was that night, the big event before the big event of the All-Star Game the next night. The Derby included Barry Bonds, Sammy Sosa, Rafael Palmiero and Miguel Tejada. They cracked home runs like slam dunks across the TV screen. "Okay, but you have to listen to *Cold Sassy Tree*," Leslie said to the boys. And to Phil, "You haven't read your science book, have you?"

Will put down his Coke too quickly. "Why we gots to? You makin us listen but it Ripton's work. We not sayin nothin but it ain't fair," he said, looking for affirmation, gravitas to his concern.

"It's good for everyone. It builds your vocabulary," Leslie was undaunted.

"But we not listenin, Leslie. You, Ripton and Mike be, but we not. Not Morgan. That the truf."

They didn't wear headphones during the daily half hour, didn't talk and when I turned back they were looking out the windows or somewhere in the car. I thought they were listening. It was easier to than not.

"That voice, I can't take it," Kindu said.

"You're not reading your book," Leslie said to Phil.

"Why we gots to? This like Miami."

"You're running out of time," I said.

"We watchin the Home Run Derby."

"I expect everyone to listen to *Cold Sassy Tree*, and Phil, I expect you to read, before that TV show."

"We ain't got time. I'm tryin ta tell ya."

"No?"

Phil shook his head.

I faced Ripton. "You have to listen."

"We can't, the derby's starting."

"You're going to do what your mother says. Phil, you're going to read. If you don't, I'm sending you home." I walked across to the inn, asked at the front desk for the key to the boys' room. A great wind had blown through there, the same as down the whole East Coast. I unplugged the television, unscrewed the cable connection, bunched the wires so I wouldn't trip, propped the door open, in anger lifted what was too large and waddled around the pool and guests in their lounge chairs, up the two steps to the porch of the Victorian main house and put the TV on the front desk before the confused woman there. "Don't give this back to my children," I patted the TV and gave her the room key.

"Where you at?" Kindu asked when I sat down.

I realized I was disheveled, breathing hard, sweating through my tee. I wiped my forehead and calmed by breath. "I took the TV out of your room."

"What?" Phil and Will glared.

"Mike, man. Strongest man in the world," Kindu gave an honest million-dollar smile.

"You're not getting it back till you listen to *Cold Sassy Tree* and Phil reads."

I followed their eyes to the TV on the bar beside the bottles of tequila and rum beneath the thatched roof. I walked to the bartender and pointed to my boys. They were watching, but looked away. "My sons haven't done their homework," I told him. He looked to our table. Leslie and Morgan watched. The others stole glances. "I took their TV away. If they try to watch the Home Run Derby here—" I wrote my cell number on a napkin and slid it across the mahogany bar. The man nodded.

"Jesus, Mike," Phil said when I sat down.

The others were silent.

"Good luck," I ate and ignored them.

The boys listened to *Cold Sassy Tree*, or not. Phil held his science book for half an hour by the pool as the others swam. He hardly turned the pages. The boys carried the TV back to their room. The home runs went on for hours.

The next morning Leslie suggested going to one of the wreckers museums and Hemingway's house. Ripton but not the others had heard of him; he remembered our reading the book about the fish. The boys wanted to do nothing, to do boy things. They spent the day at tee shirt, trinket and souvenir stores along Duval Street, hunting for girls around the pool and sitting by the TV. Ripton switched the channel from a show Phil was watching, Phil demanded and Ripton refused to turn it back. "My parents are paying."

"Fuck you," Phil grabbed the controller.

Ripton pulled it back and Phil pushed him away. Ripton pulled harder and Phil punched him in the face. His nose started bleeding and he ran for Leslie.

Red was on the white sheets of a bed. Phil was laughing with Morgan at the TV, dismissing our concern. Ripton demanded we send him home. Kindu and Will thought both boys were to blame. "You run to Mommy?" Phil taunted.

Ripton demanded that we should be his parents alone. We rebuked both boys and started seven hours north along the west coast the next morning to my parents in Sarasota. We thought we'd visit for dinner and find a hotel, sensitive to my father's old rage regarding unwanted guests, but he'd calmed into retirement. My parents had borrowed inflatable mattresses, rearranged their house and insisted we stay.

We called Juan and left another voice mail.

Carlos, keeping daily track, understanding we'd rounded Florida, demanded we come home.

We could, but were a few days ahead of schedule and told the boys New Orleans wasn't far. Will insisted on going back to New York. He denied it was on account of his girlfriend, but hearing "Baby" this and "Baby" that on hushed phone calls several times

daily told a different truth. Morgan didn't care. The others knew the
Saints and Hornets. "The Big Easy," Phil declared. "Mardi Gras. Girls
is crazy." That was February or March but the boys were sold. We
clocked miles through the Panhandle till restlessness overcame the
back of the Volvo and we picked a motel off the highway. We didn't
try to find out about the town we were in and walked across the
feeder road to another Ruby Tuesday, T.G.I. Friday's or Denny's, taking turns with the dog; in and out of the car with our stuff, in and
out of another hotel. The office complained the next morning that
our boys were loud into the night.

They slept as we drove the last 150 miles past much water into
New Orleans. "Mardi Gras," Phil mumbled waking when we slowed
to our first stoplight.  We checked into a titanic hotel beside the
French Quarter, endless halls to thousands of rooms, then took the
dog and boys outside through Royal and Chartres streets to lunch.
We walked to the Mississippi and went for a riverboat tour on a
paddle-wheeler called the *Cajun Queen*. I'd taken a ride one time
twenty years before when I'd been in New Orleans, more than the
boys' lifetime. "*Down here we call 'em niggers*," a man said when I
stopped at a Jim Crow pair of Aunt Jemima and Uncle Ben ceramic
salt-and-pepper shakers behind a window of souvenirs on my way
off the boat. I turned around. He was short like me, thin, light brown
haired, a pencil moustache, white skin burned red.

"That's old school," Will said.

"Racism ain't gone, Five," Kindu told him.

"I guess, rah? I'd deck that nigga."

"I don't know? My moms tells stories about the South."

Our way home was a line into it, to Philadelphia, Mississippi,
through Selma, Montgomery, Birmingham. "*I am in Birmingham because injustice is here*," Martin Luther King Jr. wrote to its White
clergy from a jail cell in 1963. The places along the line we'd drive
should matter to our strange accidental family. Freedom Summer,
Mississippi burning had to be deeper than PlayStation 2. I called a
friend, Diane, who'd grown up in Birmingham. She'd won a Pulitzer
for *Carry Me Home*, about her hometown and family during the

civil rights revolution. I told her we were in New Orleans en route to Birmingham and asked where we should visit.

"When are you going?" she asked.

"Tuesday," figuring two nights in New Orleans and another day driving.

"Can I show you around?" She was arriving from New York the day before.

We watched our boys, momentarily Tom Sawyers and Huck Finns, arguing about the Yankees and Red Sox. We left them to their own for the afternoon, took them to the French Quarter again for dinner, set a cot in our room for Morgan as the others ironed their casual clothes and gave them evening pocket money again.

The next morning was overcast. The guys got up for lunch and we walked through the mist and mauve to St. Louis Cemetery No. 1, Leslie reading about bodies floating after floods in early New Orleans, then laying brick and plaster for tombs and the interment of thousands in these decaying buildings in a city of dead. This was a year before Hurricane Katrina.

"Ig-Nai-Tee-Us Riley? Nigga famous?" Phil read the name from a bronze statue under the clock of what used to be the D. H. Holmes Department Store across from our hotel. The odd-looking man wore a hunting cap, baggy clothes and carried a shopping bag as his scarf blew in the wind.

I tried to explain *A Confederacy of Dunces*.

"Nigga killed hisself for a book?" Phil was mocking.

"Nigga whack," Will said.

"White peoples," Phil agreed.

As we rode north into Alabama I thought of Reverend King's words, wondering what they would mean to the boys when we came to the places that lay before us: "*Go back to Mississippi, go back to Alabama, go back to South Carolina, go back to Georgia, go back to Louisiana.*" The FBI found James Chaney, Michael Schwerner and Andrew Goodman in Olen Burrage's earthen dam. "Nothing educational, Dad," Ripton continued to insist. "*I have a dream that one day even the state of Mississippi, a state sweltering with the heat of injustice, sweltering with the heat of oppression, will be transformed into an oasis of freedom and justice."*

"Ten minutes," Leslie reminded the boys to turn off their electronics when we crossed the Neshoba County line on the way to Philadelphia, Mississippi. "Ten minutes," she said again. *Five minutes to get dressed, Five minutes to the bus.* We were close to Mount Nebo Missionary Baptist Church. *"And Moses went up from the Plains of Moab, the top of Pisgah, which is opposite Jericho."* Atop Mt. Nebo. The parishioners alone welcomed Chaney, Goodman and Schwerner in Philadelphia. *"I have let you see it with your own eyes, but you shall not go there . . . Moses the servant of the Lord, died there in the land of Moab."*

"Where do civil rights come from?" I asked when the boys stopped their music and turned off the video games.

They had no interest in small Mississippi towns. Or my question.

"From the government," Kindu said because the silence grew increasingly awkward.

"The government just gives rights?"

"Of course!" Phil was shutting me up. *"At the time of my brother's murder, it was not fashionable . . . to try a white man for killing a black man and two Jews,"* I read Ben Chaney about his brother, Goodman and Schwerner. Mt. Nebo had invited them to Philadelphia to organize a literacy campaign as a prelude to voter registration against the Jim Crow tool of literacy testing. On June 21, 1964, the three drove out to investigate the fire bombing of Mt. Zion Methodist Church, ten miles from town. They were stopped in their blue Ford station wagon by Neshoba County deputy Cecil Price at about 5:00 p.m., after they'd left the church. He brought them to the Philadelphia jail, kept them in custody for some hours while the Klu Klux Klan organized, then escorted them to the edge of Neshoba County at about 10:30 and saw them off towards Meridian. Their station wagon was found two days later. Mississippi's governor called the disappearance a hoax. Local police and the state's attorney general did nothing. The FBI insisted on investigating and was met with silence. Until one or more informants spoke and the three bodies were found forty-four days later. The Jews had each been shot in the heart. The Black man had been chain-whipped, mutilated, then shot three times. The State of Mississippi dismissed forming a grand jury. Attorney General Robert F. Kennedy directed the FBI to pursue civil rights charges. Eighteen men were arrested and charged with conspiracy to deprive the murdered men of their civil rights. Eight were acquitted. Seven were convicted on civil rights violations, none serving more than six years. Three trials ended in hung juries, including that of Edgar Ray "Preacher" Killen, a sawmill operator and part-time Baptist preacher, organizer of the murders. The one holdout on Killen's jury said she could never convict a preacher.

Of the light sentences, Judge Harold Cox, who'd earlier thrown out the arrests, said, *"They killed one nigger, one Jew and a white man. I gave them* [the convicted] *what I thought they deserved."* Not much.

"That's not right," Will said.

"Those men live here. Preacher Killen walks these streets. They tied James Chaney up, cut off his fingers one by one for trying to teach Black people to read, whipped him with a chain till the metal went into his brain then shot him three times. He was buried in Meridian, not far from here. His grave is vandalized, the headstone thrown into the river, the eternal light shot out," I told the boys.

"That's not right," Will said a second time.

I wondered at Cox, after an entire murder trial still unaware whether Schwerner and Goodman were both White Jews.

We parked in front of Old Benwalt Coffee Shop for lunch, facing the tree- and bench-lined square beside city hall. White people watched us eat. We walked to the chamber of commerce for a town map and asked about Mt. Nebo. "Pritcher Killen," the man there kept repeating. Pritcher Killen could have been one of the men sitting on a bench in the square, having a cheese sandwich in Old Benwalt Coffee Shop. Nothing on the map, no tourist signs indicated the church. Our *Lonely Planet* said to drive a few hundred yards one way then a few hundred yards another. A one-story church was built on a hill in an unassuming neighborhood. A granite gravestone stood as a memorial on the church's side where someone had left a fresh bouquet of purple impatiens, black-eyed susans, daisies and fern. A photograph of each boy was set in the headstone, his name, date of birth, June 21, 1964. My boys' lips moved as they figured ages. Goodman was twenty, Chaney twenty-one, Schwerner, the old man of the group, the one Klu Klux Klansmen went hunting, was twenty-four. He'd lived on the Lower East Side before moving to Mississippi. Phil was nineteen. Kindu and Will were each twenty.

We drove ten miles to Mt. Zion Methodist Church, a way of verdurous lawns and tidy one-story homes along a country road leading to other country roads. I have a picture, everyone and the dog in the sun beneath a blue and yellow painted metal plaque next to the road outside the church:

## FREEDOM SUMMER MURDERS

On June 21, 1964, voting rights
activists James Chaney, Andrew
Goodman, and Michael Schwerner, who
had come here to investigate the
burning of Mt. Zion Church, were
murdered. Victims of a Klan conspiracy,
their deaths provoked national
outrage and led to the first
successful federal prosecution of a
civil rights case in Mississippi.

"But no one for murder?" Kindu was trying to figure the nuance.

"Right. And while they looked for these three," I pointed to the sign, "they found eight bodies of Black people nobody investigated. Schwerner's wife said the government got involved because Schwerner and Goodman were White."

"You said they was Jews?" Will asked.

"From New York," I answered.

"Like us," Kindu said.

"You Black, nigga," Phil said.

"I'm half Jewish. That's what I tell people at college. I got my yarmulke."

A door slammed and an older man crossed his lawn and the road to us. He came slowly, long past Freedom Summer with a fitting stiffness of age, medium height and strong. He told us it was a nice day. He asked how we were doing. Did we have questions?

"Mike tolt us a lot," Phil answered, meaning too much.

"You're from New York?" he'd seen our plates.

"Yes, Sir," Kindu answered.

"I'm from Staten Island." He'd retired from construction work and moved to Neshoba County, where his mother was born and his grandparents always lived. He spoke to us about Freedom Summer anyways, telling us how the Klan came to Mt. Zion on Memorial Day looking for Schwerner, who'd convinced the church to allow a freedom school there. They beat parishioners, some so badly they were hospitalized, came back that night and burned the building to the ground.

We left for Birmingham. I wanted to go through Selma across the Edmund Pettus Bridge to Montgomery, where Martin Luther King Jr. and Ralph Abernathy linked arms to face billy clubs, tear gas and the bullwhips of Alabama's state and local police on Bloody Sunday, March 7, 1965. A White minister was killed on the next march. Abraham Joshua Heschel's feet prayed—but in the third march, when celebrities participated. But the map said it was too far to drive my way because Diane would be waiting the next morning in front of Birmingham's Sixteenth Street Baptist Church.

She was standing beside her car in front when we arrived a few minutes late. She pointed to the Birmingham Civil Rights Institute and the freedom walk in Kelly Ingram Park, then told us the history of the church. Three White men planted nineteen sticks of dynamite beside the women's restroom on Sunday, September 15, 1963. It was filled with girls preparing for choir. Four were killed. Diane showed us a stained-glass window of a crucified Black Jesus in the front wall. It was stunning from inside, facing south to the sun and sky.

"Jesus wasn't Black," Will was doubtful.

"That's right," Phil agreed.

"What was he?" Diane asked, her blond hair and pug nose that suddenly seemed identical to Morgan's, her voice lilting more Southern than when she was home in New York.

"White," Phil answered.

"He was a Jew, that's White," Will explained.

"In the Middle East, two thousand years ago, Jews weren't White," I said.

"You're White," Phil answered.

I tried to understand why it so bothered Will that the glass Jesus was Black.

Diane took us to the freedom walk across the street, a loop through fire hoses and German shepherds that Bull Connor and his police turned on Black children of Birmingham. Dogs lunged, teeth bared. "Children protested, two thousand were arrested in two days," Diane explained why kids became activists. I watched our boys' faces imagining themselves. I thought of the pain parents and civil rights leaders must have felt sending children to danger.

We walked across the street, past the statue of Reverend Fred Shuttlesworth in suit and tie standing in front of the Birmingham Civil Rights Institute. Diane stopped. "He's the hero of my book." I didn't know who he was. "Pastor of the Bethel Baptist Church, a founder of the SCLC," Diane explained, the Southern Christian Leadership Conference, famous for Martin Luther King Jr. and Ralph Abernathy. "He led the effort to desegregate Birmingham."

Jim Crow memorabilia were displayed throughout the beginning exhibits of the museum. Rastus advertisements for Cream of Wheat. COLORED signs for water fountains, Klu Klux Klan robes and hoods, a *Black Jack* oil can, blackface bellhop cookie jars, shackles, whips, photographs of lynched men hanging from trees. A Freedom Ride bus had been re-created. The cell where Martin Luther King wrote "*Let-*

*ter from a Birmingham Jail"* was rebuilt. The boys touched the bars, looked inside at the small bed, a newspaper folded there, the toilet. Diane walked us a few blocks afterwards through the civil rights district and suggested her favorite Southern food place, Nikki's West, for lunch. I kept the dog on my lap without a seatbelt and rode with Diane as she spoke about the day before Christmas, 1956, when sixteen sticks of dynamite exploded outside Reverend Shuttlesworth's bedroom window as he sat in bed. The house was destroyed yet he walked out safe. A police officer belonging to the Klan told him, *"If I were you I'd get out of town as quick as I could."* Shuttlesworth told him to tell the Klan, *"I wasn't saved to run."* They attacked Shuttlesworth and his wife the next year when the two tried to enroll their children in an all-White Birmingham public school, stabbing his wife, chain whipping and beating Shuttlesworth unconscious with brass knuckles. A bomb was secreted beside him the next year, discovered by a church member and rushed away before it exploded. "Shuttlesworth was fearless. Abernathy supported Reagan, for God's sake." Diane said Shuttlesworth had moved to Cincinnati decades earlier and became pastor of a Baptist church there.

I went last in the food line so I could pay, cold to hot items, drinks and desserts, the young woman at the register waiting, ringing up fried chicken, collard greens, candied yams, barbeque ribs, corn bread, lima beans, Coca-Colas, Sprites, ice teas and lemonades.

Diane spoke more with the boys about why Shuttlesworth organized Birmingham's civil rights protests around teenagers. She looked across the room at one point and her expression froze, her head tilted, eyes narrowed then opened. "Reverend Shuttlesworth!"

An older man in suit and tie, closely barbered and gray, looked up to his name, recognized Diane, stood and hugged her in surprise. "Diane," holding her gently away. "Why are you in Birminham?"

"Visiting my family, starting a new book. Why are you here?"

"A conference. You deserve all the honor, Diane." He was with a small table of middle-aged women, Black and White.

"Let me introduce you to my friends," Diane said, explaining we were a family as Reverend Shuttlesworth shook our hands.

"Are you enjoying Birminham?" he asked the boys.

"Yes, Sir," Kindu answered.

"What brought you here?"

"Mike wanted us to see the civil rights places," Will answered.

"What have you seen?"

Kindu told him about the Sixteenth Street Baptist Church and the civil rights museum.

"You the man who statue we seen?" Phil asked.

Shuttlesworth smiled shyly.

The boys told him about Philadelphia, Mississippi, New Orleans, Miami Beach; they had noticed the architecture of Savannah, the slave market in Charleston, my lecture at Independence Hall.

"Too much was educational," Ripton made a face.

"That's the truf," Phil agreed.

"Like the Civil Rights Institute?" Shuttlesworth twinkled.

"No, no, that's cool," Phil said, "but Colonial Williamsburg."

"OHYEAH," Ripton agreed, running the sounds together. "Dad had to lecture about everything."

Shuttlesworth looked sympathetic, as if he'd suffered parental educational lectures. "Like what?" he asked.

"Everything wasn't that way," Ripton hesitated. "Pretend, like . . ."

"There ain't no slaves," Will finished.

Shuttlesworth was quiet a moment then spoke, his voice staying quiet. "We're afraid of ourselves. What's inside. We want history to be pretty, so it doesn't scare us. The White ministers here, in Birminham, wanted us to pretend everything was pretty, like that. But you have to stand up for what you believe. You can be afraid, but you have to stand up. You understand?" he shook the boys' hands, wished us a good trip, kissed Diane and sat back with his guests.

We made Gettysburg by nightfall. Kindu called his mother on the way and told her we'd met Reverend Shuttlesworth. She said how lucky we were.

We toured the battlefields and were in New York by dinnertime on July 25. Carlos waited outside. "It was mad borin, yo," he kept repeating, though he was batting fourth for Youth Service.

Morgan, our baby, but eleven and a half years old, nearly Carlos' age when we first met the bigger boys, insisted at the beginning of summer that he wanted to return to the skating camp in Pennsylvania. Leslie had registered and paid. But on the way from Birmingham, two weeks before camp, Morgan started whispering to Leslie that we'd been away too long. He wanted to hang out with his friends, to not go away again.

He remained silent and stoic with me.

"If he's not going to be happy, we shouldn't force him," Leslie said.

"We paid cause he said he wanted to go. That's a commitment."

I drove him to Pennsylvania and he'd made good friends when he called two days later. He predicted he'd be doing backward summersaults when we picked him up at the end of the week. He did, one after the other as Leslie, Ripton and I watched, predicting what he'd do by the end of the next summer.

*Next summer;* we'd always had next summers with our kids, before and after Tompkins Square. We'd take Morgan to camp the next summer, he'd do new tricks. And all the boys would be older.

# CHAPTER THIRTEEN

# CARLOS | *Summer 2004*

Coach O'Keefe called Carlos while we were traveling and offered him a two-week junior counselor job at Cooperstown Baseball Camp. "You sure you want to stop Youth Service?" I asked because he'd been doing well and YSL was preparing for the Williamsport baseball tournament, held in the birthplace of Little League. He said Mel Zitter used him too often as a middle-inning reliever and too little as a batter. "That's bullshit. I ain't gonna make it as a pitcher," he grew shrill.

"Scouts are gonna be there," I reminded him, a young player's catnip.

He agreed the tournament made sense. I drove him to Cooperstown and he came home by bus two weeks later announcing Coach O'Keefe said he could play college ball in St. Louis. I pointed out what he was ignoring—the YSL bus leaving in the morning. "I'm gonna practice hittin off a tee in the East River," he said.

"Scouts—"

"I don't care bout scouts."

"You made a promise to your team."

"I didn't promise nothin."

"You joined a team. You promised your best to help them win."

"Fuck 'em. Mel doesn't wanna let me bat. I gotta look out for my-self. I tolt you, pitchin is bullshit."

"If you don't go, you're out of Youth Service. You're cutting off Queensboro"—a community college in the city with a Division One team his coaches wanted him to attend. They'd find a team in Texas, Oklahoma or elsewhere in baseball country afterwards willing to nurture a major league dream.

"You ain't listenin. I don't care. Coach says I can play in Missouri."

A YSL coach called and Carlos refused the phone.

"I don't like quitters."

"They don't have Spanish kids in Missouri. Coach says I'll tear it up."

"Call Mel, tell him why you're not going."

"You're a clown."

I walked away.

Carlos told his new plan to Leslie: he'd go to BMCC for a semes-ter then transfer to whatever college near St. Louis Coach O'Keefe arranged.

"You're not going to be able to play fall ball," I said the next day about BMCC over Queensboro. "You'll get rusty."

"I don't care."

"I'm not paying," I threatened about college in St. Louis, but only to Leslie when we were alone.

"He says he's getting a scholarship," Leslie said.

"You don't get full scholarship to a community college in baseball."

Carlos and I ignored each other with the concentration of two an-noyed people in one small place. I stayed writing at the kitchen table and rode my exercise bike beside it to the Yankees on TV while he came inches away to pour glasses of milk from the refrigerator, take plates behind me on the wire shelves and heat Hot Pockets in the microwave. We pretended the other wasn't there.

But Yankee moments good and bad became the seed crystal over the week between us, a Mariano save, what Paulie would have done during an at bat versus some new player I wouldn't accept. "They done real well, almost to the World Series," Carlos said one evening.

I nodded. We hungered for the old Yankees.

"You and me's too much alike. Like wif my moms. That's why we argue."

Coach O'Keefe put Carlos in touch with Coach Gober at a St. Charles community college somewhere outside St. Louis, who offered him a partial scholarship and the opportunity to play in the spring after he finished the semester at BMCC, if he passed the GED.

---

Carlos, Phil and Kindu, his last week home before returning to Morrisville, pranced towards me at the kitchen table and I knew in less than an instant that they'd waited for Leslie to go upstairs.

"What? I asked.

Kindu spun around into his round-shouldered, stiff torso, straight-armed shuffle out the kitchen and immediately back.

"YoMike—" Carlos pretended being official but broke down laughing.

"Mike," Phil started in his forced nasal way of beginning a scam.

"You're gonna scam me."

"That's hurts," he deadpanned.

"Juan has to move in," Carlos said.

"The Rosegardens," Kindu said.

"He needs the Leslie-Michael treatment," Carlos said.

Juan had been working in a bar inside Newark International Airport and living at Will's since his mother kicked him out again.

"He needs to be here, you'll make him do things. He wants to go to college," Phil said.

I imagined the apartment, figuring where another boy could sleep, though Kindu was leaving back to college. We couldn't say *no*. The boys already knew. I wondered what I'd say to Leslie.

"You'll be quiet at night?" I asked Carlos and Phil.

They'd keep Ripton and Morgan up on school nights. They'd stay in the small room behind the living room, pretending to sleep till I went upstairs, then come out. I'd heard them on cell phones behind the door too many times to think otherwise. I'd come down to them laughing and shouting around the dining room table, no way for Ripton and Morgan to sleep. Leslie pronounced 10:00 p.m. to be everyone's bedtime. But I couldn't enforce that.

Our sons adored the bigger boys with the rough rapture reserved for older brothers. Ripton and Morgan never decided books were captivating and grades worth the costs of striving. My Talmud scholars in Yankee Stadium, the scholar athletes, weren't making daylight; the older ones' disregard for books and school colored things. Leslie and I were old and out of touch, our sons were certain of that. And though Morgan never spoke about it, Ripton did tell us in his deepest, infrequent rage that he wasn't like us, he wasn't a *nerd*, he wasn't a *braniac*, he'd been adopted, he was an athlete, he didn't like to read books, he didn't care about the things we did.

There would be dirty dishes left around, more crumbs spilled here and there. More food to buy. More clothes scattered. We didn't plan where Juan would sleep or keep his things. The boys slept where they did, shared beds how they did. Our rules remained to call by eight o'clock if not coming back on a school night and otherwise be home by eight-thirty and in bed by ten, to call by nine o'clock on a weekend night if not coming home and otherwise be there and in bed by midnight, to put their dishes at least in the sink if not the dishwasher, lift the toilet seat and pee into the water rather than onto the rim or floor, make a note in the book on the counter if you ate or drank the last of anything. Those were our broad strokes.

───────────────

We were late but Kindu kept climbing the iron ladder into the loft between the kitchen and TV room where he'd slept the summer, carrying down boxes of sneakers I didn't know were up there. "We gotta get going," I kept complaining because I was driving back and forth to Morrisville and didn't want to be on the highway late.

"I know, Mike, I know," Kindu said in his way, ignoring me.

"Kindu, dogs," Carlos was smiling. "You nevva ready."

Which was true.

"How many shoes do you have?" I asked in deepening disappointment.

He didn't answer, looked down, walked past to stack more sneaker boxes outside in the hallway.

"Who bought these?" I asked because he hadn't earned anything through the summer.

"My brothers," he walked past again. The same drug money as the shoes we'd brought back to New York. Kindu didn't ask us for help with his expenses. I didn't think about his brothers' earnings, but knew. He stacked eighteen pairs of sneakers in front of the elevator, a shoe store we packed in the back of the Volvo with the rear seat folded away. Kindu brought down the small TV his roommate had given him.

"You don't need the TV, when are you going to watch it?" I tried like I had at the beginning of summer.

"Yankee games, Mike," and he wouldn't hear any arguments.

We pushed his luggage into the roof-rack carrier and the TV onto the middle seats.

I played Savage Garden as we drove. I couldn't help liking the slow and naïve optimism of "*I Want You*" segueing into the fast and naïve optimism of "*Truly Madly Deeply.*" Kindu had made sure earlier in the summer that I knew the lyrics to "*Universe.*" We stopped for lunch in a small deco diner off the square beside the white church in a small town I didn't know where. The booths were full and we took seats at the counter. Kindu was the only dark-skinned person there, including the dishwasher. He left his dark-tinted aviator sunglasses on as we ate. Customers tried to hide their glances our way. "*Universe*" chanced onto the stereo as we drove into Morrisville, passed its few streets and stopped at his dorm. That's the truth.

*You will only end up lost in loneliness*
*And wake up with the words already on your lips.*
*So I'll let you go, baby.*
*So I'll let you go . . .*

Tears started down my cheeks during the first line, overcome with pride and passing life. I was leaving my son at college. Even with eighteen pairs of sneakers and a small TV.

───────────────

As with Kindu, Carlos couldn't go to a college he'd never seen. He had a long weekend off from BMCC for the upcoming presidential elections and I was surprised to realize four years had passed since his shock that the American presidents hadn't all been Jews. I suggested driving to St. Louis. It was sixteen hours, not including gas, food, bathrooms and stretching. I thought we could spend two nights and days afterwards in Cleveland working the election, because Ohio was predicted to be an important swing state. Coach Gober recommended a hotel near the St. Charles campus. We drove till I was too tired, found a motel by the road and started early enough the next day to knock on Coach Gober's open door by mid-morning.

He stood from behind a gray metal and wood-grain-vinyl-topped desk, looking down on me and Carlos, fading into middle age with what I saw were beer weekends. He was light freckled and his thinning hair was once blond. He shook Carlos' hand then extended it to me while keeping his eyes on his new acquisition. Coach Gober had no choice over office furniture—it was the same in the others we'd passed—but the plastic-framed certificates of achievement hanging on his walls, the neatly stacked small number of folders on his desk and other signs of emptiness cried out to me not to leave Carlos in his care.

Gober never became aware of me. He sat behind his desk with thin bravado. I watched his hands flurry. I could have asked whether

his Cougars had been winning, where players transferred after completing their associates degrees, if any had gone to the minors and,
however unlikely, the majors. I didn't ask because they didn't matter.
I'd asked Carlos at the inopportune time when he first mentioned
Gober. He didn't know and didn't plan to find out. O'Keefe's recommendation was all that he believed in.

"Fast hands," Gober said to Carlos clocking his bat speed at
ninety-seven miles per hour, he said faster than the average major
league player. "You swing like Pujols when he was your age," the major league star who'd played community college ball in the same
league with St. Charles. "You'll be scouted. You'll get drafted one of
your years." Pujols was drafted from community college. Then I existed for a moment. Coach Gober turned to me. "I'm expecting
great things from him."

He told us how to get to the motel and told Carlos one of his
players would pick him up in an hour. Then he was gone. I drove
along the strip-mall-lined road back to the expressway looping St.
Louis and off at the exit Gober said, onto a feeder road unlike any
road I'd imagined, paralleling the highway leading nowhere other
than mall parking lots to our right and an interstice of strip malls to
our left shoehorned between it and the expressway. Our motel
would be there. It unfortunately was, a one-story structure sharing a
parking lot with a one-story restaurant. We unpacked and waited in
the parking lot till a blue Ford pickup turned in. Carlos recognized
the driver, a junior coach from Cooperstown. The young man rolled
down the window and shook hands fiercely with Carlos, who
climbed in, and they left. I asked the office clerk to recommend a
place for lunch and she said the food was good in the restaurant on
the other side of the parking lot. The young hostess welcomed me
with a wide smile of good teeth. "One?" she asked when I let the
door shut behind me into air conditioning and soft light. The few
windows had been draped. I passed thick wood tables and chairs, circles of wood stools at high tables, across a wide plank wood floor
scraped free of stain. The rest was invisible colors and the glare of
neon beer signs. I scanned the menu for Caesar salad and lost myself

among Mild, Medium, Hot, Abusive, Nuclear, Suicidal, Honey Mustard or BBQ chicken wings, wondering what these meant in Missouri and why Suicidal was worse than Nuclear. "Care for a beverage?" I jumped at hearing the waitress, ordered hot chicken wings, walked back to our room and read, walked across the feeder road and mall parking lot to a health club, phoned Carlos near dinner and left a message. I didn't hear from him, tried again when I'd grown hungry and left another message. I didn't want to drive but didn't want the chicken wings a second time and walked across another mall parking lot to a T.G.I. Friday's, complained to Leslie when we spoke and woke the next morning to Carlos shaking my shoulder, "I'm goin to a workout wif Coach."

"Okay," I answered in that moment of waking, trying to remember why I was in a dark and stale place. "Ask him about dinner," I added.

I drove later to a store calling itself a NEW YORK DELI in a strip mall for a bad coffee and muffin, called Leslie, wrote, called Leslie, walked to the exercise club where I'd been the day before and drove to downtown St. Charles along the Mississippi River for lunch, read the tourist sign where Clarke finally met Lewis to set off together with thirty-two men in three pirogues, ordered a coffee in a sidewalk café and wrote. I tried Carlos in the late afternoon, stayed in St. Charles for dinner, went back to the motel, packed, set my cell phone, pulled the drapes and stared at a gray ceiling with parking lot light gushing in. I felt sorry for myself, abandoned, and wasn't wise enough to realize I was the adult. I should have been clear about expectations for our trip. I reset my phone to wake up earlier. I was in a soft sleep, didn't look to see what time it was and neither of us said anything when Carlos came back. I woke quietly to my phone, knew exactly where I was, washed, ate the muffin and drank the coffee I'd brought back from St. Charles, checked out, put my suitcase in the trunk, came back to the room, turned on the lights in what was still dark and said, "I'm leaving in five minutes. I don't care if you stay or come," walked to the car, started the engine when five minutes had passed, shifted to reverse and Carlos opened the door, threw his bag over the seat into the back and got in. We didn't speak. I drove some hours till I needed a bathroom then started the gas pump and looked in to Carlos, motionless and staring ahead. "I'm leaving when the tank is filled, whether you're here or not," and walked to the store. I passed him inside. He came running out with a juice and cookies as I was starting the car. I stopped for gas again later, we danced the same while I bought a sandwich, coffee and water then kept driving. It took ten hours to Cleveland and I waited till the exit for our hotel, then, "I'm not your chauffeur," I pushed words like breaking a vow of silence. "You want me to be your father, I'm your father. You don't leave me sitting in a hotel room for two days. I wouldn't do that to you."

"But you write alone. You wanna be alone. I don't know what your problem is."

I passed strip malls, America was the same, looking for the street to the hotel. "I don't have to drive sixteen hours, leave Leslie and everyone and sit in some shit-ass motel and walk around shopping malls. Don't treat the next person who tries to help you like this."

"What you talkin bout? You bein stupid, Bee."

"*Bee*" had become his tick when particularly grim. The trip, my plan, this drive was a disaster I'd created in fury and didn't know how to get us out of. I turned onto a winding street up past more parking lots, watching the odometer not to miss the hotel. "Did you ask what I was doing? Did you make sure that coach invited me to dinner?" I parked near the entrance.

Carlos ground his teeth, his jaw strained. He clenched his fists, his flexors and biceps bulged, his shoulders and neck locked and its veins pushed with each heartbeat and grinding.

"Look at me when I talk to you."

He wouldn't.

I took hold of his shoulder, "Look at me."

He flushed dark red and started shaking, his shoulders, neck and head, sweat beading from his forehead. "Let go of me, Mike," he spat through tight teeth. "Let go of me." I felt his power for the first time, frightening strength grown up, the young shortstop who'd thrown to first base, our *beast*. I'd never taunted such strength in rage. We loved each other, we were both flawed, he'd never hurt me and I pushed him. I slid my hand to his forearm and gripped harder. "Look at me when I'm talking to you," I heard myself demand, echoing my father.

Carlos shook, muscles bulging, ready to lash out and I wouldn't take my hand away, watching the scene from above but there with him. "If you were anybody," through clenched teeth, quivering, spitting, louder and I understood the danger and safety, "if you were anybody, Bee, I'd flatten you, Bee, I'd fuckin flatten you," his spit to the windshield, looking ahead.

His shaking would soon break to silent tears then a muffled crying pretending not to. I knew that, so took my bag, went to the room and my cell phone rang. "Michael?" Leslie asked in her voice digging towards disapproval of how I'd dealt with Morgan and Ripton. "Carlos is crying, Michael. He's trying to get back to New York. He's standing on a highway and doesn't know where he is. What's going on?"

I tried to explain. But nothing I would say could be right because I was wrong. He and I both were, but Carlos was the child. My poor judgment, my lack of control. Leslie didn't like when I went away. She said our sons had hard times. Her inventory was long when she was on her own. Waking Ripton, Morgan, Phil and Juan in the morning, feeding our younger two, making sure they dressed, shouting off the minutes till the bus turned the corner. She'd get Ripton down the elevator, walk Mr. Jenkins and Morgan to school then bring the dog home. She'd push the bigger boys into their days, ride her bike to work and back to the Earth School on time to meet Morgan. She'd take the dog out when she got home, unpack any groceries that had arrived, ask our sons what they wanted to order for dinner and ask about their homework. She'd do dishes and walk the dog one last time or maybe ask the bigger boys to, but never Ripton and Morgan because she'd read it was wrong to ask one's children to walk the family dog. (Besides, they were too young; even as he grew past the age when we'd first asked the bigger boys to take out Mr.

Jenkins, Ripton remained *too young*.) She had to get our sons to bed on time, make sure the bigger boys were quiet in the back room and start everything over again the next morning. Leslie hadn't wanted me to stop in Cleveland. "He's a boy, Michael. He's calling me, he's calling his mommy, don't you get it? Find him."

"But—"

"He wants his mommy."

------

Carlos and his suitcase were gone. I drove the way we'd come, down the turns till I saw him beside one of the corners talking on his cell phone. I came closer but he recognized the car, picked up his bag and stepped over a curb into a shopping mall parking lot. I lost him between vans and SUVs, drove into the lot and saw him crossing the road. I turned around and caught up. "Leslie said you're going to New York," I spoke through the window keeping pace to his walking with the bag over his shoulder packed with his baseball things. It had to have been heavy.

He slowed, breathing hard, looking down. "My moms said I shoulda lookted out for you," he mumbled to the ground.

"Do you know which way New York is?"

He stopped, shrugged and put down the bag, his face dripping, his tee wet and dark.

"I'm sorry."

"YoMike, you're an asshole, you know that?"

"I know. We're both assholes but Leslie says I'm supposed to know better. You hungry?" Of course he was, he'd eaten almost nothing since Missouri. We walked into the Denny's we were facing. He told me about the Cougars and we worked the presidential elections for two days, door to door in poor African American neighborhoods, dropping off campaign literature, talking with people who answered our knocks or rings, asking if they planned to vote, encouraging them if they hesitated. We were poll watchers till closing in a Baptist church in one of those neighborhoods. Both of us, shy among people we didn't know, were uncomfortable. I'm not sure if Carlos was proud. We watched the results in a big room with hundreds of others who'd come to do what we had. Our fellow volunteers were almost all White and a generation younger than me. Our candidate lost. "America's whack," Carlos said as I turned off the light to our hotel room. My eyes adjusted to the light from the parking lot and I saw him in the bed across from mine, staring up at the ceiling. I'd pushed things too far between us, though I'd also do it again. But for that moment, coming through tension to calm had left us trusting.

"YoMike, I been thinkin."

"Yeah?"

"I love you, you and Leslie, you know that, rah?"

"We love you too. I love you."

# CHAPTER FOURTEEN

# HIGHWAYS
# AND AIRPORTS

*December 2004*

"Only losers stay," Ripton answered.

I'd asked again why he wanted to leave. We liked his teachers and they liked him. Madame Perry was no longer his advisor, but his next was equally fitting. The school culture was humble. At parent-student potluck dinners in one family home or another, what people did for a living was never the first question.

"It's too small," Ripton humored me with the same explanation. He played on the basketball team and particularly seriously on the baseball team. With twenty-five to thirty children per grade, Ripton was certain they didn't have enough boys in middle school and later in high school to field good teams. "We suck. They let every kid play," he was cynical about the Quaker middle-school philosophy of giving playing time to any kid who showed up. "How can we win? And you know I want to play football." Because, beside being small, BFS didn't allow football on account of the violence. "That's BULL-shit." It didn't help that his school was in downtown Brooklyn, sur-rounded by urban density rather than playing fields. "Only losers stay," he repeated.

The principal distributed a memo announcing that BFS had raised sufficient funds, signed a lease for a space around the corner and down a block from the school and was renovating it to open in the autumn as a new high school. Preschool (beginning as early as twenty months) through twelfth grade were till then in the same building. Over half the children left at the end of eighth grade, including, it seemed, nearly all who'd been there from elementary school. New kids were added, grade sizes remained the same.

With the new high school, the principal was determined to break the cycle of children leaving and intended to grow each grade to fifty or sixty students. He sent out a second memo notifying parents that BFS would hereon provide only the minimum required for a student to transfer, a transcript and basic letters, no longer the extra assistance that might be needed to go elsewhere.

As it had been with the Earth School, Ripton didn't realize how content he was. The peace we'd sensed with Madame Perry seemed to genuinely be that of the school. We wanted him to stay, but Leslie agreed to call the admissions offices of the larger schools he wanted, with campuses surrounded by playing fields, to be told what she knew; ninth grade wasn't an intake year. These were elite schools. They didn't have mass migrations. Students might fail out, move away or go elsewhere in the city, but openings were unpredictable and few. Ripton didn't have the highest grades. He'd receive nice but not glowing letters of recommendation. The elite schools topped up their endowments, recruited students, bragged and in all other ways leveraged their graduates sent to Harvard and Yale. Ripton wasn't compelled that way.

I was still taking my place at the table by the front of Casimir each Monday, the doors recently slid open for summer. John Howard came more often than not, Kindu when he was home, Ripton and other bigger boys often, Leslie sometimes for the first hour to play games of Uno.

"*You have the horsepower,*" John encouraged Ripton week after week. He'd scored in the highest percentiles on a national exam and mail arrived from Johns Hopkins offering him a summer of advanced studies. But Ripton had stayed home to play baseball and, as he said, *"be a normal kid"* nearly six years from when we'd met the boys in Tompkins Square. John gave him books to read about poker. He gave Frank Herbert's *Dune* trilogy. The books stayed on our shelves. Ripton said he didn't have the patience to read. He didn't have the patience to study a school lesson more than once.

But the score gave him and reluctantly us hope he might be accepted at one of the schools fitting what he wanted. Leslie called Fieldston School and Poly Prep Country Day School, where we'd applied the first time, and Riverdale Country School. The three had extraordinary playing fields.

No place encouraged her to apply.

"Only losers stay," Ripton persisted.

Nursing the illusion he'd been wait-listed two school years earlier, because Leslie and her sister had graduated from there, because we, her sister and parents still contributed, we hoped he had a better chance at Fieldston than any other place and asked for an application in case space opened. We filled out what we could, then needed Ripton's grades and recommendations from BFS. I called the princi pal and asked to meet. I rode my bike down Essex, to the Manhattan Bridge where the boys had gawked at the breasts of an Indian girl beside a pioneer boy when Leslie and I first took three cabs and boys we hardly knew to Chinatown for dinner. Of course we hadn't considered the trajectory of years that night, and had our hands full with boys spinning the lazy Susan too fast and shouting to the waiter across the crowded restaurant. And deciding, accidentally, that we needed to buy them all books. They were children; they needed and deserved much more than books. Some needed to move in and eventually grow to be able to move out. I pedaled beneath the arches of the bridge onto the bikeway to Brooklyn along Jay past Tillary to Willoughby where the high school would be and Ripton came up from the subway each morning, walking my bike shoulder to shoulder with pedestrians the block to Pearl Street. I explained to the principal that Leslie and I would stay at BFS forever. But Ripton dreamed of a school surrounded by sports fields. He knew and wanted Ripton to understand that a good pitcher was transferring into the school next year.

Fieldston called to schedule an interview. Leslie didn't want to take Ripton. She'd been disillusioned, was certain nothing good would come of it. He and I reported to the admissions office and were assigned a nervous junior from a family of modest means to walk us through the campus. Ripton wanted to see the gyms, basketball courts, indoor and outdoor pools, baseball and football fields. Our young man, Black from Queens, told us about girls' and boys' lacrosse, volley ball, ice hockey, golf, crew and Ultimate Frisbee teams. The crew rowed on the Hudson. The young man left us in an auditorium filled with other applicants and their seemingly formidable parents, I thought investment bankers, Fortune 500 CEOs and ambassadors. We listened to inspirations delivered by a rainbow of juniors and seniors about the wonder of the Fieldston family from prekindergarten through high school or transferring from a public school in the Bronx or Queens in seventh grade, afraid of fitting in, a class step up, realizing the rapture. Our speakers were Asian, Black, Latina and a very middle-class White teenager from the Bronx open about his scholarship. They had me cheering for the adventure, the best America had to offer. I had to remember the unpresented reality, the children of those investment bankers, hedge fund managers, real estate developers and high-powered attorneys, rich, largely White, class intolerant and re-creating the discrimination we dreamed of breaking. That's why Leslie hadn't wanted to go back.

The head of Admissions introduced herself in the waiting room and took Ripton to her office for his fifteen minutes. My fifteen minutes came next. "He's quite a nice young man," she was kind as we sat. I looked at the photographs standing on her bookcase shelves, a young professional African American with her young professional African American husband, other photographs with her mother and apparently no children. "I went to BFS. It was lovely," she explained, which seemed in her voice a natural step moving to Fieldston. "I understand wanting a larger school." I nodded for Ripton's wants. "But

I'm confused. On your son's application, he has one brother. But he was talking about 'my brothers,' and he said six?"

"She really liked me," Ripton said as we drove home. He was proud.

We'd hear from Fieldston in February.

---

I liked the front window of a skateboard shop opened nearby along a route I pedaled often, and walked there one day to buy sneakers to replace the pair I had. They were my only ones, with holes in each sole that leaked when it rained. The storekeeper was busy selling a board to a kid not much younger than he. Listening to them discuss boards, trucks and wheels warmed me with the same affection I spoke about bikes and skiing. I liked watching skateboarders tilt and glide and decided to buy a board too. The extra exercise could only help.

The storekeeper treated me like a tottering man, sold me a beginning board and things were perfect as I walked home till I tried keeping my balance rolling a few feet on the sidewalk in front of the Christodora.

"Yasurethatsagoodidea?" Dennis asked.

Morgan came out the front door to me falling. He burst in amusement, covering his mouth in embarrassment at his father. He went to the corner grocer for a dollar old-fashioned bottle of Coca-Cola and a turkey sandwich on a hard roll with lettuce, tomato and mayonnaise, his dinner, came back and asked to try my board. We walked onto the baseball field in Tompkins Square towards the backstop around home plate. Skateboarders were grinding on rails and launching themselves from ramps they carried into the park each day and locked to streetlamps and signposts outside when the park closed. It was as if our boys and baseball had never existed. Morgan and I avoided them. We'd come for the smooth skim-coated infield, passed first base where Ripton played for moments the first day and managed his way back after. He'd made himself an excellent first baseman. We stopped at home plate. The grayish blue and Mets orange of the infield had faded, the smoothness scoured in years of jumps and missed tricks. Morgan lay down on my skateboard and paddled towards the pitcher's place. Skateboarders did part, seeing his beginning. The once clear "X" was potted and hard to see. I hadn't thought of the older and taller captain in years. I didn't see them on the street. We'd dropped out of touch with Dakota but heard from Ricky that he was growing fine, in a school for children with learning disabilities. Ricky had followed Carlos into Youth Service, was a pitcher and determined to make it there. The boys played catch with him sometimes in the East River fields. Morgan sat up and paddled back to home plate, stopped and stood there, keeping his balance. "I'm gonna skate," he said.

"Do you want me to hold you?"

My doting was a second embarrassment. He made a face, pushed off and rolled smoothly to second base, where the two captains had screamed at each other as we walked onto the field, where the boy who would become Ricky rounded slowly while Dakota groped behind the center field American elm for the baseball. Then Morgan skated to home.

He'd been walking home alone from school since the beginning of the year, older and wiser than I could have imagined, stopping at the hotdog store on Seventh Street, stopping in the playground along Avenue B, spending time with his friends. He came home for my skateboard the next day and went to Tompkins Square, again the next and through the weekend and the following week and started rolling through our neighborhood. He began kick flips and ollies. We gave him a cell phone as he rolled farther away. He was with friends beneath the FDR expressway along the East River—where the coach had banished Ricky from the van. He was with friends beneath the Brooklyn Bridge. Lower Manhattan was his village.

We spoke with him about middle school for the next year. He wanted to go upstairs rather than Brooklyn, to keep his 433 steps rather than the bus and subway his brother rode each day. He wanted to stay with his friends.

"You won't lose them," I assured him.

Leslie said the same.

He knew better. His sadness grew to desperation. If Morgan could get in, attending another school in another borough would strain his friendships much more than if he continued upstairs to Tompkins Square Middle School. Mark Pingatore let me tour again. He still dreamed of a high school as his first graduating classes struggled to find spots elsewhere. His teachers were still young and devoted. Tompkins Square still shared its library with the Earth School and PS 64. It was understocked and closed some days. The computer room had few computers. The school had no sports, few other after-school activities, classes were crowded and noisy. Dismissal was loud. BFS had a maximum of fifteen kids per class. It had resources, not the sorts of Fieldston, but sufficient. We'd try for Morgan to be accepted there.

---

Leslie had taken Ripton and Will to Paragon. Morgan was out skating for the afternoon. I sat writing at the kitchen table, intermittently watching the sink nearly filled with glasses, plates, cereal bowls and silverware from the boys' breakfast and lunch, from their dinner the night before. Bread crumbs were piled and strewn like sand across the butcher-block divider. A few plates had been abandoned on the table. Near or empty Gatorade bottles, Sprite cans, an empty milk carton and another of orange juice were abandoned around the sink. I was frustrated with the neglect when Carlos came from the living room carrying a plate, put it on the pile in the sink, took another from the shelves behind me and started rummaging through the refrigerator.

"We ain't got nothin to eat," he complained.

"There's ham and cheese." Leslie had been keeping the bigger boys supplied with cold cuts.

"Someone ate the bread."

Those were the crumbs. "Here's money, go down to the store," I handed him enough for a loaf.

He did, to the greengrocer, ate his sandwich with mayonnaise and set the new plate on top of the old on top of the others in the sink.

"It would be nice if you'd help with the dishes," I said as he started away.

He turned back, his voice already tight. "Ripton don't. You don't make Morgan."

"Leslie and I do them all the time."

"I hate dishes. You don't ask your kids."

"I'm asking for your help, for the house."

"You don't make Ripton."

"I'm asking you."

Carlos turned to the sink, sponge-washed the two plates and knife he'd used, put them in the rack beside the sink and started off.

"What about those?" I meant the farrago.

"I ain't used 'em. Tell your kids."

We were in our call and response of an escalating argument. I didn't want the acceleration, yet did. "You don't want to help in the house?"

"I guess not," and Carlos walked away to the living room.

I stewed. I took deep breaths. I tried to make them slow. I couldn't stop feeling his disrespect. The insult throbbed. "You don't want to be part of the house?" I shouted to the living room, walked to the passageway beneath the mezzanine and reached for the Triple Crown trophy he'd recently brought home and put on display. It came higher than three feet, a trinity of candy cane columns in blue and gold rising from a marble base to marble spandrels tied by a golden crown, every boy's dream: *2003 FELIX MILLAN L.L. EAST RIVER TIDES, TRIPLE CROWN AWARD, CARLOS SUAREZ*. I bent for the Gold Glove: *2003 FELIX MILLAN L.L., EST. 1977, DIST 23, MANNY RODRIGUEZ PRES., GOLD GLOVE AWARD, CARLOS SUAREZ*. I took them to the front door and dropped Carlos' trophies into the hallway.

I wanted to let go gently. I did, to the carpet. The Gold Glove nestled on its side. The Triple Crown landed on its marble base and skidded. Its height said it would never stand. I'd made a terrible mistake and the base gave way slowly sideways till there was no room left for grace and the crown slapped the floor, snapped and rolled away. Sometimes you don't understand how precious something is till you watch it break.

"Where my trophies?" Carlos shouted from the place they'd been, no calm to his voice. "YoMike?" He didn't know I was at the door. "Where you at?"

"Here."

He hurried to see me still holding it open, confusion a cloud across his face to fear.

"Carlos—"

He stepped past me into the hall. "*Coño!*" Then more words in shrieks I couldn't understand. He picked up the Triple Crown, picked up the broken crown, held the two in two hands, his face empty then threw the trophy to the floor with a force to break it to pieces. He threw the Gold Glove the same. He stomped on the shards.

"Stop," I said. I couldn't watch. "Stop," I screamed. He didn't hear me. He stomped and smashed and stomped on what he'd smashed.

He looked up, hurt, when the pieces were small.

"I'm sorry."

He walked past me into the apartment, into the TV room, into the bathroom and shut the door.

"Carlos?" I tried the handle. He'd locked it. He ran water in the sink. "Carlos?"

"Michael?" Leslie called from the hallway, then from the kitchen. Ripton, Will and she had Paragon bags. "What happened?"

I couldn't say.

"Where's Carlos?"

I turned back to the TV room and the locked door. "Carlos, let's talk."

"Go away." He was crying.

"Carlos, please. Open the door."

"You know," his voice broke, "I'm stupid. I know better. This is what happens. I believe it. I think I found a family, they love me, but who am I? I'm stupid."

"You're not stupid. I promise, I'll never do anything like this again. This is your home. I promise."

Leslie, Ripton and Will stood at the doorway, listening.

"It's not, you'll see."

Carlos wouldn't open the door. He wailed and I waited. After a while I walked past Leslie and the boys, only able to glance at her. I picked up the pieces that had been trophies, dreaming of a way to make something of them Carlos would smile at.

I couldn't imagine ever again doing something so hurtful.

---

The gun game and WWF wrestling had become long-ago adventures. The boys bragged to guests about launching themselves from the mezzanine down to the stuffed dogs, about running and shooting through the apartment in the dark. But they were older and those had been children's games. Hundreds of fingerprints, smudged handprints and a few complete ones in black paint were preserved perfectly along what had been white plaster wrapping the outside of the spiral stairs from the living room to the mezzanine. The boys sometimes matched their hands over how small they once were. A wide smear a foot and a half from the lip of the mezzanine knee wall had been made by heel scuffs of children readying to fly and unwashed hands wrapped the edge.

We cleared piles of toys from there, found good homes for Lego and board games. We took armfuls of pistols and rifles with flashlights taped to their barrels to the compactor room.

I put aquariums beside two windows in the living room; it seemed they would be safe from having no quite young children anymore. But Phil fell against the largest, one evening, roughhousing with Will and Kindu, forcing seams of glass apart and water rushed to the floor. We positioned bowls and pots beneath, netted fish, moved plants, dried and cleaned the best we could. The boys and I carried the tank to the terrace and emptied it. I explained how to fix the seams and bought the single-sided razor blades, a tube of silicone and gun they'd need. The boys did nothing through weeks of prodding beside make promises for repairs they never delivered.

I pouted my way to the terrace on a Saturday morning and started scraping near Kindu wrapped asleep on the blue chair and ottoman. "What you doin?" he woke up to my grunts.

"Do a job big or small, do it right or not at all."

"What?"

"Do a job big or small, do it right or not at all," I scraped into a seam.

"We do that, Mike," he looked through sleepy eyes.

He woke Will and Phil. Carlos came to watch.

"Let us do it," Will insisted.

"I'm tired of waiting for you. Do a job big or small, do it right or not at all."

"YoMike, let 'em do it," Carlos took my shoulder.

The boys and I repaired the aquarium together. I chanted my mantra.

"A job big or small, don't do it at all," Kindu chanted as he was beading silicone.

"A job big or small, don't do it at all," Phil repeated.

------

"Duckin n' dodgin Momma Gruss, what you think?" Kindu smiled when we couldn't find Phil after Leslie had asked him to help with something around the house. That was Phil, our boy with a fourth sense for duckin n' dodgin me or Momma Gruss (Kindu's nickname for Leslie when she pushed for something to be done. Carlos called her *"the L train"* at those times, the first letter of her name for the similarly named L subway train running across Lower Manhattan).

We really couldn't figure what was going on with him. He was presumably taking three courses at BMCC, 60 percent of a full load. And he was taking the night school science lab. He sometimes studied with Leslie at the dining room table and I helped edit papers he had to turn in. Leslie woke him in the mornings. We kept him and

the other boys fed, gave him and the others MetroCards for the subways and buses. We guaranteed their cell phone accounts or put
them on our own. Phil did occasionally show us quizzes and tests
he'd taken. But no matter how much we asked, how much we con-
centrated on digging out an answer, he was magnificently elusive at
telling us his course grades. I had the sense afterwards of something
disappearing, hiding away and Phil's smile lingering, his nasal tone
flat in my ears.

He apparently completed the science lab and with that graduated
Norman Thomas. He said with honors and insisted on taking us to
dinner with his girlfriend at an Italian restaurant around the corner.
We didn't want him to spend the money. He insisted with abandon
and dressed splivy. His girlfriend, his mother's best friend's daughter
from home in the Dominican, was equally resplendent. She was
large, kind and smiling. We were two couples celebrating Phil's high
school success accomplished through his hard work, through Leslie,
Misses Kaplan and Green and the Bellevue co-op. He'd passed three
BMCC courses and was accepted there full time for the spring semester. Apparently.

<hr />

Carlos phoned the number for GED results. He passed. Next steps
were possible.

<hr />

The *"Leslie and Michael treatment"* didn't feel like a resounding success with Juan. At least he woke up while it was still morning and
went to the Door for college counseling. He was accepted to Mohawk Valley Community College, in Utica, forty-five minutes from
Kindu Upstate. He didn't accept our house rules. He acted hurt and
explained why we weren't clear when we complained about something wrong. But we were. *"You have to be home by eight o'clock,"* I'd
say when he came in much later, past Ripton and Morgan's bedtime.

I called time after time to voice mail, out of range or he'd turned his phone off.

"*I couldn't call,*" he'd answer.

Juan came home after I'd gone to bed one Thursday unable to reach him. Leslie grounded him the next morning, telling him to come home after work. He did. Leslie and I went out to dinner and saw him in the lobby on his way out at 8:30 p.m. as we were on our way in.

"Where you going?" Leslie knew the answer.

"Out," his face was set at tense.

"But you're grounded." We'd never grounded a child.

"I'm goin out," and he did through the two of us beside the front door, so close between that he had to twist his shoulders. He was the most damaged, like an empty soda can, thin skinned. You knew he'd never be fine. Not overall, not ever, always looking for reasons to be slighted. To be crushed and thrown away. Carlos asked why he was that way. I explained being abandoned from one family to another, being told he was conceived in date rape, having a stepfather murdered—

"It was the same wif me, ain't no different," Carlos showed no patience. "My moms says my dads raped her, my biological dad, and my dad was kilt, my moms sendin me to my grandmother. I ain't tolt you, but my moms and dads got into drugs and Social Services took-ted me and Carmello, wc was the youngest then, we lived with my uncle. My sister was thirteen and pregnant wif Mosesto, that's who she had her first three kids wif and she moved wif him. We was wif him for two years before we come back. When I was nine, ten, eleven, she was throwin me out all the time. I tolt you about the shopping cart to my grandmother's. She tookted me back when my grandmom needed money to feed me. She always told me I have a bad attitude, she has a bad attitude and we can't live together. Hidin at my grandmothers, livin with my moms brother, I can be in a room all day alone watchin TV. YoMike, I don't know what I done, I don't know why my moms hates me. I tell you this . . ." he paused, took a breath into what would come because it seemed harder, hesitated a moment more then launched himself to words, "She'd love me if I'd steal somethin. That what peoples do. Steal credit cards, numbers. What you think? I should do that? Get me two names and social security numbers? Scammin like that?"

We sat at the kitchen table understanding we could tell Juan to leave because he refused to live by our house rules. Or we could tolerate five weeks until he left for college. We absolutely didn't want him to be a destructive example to Ripton and Morgan, disrespecting us openly.

A week earlier, Leslie, Juan and Will had been sitting at the kitchen table while I scraped and cut carrots at the sink. Will was talking about Mohawk Valley as if we knew he was transferring there.

"You're going with Juan?" I asked.

He looked as if I'd crafted an insult.

"Do they have criminal justice?" Leslie asked, because he'd wanted to major in that, John Jay's specialty, and become a city policeman.

"I don't know," he was lackadaisical.

"How can't you know?" I wasn't.

He didn't know.

"Did you break up with Angie?"

He hadn't. "I'll study better if I leave. Like Kindu."

"But you did well?—right? That's what you said." About his semester at John Jay.

"Of course," in his softness of "*Ollrrot*." "I passed my classes."

"You're too smart to pass, you should be getting As."

"It's hard, Michael."

"It's not. You can study with Leslie. We want you here."

Will turned away, wanting nothing of the conversation. I turned to my vegetables. He and Juan spoke about a friend we didn't know, new sneakers, testing in a couple of weeks at Mohawk Valley and then the start of the semester. The semester was a month and a half away. Kindu would be home for the Christmas through New Year break. I'd planned to take Juan and Will to Mohawk Valley when I took Kindu to Morrisville. I turned from the sink. "What testing?"

"Figurin what classes we suppose'ta take," Will answered; whether they were ready for community college courses or would be required to take remedial classes. Mr. David had explained only part of the failure process to Kindu and me. The remedial class route was wrought with defeat, a cul-de-sac from which academically unprepared students never emerged to regular classes and graduation.

"You need to take it there?"

They said they did.

"How are you getting there?"

The boys stared at me, what might have been equal parts hurt and meekness. "You don't wanna drive us, Mike?" Will asked. I tried to place his look—Ripton asking Leslie to drive him the few blocks to Paragon when I was in the same room, knowingly inappropriate.

"*And* when the semester starts?" They nodded, expecting two long trips within a few weeks. I don't know how soccer moms feel, but I probably wasn't as kind. I thought of what I cooked and they wouldn't eat, paying for Chinese and pizza delivery night after night, not cleaning up after themselves.

"Mike and Leslie treat us differently, dogs," Juan was dejected.

"What do you mean?" I didn't like the accusation, perhaps because there was truth to it.

"You tookted Kindu to Morrisville. You takin him up. You tookted Carlos to Missouri."

"But back and forth like a yo-yo?"

They looked at Leslie and me with bashfulness and rage. I tried reminding myself that they were teenagers. Ripton and Morgan would be no different. They put no value on my time. Carlos and Kindu took more care for our home. They took more care for us and our children. They were the first to move in. They were more responsible.

"What you mean?"

"I'm really busy."

"Mike and Leslie treat us different," Juan repeated.

We did, with deeper levels of trust and affection, with comfort towards the others.

"We love you," Leslie looked at them with the clarity of a medical diagnosis. "Parents love all their children differently."

She was honest.

"That's bullshit, Leslie," Juan answered. "You like them more, say so. You treat Ripton and Morgan different. You never make them walk the dog, you never yell at them to clean up nothin, but us, you make us do everythin."

"We do treat you differently. We love you, but you aren't our children and you aren't Carlos and Kindu."

I cringed. I wished she hadn't said it, especially the last part, that could never be unsaid.

"We and Phil second class, dogs," Juan said to Will.

"You don't take the same responsibility, Juan," Leslie told him. She was right, but I wouldn't have said it. Her words made me want to shelter Will and Juan.

"Can't you take that test down here?" I tried to find a solution.

"I don't know," Will said, shocked, having heard an unwanted answer to a question he probably wished hadn't been asked.

"I don't know," Juan said.

"Call the college tomorrow morning and find out, okay?"

The night was empty. Mohawk Valley told them the evaluation could be taken in New York if administered in a school. The boys asked me to call that middle school principal I knew. I gave them Mark Pingatore's number and told them where he was inside the PS 64 building. They said he wouldn't return their call. I asked them to call again or go to his office. Days went by. They said they couldn't reach him. When I called he said he'd administer the test.

I asked Will and Juan to arrange for Mohawk Valley to send the exams to Tompkins Square Middle School. They couldn't get through, then did, then had to prove the destination was a school and couldn't figure out how to do that. I arranged for the test to be mailed to Mark Pingatore. I asked Juan and Will to coordinate with Mark's office to proctor the exam, as their college required. They tried but couldn't reach him. I called, Mark answered and the three of us went to him for the boys' exam. Mark sealed the envelope afterwards, wrote his signature crossing the line between back flap and panel and handed it to us to mail to the school. I gave it to Juan and

Will. They didn't go to the post office the next day or the next. I called Mohawk Valley because I wanted to understand deadlines. A woman in the admissions office told me it was too late to mail the exam. We'd need to take it when we came Upstate.

---

It was Leslie's idea, something I wished I'd thought of and wouldn't have had the management skill to pull off. Phil, but not any of the other bigger boys, had a passport. None had a driver's license. Every person of age should have these things. Will, we discovered, wasn't even a citizen. He'd been living in New York as a foreign resident since a boy. As soon as we learned about Will, we saw a *New York Times* article about a middle-aged man being deported to an African country he'd come from when young. He'd become a resident, like Will, but never a citizen. He was issued a citation for speeding, then another for jaywalking or perhaps marching at a protest rally and two or three violations without citizenship meant he was a threat to the well-being of the country. His children and grandchildren were born here. He didn't speak the language of or have anyone where he was going. We downloaded citizenship forms for Will and passport applications for Carlos, Kindu and Juan. We printed the driving instruction book the boys needed to read for the permit exam. Leslie sat with them to fill out forms and marked the days on the calendar when they agreed to register at DMV for the test. Applicants had to provide various documents each worth determined points to prove New York residence and legal existence. A baptism certificate, an elementary school report card, an electric bill, a pay stub. Each boy established his existence and passed the written test enabling him to drive sitting beside a licensed adult, save Kindu, who couldn't produce sufficient proof. Leslie sent him back with more documents. She followed up as avidly as he tried to avoid letting anyone know what happened at DMV. Which seemed always needing more documents. He looked everywhere for his high school ID. I helped and we couldn't find it. He asked for my help again finding a middle-school year book he'd shown us once with a picture of him in the eighth-grade graduating class wearing a button-down shirt and tie. We searched shelves and found it, photocopied the page with his picture and the cover. We woke Kindu the next morning to get to DMV early. He waited an hour, approached the woman at her window and the computer system crashed. He waited another hour for it to come up, then left to return with his documents early the next morning and was again turned away as insufficiently evidenced. I insisted that he let me go through his folder of documents, something he'd refused till then. Adding a pay stub provided enough identification points, by my reckoning, to qualify for the permit exam. He and a couple of the other boys had worked briefly filing in Leslie's office. I asked him to call her to bring home a pay stub that day so he could go back to the DMV the next morning. He refused, preferring to ask Leslie when she came home. I called in spite of his anger, she brought home a stub, Kindu returned to DMV and after his seventh or eighth trip was approved as a bona fide state resident of sufficient age, took the written test and passed.

The boys needed to complete a five-hour driver's safety course, then except for Phil, who ill-begottenly knew, learn how to drive. I didn't have the courage to teach them. Leslie found a driving school in Chinatown, paid and the boys took lessons.

Phil, Juan and Carlos passed the road test. Their licenses arrived in our mail. Will and Kindu failed. Leslie pushed them to immediately sign up for another round of driving classes. Will did and Kindu ignored her, finally did, they took classes and the road test, Will passed and Kindu failed. Leslie insisted and Kindu resisted signing up for classes again.

Days later, newly licensed, Will was driving Kindu to Port Authority to catch a bus back to school, navigating East Eleventh Street between double-parked cars on the driver's side and a construction Dumpster on Kindu's, asked if there was space to shy his way and Kindu assured there was. Will ripped off the side mirror and crushed the front passenger door of the Volvo into the Dumpster. We paid nearly two thousand dollars to repair the damage.

Leslie insisted Kindu sign up for driving classes over the Christmas through New Year's break. His teacher, the same elderly frail man from China who'd taught each of the boys, spoke English haltingly, knew the bigger boys' parents were White Jews in addition to each of their mothers and was confused by this story, went with Kindu after they finished the third round of lessons to the remote area of Brooklyn where exams were given and waited by the side of the road as Kindu drove off with the examiner. Failing a third time would require him to wait months before being allowed to take the exam again. Kindu came back to pick his teacher up, a newly licensed driver. Nearly a week later, a letter arrived for Kindu from Geico, the car insurance company.

"What do you think that is?" Leslie pointed me to it. I assumed Geico was fishing for new clients. "I don't think so," she disagreed.

I thought she was too suspicious. Geico had acutely smart owners. They must send prospecting letters to anyone issued a new license.

The next day, Ripton and Kindu wanted to take a cab to the batting cages at Chelsea Piers where we used to take Morgan to skate. We suggested Kindu drive the Volvo. He arrived safely, pulled into the ground-level parking beneath the complex, searched up and down the aisles for an open space among the angled cars, vans and SUVs, found a spot and crushed the driver's door against the car he was trying to pivot around. I wondered, when he whispered to Leslie afterwards because he was afraid to tell me, how he could be a good center fielder, judge the flight of balls to running catches, have a fine batting average and not be able to steer a car. The damage was eighteen hundred dollars.

Leslie, persistent, asked Kindu about the Geico letter left sitting on the butcher-block divider in the kitchen. She told me afterwards that Jamar and Fuquan had purchased a car, listed it in Kindu's name because he was the only one with a license, gave him the money for insurance and Geico mailed the papers.

Kindu told me that Jamar, three years older, had a driver's permit. Fuquan, a year older, had nothing. The car was parked in a garage in Brooklyn, Queens or the Bronx. His brothers were waiting for Kindu to sign the documents.

"It's fraud. I'm not letting you do it," I said.

"Mike—" he stopped, a look on his face I couldn't read. Leslie had told me he didn't want to take the insurance. I couldn't tell. "Mike—" he stopped again.

"Who's gonna drive it?"

"They friends."

"Sure. You believe that?" He shrugged. Of course he didn't. "Leslie said you don't want to do it."

"Theys my brothers. Theys what I got."

"You have us. You have Elaine. Your cousins. Does Elaine know?"

He shook his head. Of course not. "I tolt 'em Leslie and you gonna see the letter comes and ain't gonna like it. They say don't matter, blood thicker than water. I got to, all the things they done. Gives me money when I need it."

Leslie understood the envelope.

"Give me Jamar's number." He wouldn't. "I have to call him. You can't do it."

"What you gonna say?"

I explained. He gave me Jamar's number. I'd met him a year or so before, when Kindu asked because Jamar wanted to get out of drug dealing. We sat in a newly opened Japanese tearoom on the second floor of a two-story building on Ninth Street nodding towards traditional tearooms with stone, wood, rope lashing in place of nails, tatami mats, ikebana flower arrangements and mountains of salt in little bowls by both sides of the front threshold to keep evil spirits at bay. The owner had built a classic ceremonial teahouse inside. The uniformed woman handed us menus offering several varieties of puer, white teas, a variety of oolongs, many green teas, harder to find or especially good black teas, herbal teas, various cold tea drinks, Japanese and Japanese-influenced finger foods and desserts. "Do you like tea?" I asked.

"They got Lipton?"

They didn't. The waitress recommended what was closest.

Jamar was young, deferential, larger than Kindu, not taller, seemingly not stronger but wider, more filled with water and air, more

full of age and a feeling not quite healthy. He glistened in rock earrings, substantial gold rings for nearly each finger and gold necklaces
wound within themselves. He wore a white Puma velour tracksuit
with red piping, a zip top and elastic-waisted pants with white socks,
white high-top Jordans and red laces, a red Puma tee with a white
leaping cat across the left breast to his right, a white Yankees baseball cap with the classic interlocking NY logo in fire engine red. Its
front panel was broadly straight, the brim flat as if on a store shelf, a
gold foil label larger than a Morgan dollar on top and a silver foil label the size of a quarter on the bottom. Pure Yankees baseball caps
were darkest blue with a white embroidered logo.

I knew Jamar was three years older than Kindu yet had expected
someone my age. "What? Excuse me? I'm sorry? I didn't hear.
Could you say that again?" I repeated too often. I better understood
someone from London or South Africa than Jamar, from a few
blocks away and whose brother lived in our family. They were un-
mistakably from the same parents. I was happy and saddened by
how far Kindu had come. It had to hurt to visit home every day. I'd
never realized he'd learned to speak differently. I wondered if he
slipped into another voice there. With hard work, Kindu would
continue on to a four-year degree after Morrisville and a middle-
class life, a gap growing greater between him and his family. Only
Kindu of the six brothers in Elaine's family didn't sell drugs on
Broome Street. Maybe he wouldn't have, regardless. Each of the
other boys had spent time in jail already, Jamar three of the past six
years. He wanted to be a good father to the son he had with a former girlfriend, but in addition to the hurdles of incarceration, the
mother accused Jamar of abuse whenever he tried to visit his boy.
Fuquan was apparently a marked man in prison, to be hurt or killed
if he went back. When he went back, I guessed. Fuquan had a
young daughter with a girlfriend. The next generation was already
here, parented by children.

Jamar handed me a resume. It didn't show jail, drug-dealing skills,
education, computer knowledge, an email address, volunteer work
or much of anything except disconnected short stints of building

demolition work. He wanted to get a job, learn another skill, anything to get out of drug dealing so he wouldn't end up in jail again. The stretches would get longer, then he might not get out again. He might die like his dad. I made changes while we drank our teas. He said a friend would edit them on her computer and he'd get the resume back to me in a day. I set up an appointment at a neighborhood organization that helped train and find jobs for people coming out of the prison system. Jamar kept it. He didn't get his resume back to me. He didn't call me. I don't know if he listened to my voice-mail messages. The woman running the job training program said he expected immediate results, as in *tomorrow*. He didn't have the patience for programs and the search for work. She doubted he'd be back.

She was right.

I met with Fuquan once near the same time. We agreed on a time at a diner on Delancey. I locked my bike in a snow bank and looked through the window to a flash of confusion, wondering why Kindu was sitting inside. The two were identical, except when I came closer; the broad corner of Fuquan's mouth was pulpy and raw. And there was something hard about him. I remembered the story of the brothers chasing someone who'd cut Fuquan, beating the man near the Williamsburg Bridge, something about a gun. His jewelry was the same as Jamar's save a Madonna Mary Mother medal. He said it was twenty-four-caret gold, cost ten thousand dollars and, he assured me, was a bargain. Its gold chain was thick. He was dressed in a lime green version of Jamar's white. He wore lime green and orange Jordans. His Yankee cap was lime green with an orange logo. I had no easier time understanding Fuquan, not the individual words, but what he meant with ones and combinations. He wanted to talk about raising money to pay for his music studio time.

> *Man, it wasn't suppose to be that way*
> *Every time I close my eyes all I do is see that day*
> *Mom dukes in the hospital dying of AIDS,*
> *Pops locked up, we all thought he'd die in the cage*

The bigger boys listened to his rap. Carlos didn't listen to rap and he listened to Fuquan. "It's bangin," he explained.

I told John Howard at Casimir after Ripton and Kindu had left one night about sitting with Jamar and Fuquan. He asked how good Fuquan was. I said the bigger boys listened to him. One of John's friends managed an enormously popular White rapper. John asked for and I gave him a CD, which I heard nothing about. Till I asked later, to learn his younger daughter didn't think it was wonderful.

I waited till near noon, when I thought a drug dealer might be up, and left a message for Jamar. He didn't call and I tried again near seven and again before I went to bed. He'd be waiting for customers down on Broome Street. Kindu probably said something to him that night because he answered when I called near noon the next day. "What up?"

"This Geico letter to Kindu—"

"It got nofin ta do wif you. What it got ta do wif you. It Kindu," he began, livid.

I wondered what color combination Yankee hat he had on. What color sweats. "He's my son, he lives here. The letter came—"

"He my brutha, Fu's brutha, ain't got nofin do wif you. Kindu make his decision," he yelled at me.

"It's fraud—"

"Fraud?" he screamed. "How it fraud?"

I started explaining and listening. Fuquan didn't have a license or learner's permit. Jamar's permit was suspended for a speeding violation. He was required to take a course so it could be reinstated, to practice driving if he didn't know how already and take the license exam. Fuquan told me neither brother would use the car till they legally could. It was parked waiting for Kindu to sign the insurance papers I'd stuck inside a book inside my backpack. A friend would drive them. He was a good driver. They needed the car in case of emergency. Their friend would always be nearby. They wouldn't use it to pick up or deliver drugs. Drugs would never be in the car. Kindu could drive it whenever he came back to New York. "So if your friend's in an accident—"

"What you sayin? Nigga's good drivin."

"Sure. But say he's going through an intersection and a guy runs a stop sign and crashes into him. Kindu's in Morrisville, the insurance is in his name, Geico sends an inspector to our house—" I didn't say Jamar was driving, ran a stop sign with a suspended learner's permit and drugs by his side. Or Fuquan was at the wheel. Carlos told me, loving Kindu, what I'd partially figured out; sometimes his brothers called and Kindu left home to pee for Fuquan's probation tests. Kindu's lost learner's permit, as well as the Morrisville ID and old high school ID we'd been unable to find to earn points for the new permit he needed, were with Fuquan—because the two looked alike.

"Ain't got nothin do wif nothin, got it? I tellin you."

"He's a boy. I'm not allowing it."

"What you say?"

"He's a boy. I'm not allowing it."

"Kindu a grown-ass man. You ain't got nothin do wif it."

"He's my son. He lives in our house. We feed him, put a roof over his head. It's against the law. He's worked too hard, I'm not allowing it—"

"He's my blood, me and Fu, us three. I raised him up when ain't nobody. Not Elaine, me and Fu, no one tellin Kindu what to do, he helpin his bruthas. You actin like you give im somefin nobody give him. Our oldest cousin gone to college, a girl cousin goin ta college, ain't nofin—" and then he wasn't on the phone. I called back. He answered and kept speaking, "We blood, thicka than wata, he gonna do this ain't you business—" and the line was silent once more.

I called back. "Fuquan, are you—?"

"Jamar, this Jamar, Fu ain't on tha line. You don't know who you talkin wif?"

"I'm his father." I heard my awkwardness. "One of his fathers."

"I'm his real brotha. You ain't no fatha. Ain't no fraud wif us."

"It's not a contest. You love him and we love him. You want to do what's best, we have to do what's best for him. Does Elaine know about this?"

"Elaine don't care. What Elaine gotta do wif it? Don't talk about Elaine. We's family. Kindu gotta do what I say, Fu say, we the oldest—" he hung up and I didn't call back.

Kindu loathed the disapproval of his older brothers and what I recounted hurt. He wanted to be dutiful yet knew what they were asking was wrong. He'd never said a thing but I thought about what Carlos said. Kindu had called me from a Transit Authority jail a week and few days before first going to Morrisville. He'd walked between standing subway cars on the L train as it waited in the Eighth Avenue station. A transit cop walked him to the underground police station and ran a standard check for outstanding warrants. He'd never been arrested, numbered, entered into the system—Mayor Guiliani's genius of policing, numbering the dark boys. If a warrant popped up the next time the kid jumped a turnstile or looked at a cop the wrong way along Avenue D an outstanding condition already existed. A warrant came up for Kindu urinating in public when he was sixteen. He told me he'd never done such a thing. The policeman took him to the main transit jail underground at Canal Street. I was his one allowed phone call. I raced through traffic but he'd been transported to the Tombs by the time I arrived. The policeman at the counter, White, tall, couldn't tell me anything and called for the arresting officer, not as tall, White, kind, who told me Kindu was a considerate young man. He was as surprised as anyone when a warrant came up. I rode the subway before bikes and walked often between cars. Ripton and I had been on the subway not long before. A young woman then an old woman, one White and the other Black, walked between cars to us. They weren't hauled off to the Tombs. We had to get Kindu out of there. My phone wouldn't work below ground so I hurried out through the subway station, found a seat on a bench in a small park below Canal and called Leslie. She contacted a patient who was a criminal lawyer in a legal defense firm in the Bronx, who was already on her way to 110 Centre Street, the courthouse above the Tombs. Leslie set out as well. I should be on my way and we'd find each other there. It had become early evening. The bottom of the

Tombs was kept frigid because street people were picked up, people urinated and retched, it wasn't often cleaned and the police wanted to keep smells down. Prisoners passed later into the holding pens behind the fancy wood paneling of the wall against which the presiding judge sat and no one would imagine what was on the other inhospitable side. Our lawyer could see Kindu only when he was finally brought up to the holding pens. The law required a hearing within twenty-four hours. It regularly went to thirty-six or longer. Fifteen-, sixteen- and seventeen-year-olds were picked up for the range of street reasons. Our lawyer got Kindu's case moved onto the docket for that night and a message to him that we were upstairs, he had a lawyer and would be seen within a few hours. New papers in hand, our lawyer revealed that the warrant was for disorderly conduct from the past weekend, not when Kindu was sixteen, on a night and at a time he had been at Ria and Mike's with us for Friday night Sabbath dinner. We waited in the hallway between courtrooms, the place of the 1980s sitcom *Night Court* without the spirit of Mel Tormé, witty lawyers and loving criminals. A half hour past midnight a court officer came out of kindness to tell our lawyer that Kindu had been brought up to the holding pens. The smells there, she said, were the worst. Lawyers gagged and vomited. We went into the courtroom of off-white walls, cavernous ceilings, long brown wooden benches, the wall where the judge sat and accompanying furniture of jurisprudence processing, as far as we saw, underage brown males. Our lawyer confirmed that a thirteen-year-old child could be tried as an adult in capital cases. Relatively few of the arrested were legal adults. Most were male. We saw no girls or women among the brown faces sitting and waiting with their White legal aid lawyers for the White judge. One was chained wrist and ankle through an O-ring near his bellybutton, jangling as he shuffled the prisoner walk from movies. We weren't to wave or mouth words to Kindu when he was brought in wearing jeans and the long-sleeved *DANGER–EDUCATED BLACK MAN!* tee I'd thought cute and given him when he was accepted to Morrisville. Our lawyer was handed new papers, went forward to sit with Kindu and came back to us with the news that the warrant was now for something completely different. A court officer eventually called our son. He and our lawyer went before the judge, who in the matter of seconds dismissed the trail of mistaken warrants, perfunctorily awarded Kindu a six-month probationary period and released him. The shackled brown man, Kindu's age, was being extradited to Texas for capital murder, death by lethal injection or electric chair; one of the highest execution rates in the country. He wore the same braids Carlos had before Youth Service. His eyes were Phil's. We left the courtroom at 2:30 a.m. Kindu insisted on showering before eating when we got home. He put his clothes in the washing machine and I ran it. We let him sleep in the next morning. Lying in bed, I realized Kindu had become another dark boy numbered.

"Do you think the warrants were from Fuquan taking your ID?" I asked Kindu later. I imagined Fuquan stopped, handing over the cards he'd taken from Kindu, cops writing tickets.

"Mighta," he answered. His cell phone vibrated. "Jamar," he looked at the number, looked at the ground, pushed IGNORE. His phone rang again. He pushed IGNORE. His phone rang again. He pushed IGNORE. He grimaced, looking hopeless.

I felt equally so, wondering what Leslie and I had created. Kindu had endless frozen waffles and Vermont maple syrup. Carlos had endless cups of milk. Leslie and I were committed to the value of education. We hoped the bigger boys would one day earn middle-class jobs, live in middle-class neighborhoods and read books to their own children. We thought that was better than dealing on Broome Street, spending three of the past six years in a jail with the prospect of more. But I couldn't stand splitting a family. "Do you want to do the insurance?" I asked.

Kindu shook his head, his eyes back at the ground.

My cell phone rang. Jamar began yelling. He and Fuquan were the older brothers. They earned the money to support the family. They had the right to tell Kindu what to do.

Kindu, anxious, went to keep his promise to Elaine to visit home every night.

The next afternoon Kindu brought the phone to me in the kitchen. "My moms wants to talk wif you," he said.

"Don't you pay them boys no mind. Kindu told me what's goin on," Elaine said. "They doin nothin wif they lives. Kindu in college, we proud of him and we grateful to you and Mrs. Rosen."

"Jamar got angry. I told him I was Kindu's dad. I didn't mean disrespect."

"You are. I took them boys in, you took Kindu in. You treat him like your own. Ain't no competition."

"I—"

"Listen, them boys got me in trouble. Police come lookin for 'em, knockin on the door, scarin the little ones. Authority wants ta kick us out. We gots to move partments and they ain't allowed here no more. That hurts a mother. Them boys don't do nothin, ruinin our lives. They ain't gonna ruin Kindu's, that boy got chances, you hear me? Don't you pay them two no heed."

*This is the story of an adopted child,*
*whose mom was crazy and pops was wild,*
*so they sent me off to live with my aunt,*
*she's getting older now, I wish I could give her my heart.*

---

We helped Will gather evidence and Leslie helped him fill out citizenship papers, Carlos, Kindu and Juan their passport applications. She took them across the park for photographs. The passports arrived regular mail in State Department return envelopes over the course of a few days. Will's citizenship papers came and Leslie marched him to the dining room table to fill out a passport application. The passport arrived soon after. Leslie stored them all with ours in the next-to-top drawer of the small bureau in the back of the sports room.

---

From mid-December on Leslie had been making sure that Juan, Will and Carlos were outfitted for college and Kindu ready to return. She'd been shopping online for blankets, comforters, pillows, pillow-cases, sheets, comforter covers and towels. Boxes arrived every day. She took each of them on trips to Kmart and the Gap for socks, box-ers, tees, flannels, jeans, shirts and hoodies. She bought winter boots, warm coats, gloves for Will, Kindu and Carlos, mittens for Juan and winter hats. Each already owned pairs of sneakers. She bought soap, shampoo, razors and blades, condoms, hair gel, deodorant, cologne, vitamins, toothbrushes, toothpaste, Advil, Band-Aids, scissors, tweez-ers and any other essentials she and the boys could think of.

I hired a photographer to take pictures of our family before the bigger boys left. *"The family"*—that's what Carlos and Kindu then the others in spite of their frustration had been calling us.

We made sure everyone and the dog was home when the photog-rapher arrived with an assistant and an elevator full of equipment. It took them hours to set up screens, white umbrellas, flashing tripods and wires throughout the living room, then boring hours more to shoot us and hours again the next evening and the next till the allure of *"the family"* pictures was gone.

I was driving Kindu, Will and Juan to their colleges Upstate early the next morning, a Friday, beginning a trip ending one part of our lives together, opening another and changing theirs forever if they tried.

I'd have half a day or more on the road, so we asked Will to sleep over, the boys to have their Leslie-bought goods and bags stacked by the front door before they went to bed, to get enough sleep and wake up early. I wanted to be on the road by 7:00 a.m. to get Will and Juan to Mohawk Valley with enough time to deliver their evalu-ations, enroll them for classes and get them into their dorms—they were in different but supposedly nearby buildings—get Kindu back to Morrisville and me back to New York. The photographer took pictures as we ate and roasted Will and Juan.

Leslie went to bed. I stayed downstairs till 10:30 and asked the boys to go to sleep by midnight. I went down at 1:00 a.m. to remind them. The bigger boys were gone, Ripton and Morgan asleep, Kindu's and Juan's belongings draped around the apartment, including the purchases from Leslie. Will's bags, and nothing more, were in front of the door. My calls went to their voice mails. I walked upstairs and couldn't sleep, turned from one side to the other while Leslie and the dog snored, the dog woke and walked over my head to dig under the blanket beside Leslie, crawled out when he got too hot and walked back over my head to the foot of the bed, jumped off and ran down the stairs, lapped water in the greenhouse bathroom where boys had hidden in the tub for the gun game, ran on the terrace barking at the nearly full moon and probably peed, ran back in and up the doggy stairs we'd put beside the bed and laid on my stomach as I laid on my back looking at the skyline lighten. I went down at 6:00 a.m. The boys weren't back. A half hour later I heard the dog breathing and heaving and Leslie was a half flight behind wondering why I'd woken before the alarm. I told her about the night and she looked at the mess, phoned the boys and got their voice mails. We made our coffees, she read the *New York Times* and I wrote at the kitchen table till the elevator bell rang at 7:30, a half hour after I'd wanted to leave. They told us something about girls Phil made an introduction to and getting lost at a party in Long Island. I was too frustrated and tired to think. Leslie's face was stern. I understood, slowly, that they'd been at Long Island University, in Queens, not far away, and not on Long Island—though they might not have known the difference. They had no good excuse. I was afraid of falling asleep after I dropped Kindu off. "You're not sleeping in the car. I'll pull over if anyone does," I told them. I had no intention of being a chauffeur. I'd be a chauffeur but wanted company. The boys looked as if Leslie and I had lost our reason. *You beastin. Mike Oh-Dee'in*, Will's eyes said. Best friends were supposed to party all night before leaving for college.

The house a mess, the Volvo and roof-rack container jammed hodgepodge with three boys, me and their belongings, we left an hour and a half late towards Utica. I started off the road each time a boy dozed and the others woke him up. We arrived at Mohawk Valley near 2:00 p.m. and spent twenty minutes driving through the campus following various people's directions searching for the dormitory office inside an ocean of identical four-story brick buildings. The students guarding the key box there said Will and Juan needed to show proof they'd registered for classes before being allowed into their rooms. We hurried for the registrar's office and were told the boys' evaluations need to be graded before they could sign up for classes. We raced to the evaluation office where the single person there told us no one would look at the exams till Monday. I rode through a train of thought, getting Kindu to Morrisville, driving back to Utica, finding a hotel (one room or two?) and spending the weekend till the college offices opened. Leslie wouldn't be happy, I'd miss the boys, my work would back up because of Will's and Juan's ineptness. "I have to take my other son to Morrisville," I pointed to Kindu.

The woman looked at Kindu, then at Will and Juan then back at me then pulled the sleeve of her white blouse up to look at the lady-sized watch she wore to see the time she already knew. "I'll grade them," she said, waving the manila envelope of exams with Mark Pingatore's signature written across the flap and told us to hurry to the finance department to make sure the boys' tuitions were paid because offices were beginning to close. We ran to a large hall with large signs, long lines and small windows, many people crowded before. We asked someone where to start, Kindu and I took a place in the final line while Will and Juan began hurrying their papers from one line to another, one window to get an overview, another to sign for grants, another for loans then ran back to us. The woman behind our window phoned the evaluation lady, writing words and numbers on papers for the level of classes each boy could take. She warned us we needed to run to the sociology department so Will could register for criminal justice courses and to the physical education department on the other side of campus because Juan wanted coaching to be his major. The woman drew circles around the buildings on a map, wrote the names of the heads of the departments and handed me various evaluation results for the boys.

The four of us ran to the social sciences building. I wondered what would happen if the department heads weren't there, if they were busy with other students. We had half an hour to finish everything and didn't know what everything was. We knocked on one door, a woman sent us up a floor and down a hall where another person sent us across to a room where a man welcomed us kindly. He started looking at Will's evaluation results. I explained Juan and the man said the two of us should hurry to the physical education building. Kindu stayed with Will. Juan and I ran as he humored my slowness. A person in the entryway told us the department head was also the basketball coach managing the practice we heard in the gym. I walked into the middle of tall, sweating, mostly young Black men and interrupted the coach, apologizing. He blew a whistle hanging around his neck, sneakers screeched, shouts stopped and the coach called for the ball. I explained our situation. He tossed the ball to an assistant and told us to follow him to his office, a box of painted cinderblock beside the gym. The convenient times for courses were filled; Juan ended up with a schedule of earliest morning and evening classes with empty daytimes. It didn't feel like an auspicious start. But he didn't have the freedom of choice.

I called Will, agreed to meet him and Kindu at the dormitory office, the boys were given keys, we unpacked their belongings, I made their beds, we hugged, I kissed their cheeks and we said goodbye.

I left Kindu in Morrisville and started driving home, turning our pop music loud. I felt the tears of a sadness and joy every parent must feel leaving a child at college. Our home, the hours, would be emptier. Ripton had started the nine of us on an improbable journey. I had no idea of what our futures might bring, but I was terribly proud of each boy. I saw good men growing, and was grateful we'd helped this odd and remarkable group come together. We'd opened our home and become a larger family. The seven boys said so. Not a fairy tale or romance. But a family with its rough and smooth edges.

A friend had visited when the bigger boys first started staying for weekends and holidays. He was fascinated by the confusion of our home. "If you're gonna let them be here," he waved around the apartment, "it has to be unconditional. They'll test it because the way things work, disadvantaged kids are always screwed over. Teachers start nice, social workers, their mom's new boyfriends all start nice, get tired and walk away. These kids don't know it, but they're fighting for their lives. It is a matter of life and death. Especially for boys, the street kills them early, one way or another. If you let them into your family, it has to be forever."

I continued through small Upstate New York towns, past quaint Main Streets.

> *I will be strong, I will be faithful*
> *'Cause I'm counting on*
> *A new beginnin'*
> *A reason for livin'*
> *A deeper meanin yeah*

Savage Garden harmonized to the silliest words. I wondered what Kindu was doing at that exact tiniest moment, what look was on his face, what he was touching, what he was feeling. The same for Juan and Will. They were in the world, on their own. Phil planned to stay home and keep going to BMCC for at least another semester. We'd have Ripton and Morgan at home for years more. I could listen to them breathe at night.

---

Coach Gober mailed Carlos a one-way airplane ticket to St. Louis. It would have been the cheapest he could find, leaving from MacArthur Airport in the middle of Long Island. I'd never known anyone to fly from there.

Carlos packed for days. His bags were in the foyer and we planned a dinner for his last night, only Phil, Morgan, Ripton, Leslie, Carlos and me.

I woke the boys early the next morning. We ate breakfast, Leslie walked the dog to the garage and drove the car back, calling to say we should come down.

We helped each other loading Carlos' bags into the elevator and crowded around them.

"Hold on!" he shouted, rushed out and down the hall. "My batting gloves," the lucky ones he kept in his bedroom beside the television.

He didn't come back. The elevator alarm started. We had a plane to catch and I hurried down the hall. "Come on," I shouted into the apartment.

"Okay, okay, I got 'em," he shouted back. I started back down the hall.

He came to the door, stopped and turned, "Goodbye house, I love you."

# ACKNOWLEDGMENTS

Morgan, you are the least present in this book, but certainly not in our lives. You never got caught up the same in all *this*, then, except as the youngest, and that is often the hardest place to be among many brothers. You have grown to be exceptionally wise, and will be the better man for all you have understood. Follow your perception.

Ripton, thank you for bringing us onto a baseball field once upon a time; for seeing people as people. So much in our lives has come from your sight. Stay tender, please, forever, my biggest son. Keep growing into your compassion and conviction.

To both my sons, I love being your father. I love you, beyond words I can write.

To Carlos, Kindu, William, Philippe & Juan Carlos—I love being your father, too. I am proud of each of you, beyond expression. May you achieve your dreams, however they take shape as you grow. Thank you for the trust of your stories and selves. The world is here for you, I believe that. Never stop working hard. We'll work hard together. *Ganbarimasu*, as Carlos said to Mr. Valentine.

Leslie, one year after September 11, thank you for saying that writing a book was a reasonable way to spend my days, which became years. Thank you for encouraging me to tell our story, for the trust to explain what I understood as truthfully as I could. I love your indulgence, and rely on your love. Thank you, forever.

Clive Priddle wanted this book—or sufficiently pretended to. You told me about books inside books and have tried to peel close to the core of this one. You said books are collaborations. I understand this now, and am blessed to have collaborated with you.

Peter McGuigan, with unstoppable energy, said he'd find a publisher. Mary Bahr said she'd find an agent—and did so much more I nearly believe in angels. Corey Kilgannon, authentically Runyonesque, said none of the business mattered because the story was there. Gidon Kunda said to tell this story and not any other. I couldn't see that alone.

The PublicAffairs people have treated me with a love and respect for the written word I am grateful to have found: Laura Stine, Gray Cutler, Whitney Peeling, Lisa Kaufman, Pete Garceau, Niki Papadopoulos . . . thank you. Susan Weinberg and Mr. Peter Osnos—for allowing my book to come to page.

Mark Chimsky and David Groff, you gave me advice earliest, when it was hardest to hear. So too did Hiroko Waku, about scripts, movie trailers and headlines. I couldn't have gotten to half the truth myself. Wyatt "Blue" Mitchell & Bill Talen, for your caring suggestions. Robin Haller, for correcting my English.

Diane McWhorter and Sandee Brawarsky gave me time, with compassion. You did too, Roland Legiardi-Laura, and Geri Thoma. Robert Krulwich led to Jean Strouse led to Ileene Smith. Small moments for you, probably, but dry stones in a river then to me.

Thank you all for the patience and care of helping me forward, without impatience.

I outlived Drink Me, Hopscotch, Wild Lily here and there, Rapture, Gramstand & Boerum Hill Food Company. I know community changes, but it seems too fast looking back. I wanted to mark places.

Good places now to spend days: Amai, Café Orlin, Mogador, Mud, B Cup, Baked, Ciao for Now, Cha An, Fresh Salt, Sympathy for the Kettle, Chez Betty, Ninth Street Espresso (though you wouldn't hire my sons), Verdigris, Sanibel Bean, Jack's—locally owned, let people sit, are fine with refills, infusions and intended writers. George Bliss—Fritz, Jeff and Amanda at Continuum Cycles, thank you for keeping me getting around, and caring about books. So too Kirsten Cesped, Haydee Domenech, Mila Rozen, and Dr. Jo

Ann Weinrib, for the same. Daniel Bell, for keeping my Macs going. Apple and Digital Society, for making and repairing them. Arthur Brown for caring about fountain pens.

In the realm of keep going: Ernesto Ferran, Sue Grand, Marlene Burke, Sandra Shapiro. Through sometimes hard times, to live fully.

John Howard, you're not quite as *fan-Ta-STICK* as all the boys say you are. Well . . . perhaps they're right. Eric Goldberg and Carter Weiss, for sitting with me each week and deepening friendships like Thoreau blessed with his beans. Bill Bender, for letting me tell you stories early on. David Rubel for reading material and suggestions. Mike Rudell for advice. Debrah Charatan, for helping us all.

Joan Warner and the Hannah Senesh Community Day School, Michelle Harring and the Earth School, thank you for the courage and wisdom to see young male truths clearly when others wouldn't, for changing our lives in the most important way—to protect our sons—so profoundly. And Wendy Parmet, for helping us get there.

Roxanne Zazzaro, Jennifer Knies, Madame Perry, Sidney Bridges, Michael Nill, everyone at Brooklyn Friends for your concern and friendship, in friendship, in those few hard times and the more sweet.

Howard and Shirley Rosen, my parents, grew up to be kindness and a bedrock of support; the middle-aged me wants to hug the youthful you and say "Fear shall pass." And it has. Hugh Short showed me the importance of ideas, the excitement of commitment and the deficiency of most reasons for conformity—you are the best of Vermont. Brian Spooner taught as truly as anyone I've been a student of. Kim Schmahmann, thank you for showing a courage of encouragement through your woodworking and word. Ria and Mike Gruss—for welcoming me to New York, and the boys into your lives, thank you.

Jonny McGovern and Yuval Boim, we're biased fans. Thank you: Jeff the Coach, Peter Marciano, Frances Goldin, Lorna Brett Howard, Mary Spink, Margarita Lopez, Marina Torbey and Maja Patrone, Ely Weitz, Cooperstown Baseball Camp at Beaver Valley and Julie Sharratt, Coach O'Keefe, Fred Schwartz and Tracey Hummer,

Angela Goding, Anne-Marie Nieves and Keith Emmer, Peter Serling, Yuko Dokawa, Kyoko Waku for safe unagi, Rabbi Solomon Goldberg for my earliest library, Rebecca Rachael Fiske for helping me fall in love with books that summer, Jake Sherman, Erich Theophile, Neil Theise, Charles King, Dimitri Raitzin, Mrs. Zawin, Clayton Patterson, Ed Lowenthal, Hannah Brown Gordon, Vanessa Mobley, Gail Cameron Wescott and Martine Fougeron, Michael Fuquay, Michael Jesselson, Pastor Phil Trzynka, Butch Morris, Michael Small, Harish Rao, Nick Whitaker, Stella Anastasia, Bobby Valentine, Ray Chambers, Anthony Scaramucci, Larry Rocca, Leah Paulos, Michael Cecconi, Dan Thompson, Chris Yakovich, Peggy Anderson, Paul Garrin, Stewart Rosen, Jane Crotty, Kelly Hughes, David Allen, Craig Goding, Tom Newmann, Captain Doug Stewart, Shelley Kolton and Canio Pavone for the perfect bookshop.

To Ripton's and my Reading Group buddies not mentioned yet: Davon Russel, Jon Rygh, Evan Yurman, (Rabbi) Charlie Buckholtz—hugs for sharing your time, stories and understandings, for being inspirations. Let's keep reading.

To the mothers: Elaine Smith, Evelyn Velez, Brigida M. Tavarez, Nelly Vasquez, Esther Ruiz—thank you for allowing us the time with your sons, for giving us the odyssey of loving them. They always tell stories of your love and courage. We call them "our" sons with the deeper respect that they are yours.

A message in a bottle: to the birth mothers and birth fathers of Ripton and Morgan—I wonder sometimes about your moments, if your feelings travel to where mine sometimes do. Parenting in the moment of adoption is beautiful, and it is sad, it is both and we know that. Our sons, your sons, have always known they were adopted, from the earliest stories we told them about how we met, from the earliest books we read. We've always explained that you loved your babies with all your heart, with all your soul and that's why, back then, you entrusted their lives to us. They are such good young men and you certainly also must be. Know that Ripton and Morgan have grown to be good sons, and please be proud. They would smile with your approval.

Ricky, Dakota, Cam, JJ, Junito, Richie, DJ, Jamar, Fuquan, Carmelo Jr., Van and Mak, Joel and Jesus, Jason and Will, Oscar and Romeo, Gio, Harley, Justin, Matthew, all the boys from Tompkins Square who are now young men, sometimes husbands and already fathers . . . may Life shine upon you safely, warm you with peace and pride. Take care of your children, show them a way.

I apologize to anyone unmentioned who's helped me along the way of this writing. Tell me, and then a cup of coffee together, please.

Tens of people make a person's life. To my friends in the Lower East Side, in New York, Tel Aviv, elsewhere, thank you.

## A NOTE ON METHODOLOGY

When I was a student at the University of Pennsylvania, training first as a social anthropologist and later writing a doctorate involving ethnographic study, I never expected to employ the methods learned there in writing the story of my own family. But I have done so for this book. I took notes in preparation. I sometimes tape recorded dialogue and took photographs. I have, in a few places, condensed and re-sequenced scenes for the sake of narrative fluency, yet the elements were always there. On those occasions when I wasn't present, I interviewed those who were. My family knew I was writing a book about us. I left chapter drafts on the kitchen and dining room tables year after year. Everyone, except maybe Morgan when he was quite young, has read parts of it. That's how, for example, the other bigger boys first learned about Kindu's family life on Broome Street. The boys have often explained things I first didn't understand. Leslie read the full book twice, corrected errors, and questioned me on aspects of it. I want to thank all my family for their help. However, any errors are mine and mine alone.

# ABOUT THE AUTHOR

**Michael Rosen,** a community organizer, is the author of *Turning Words, Spinning Worlds*. He has been a real estate developer and investor, former CEO on Wall Street and in the public sector, as well as an assistant professor at New York University. He lives in New York with his wife, Leslie Gruss, and helps raise the extended Rosen family.

> For more information,
> photographs, and further reading:
> www.whatelsebuthome.com.